THE REFORMED PASTOR AND MODERN THOUGHT

By

CORNELIUS VAN TIL

PRESBYTERIAN AND REFORMED PUBLISHING CO.
Phillipsburg, New Jersey
1980

First Printing, 1971
Second Printing, 1974
Third Printing, 1980

ISBN: 0-87552-497-4

Library of Congress Catalogue Card No. 74-150956
Printed in the United States of America

PREFACE

This little volume is designed to aid the Reformed pastor in his work of helping high school and college students face the challenge to their faith presented in their classes on science, philosophy, and religion.

To be able to help his young people the Reformed pastor must himself have some acquaintance with modern science, modern philosophy, and modern religion. But, more than that, he must see clearly for himself that unless science, philosophy, and religion frankly build upon the authority of Christ, speaking his Word in Scripture, they can offer no coherent interpretation of life. Modern thought has repeatedly, in attempting to explain reality, shown its own incoherence.

The first chapter sets out to deal comprehensively with the relation of Christianity to modern thought. It can be read as a complete unit by itself and is, as such, the basis of what follows.

The second chapter deals with traditional Catholicism, the third with the philosophy of Immanuel Kant as the basic source of modern Protestantism, the fourth with modern Protestantism and its relation to twentieth century philosophy, the fifth with modern Catholicism, and the sixth with Ecumenism. In each case the effort is made to show the Reformed pastor how he may relate himself to these movements. The argument of the book is that only the Reformed faith can truly present the gospel as a challenge to modern unbelief.

TABLE OF CONTENTS

Chapter I

THE REFORMED PASTOR AND
THE DEFENSE OF CHRISTIANITY

I. *Introduction*

The primary purpose of this discussion is constructive, not polemical. We hope to show how the Christian view of life may most effectively be proclaimed and defended. In this connection, we have in mind the responsibilities of the young pastor who must guide his people, especially his young people, into an ever deeper grasp of the Christian faith. But the Christian faith is frequently ridiculed. It is said to deal with what is purely imaginary. It is said to be contrary to the facts of science. It is said to be logically contradictory. Appealing substitutes, which are often disguised in the words of Scripture, are offered for it.

How will the young pastor guide his flock, his young high school and college people, in the midst of this confusion? He has no time to read many books. He lives too far from the centers of Christian learning to profit from personal conversation with others of like mind who have studied these matters in depth. He needs, therefore, a criterion by which he himself may be able to distinguish truth from error. He needs, in particular, to be able to discern whether the books he reads, and those his people read, hold to historic Christianity or not. He must understand the reasons why men reject historic Christianity. He must know how to evaluate these reasons.

Is historic Christianity really out of accord with the facts of science? If it is, must he hold to his convictions in the realm of religion *in spite of* the facts of science? Are Christianity and science to be thought of as operating in independent spheres?

Again, is historic Christianity out of accord with the demands of logic? Is it really or only apparently contradictory? Does it matter whether it is contradictory? Does Christianity maintain that that which is impossible according to logic has none the less happened in fact?

The young pastor may well be baffled by all this. He cannot hope to know as much about the facts of science as the non-Christian experts in science do. He may get some help from fellow Christians whose life task it is to study science. He may get some help also from his former seminary professors. But while they are "experts" in their specialized fields of research, they may not be able to show him *how* he may settle each and every issue.

II.   *Historic Roman Catholic Apologetics*

Suppose that one day the young pastor met his friend, the priest of the local Roman Catholic parish. On former occasions they had agreed that they held "much in common." On an earlier occasion the priest had slipped him a copy of Bishop Sheen's *Religion Without God.* Sheen quotes a number of the definitions of religion given by modern so-called "Protestants." "Religion is the projection in the roaring loom of time of a concentration or unified complex of psychical values." "Faith in God is synonymous with the brave hope that the universe is friendly to the ideals of man."

The priest "knew" that all such "subjective" definitions of religion come, in the last analysis, from the "Protestant principle"—the right of private judgment in matters of religion. Luther and Calvin are really responsible, the priest was sure, for the vagaries of modern Protestantism. At this point he was interested in stressing how much Luther and Calvin had *in common* with Thomas Aquinas as over against modern subjectivism, dominated as it is by modern philosophy, which has as its father Immanuel Kant.

"We are both theist," he urged. "We believe in the same God. We believe in the objective existence of God. God is not merely a 'projection' or a 'limiting concept' as he is for the modern subjectivist. We surely ought to be able to defend our common doctrine of God together against those whose God is only 'in their minds.'

"We both believe in creation. In particular we both believe in man's creation in the image of God.

"Have we not the creeds of the early church in common? We both believe in historic Christianity. Surely we ought to be able to defend together the doctrines of creation, of providence, of the actual historicity of the life and death and resurrection of Jesus of Nazareth against those for whom Christ is nothing more than an ideal."

In some such fashion as this the priest spoke to our young pastor, explaining to him the great importance of Thomas Aquinas to the defense of Christianity. The pastor agreed to read the arguments for the existence of God formulated by St. Thomas in his *On the Truth of the Catholic Faith* (*Summa Contra Gentiles*) so that he might see how "reasonable" Christianity can be shown to be even to those who do not accept the authority either of the church or of the Scripture. He agreed also to read some of the books of such men as Etienne Gilson and Jacques Maritain, both modern Catholic philosophers.

On a later occasion, our pastor asked the priest to clarify one point for him. "Just why do I need authority and faith of any sort," he said, "if theism and even Christianity can be shown to be reasonable without them?" The priest answered that Thomas had really already answered this question, as he had shown that by reason we can only know what God *is not*. Since *all human knowledge starts from sensation,* the intellect must draw general principles from the infinite multitude of such sensations. This being the case, man attains no *positive* knowledge of God in this manner. Rather, he is only able to follow the "way of remotion" (*via remotionis* or *via negative*) whereby, in terms of the knowledge which he has, he is able to say something about God by saying what God is not. We must say, God is *not* finite; for he does *not* have a body. He has, in short, none of the limitations of man. But to this "way of remotion" must be added the "way of eminence." We must say that God is perfect in that in which man is imperfect. But if we are to make all the positive assertions about God made in Christianity, we need the authority of the church for doing so. It is not *against* reason but it is *above* reason to assert that God is triune. Granted we may say something positive about God's perfections, it still remains that we cannot assert such "mysteries" as the incarnation except on authority.

We must therefore show men, whose criterion of judgment is their own reason, that they can by themselves see that they need to believe in God as the Creator and controller of the universe. Theism is the best explanation of the facts of the world. It does better justice to the *facts* known by science than do such positions as pantheism or deism. Theism is also in better accord with *logic* than are other positions. When men have seen that theism is more probably true than other positions because it is in better accord with both fact and logic, then they will readily allow that in the realm of mystery which enshrouds all men, it is authority that must speak.

After this "clarification" by the priest our pastor was still wondering whether he could thus escape the battle of the experts. Was the priest really helping him to help himself? Or was the church, and more particularly the Pope, the expert, surrounded by a mystery which it is impossible for any man to penetrate? If natural revelation is only sufficiently clear so that at best it can merely furnish grounds for a *probable* conclusion about God's existence, and can only tell us what God is *not,* how can it be reasonable to accept the "mysteries" of the faith on authority? Does not faith then stand for acceptance on authority of those assertions which no one can know? And if so, then how can we show the "unbeliever" that our "objective" position is any better than his "subjective" one? If authority cannot be shown to be an indispensable foundation of knowledge, how can it do any good at all? If the voice of God is not so basic as the presupposition of human knowledge in the sense that all human knowledge must be built upon that knowledge which God gives to man regarding himself, man, and the world, then how can it be said to be the voice of God at all? Is the voice of God indispensable if man can live consistently and intelligibly without it?

III.   *Reformed Apologetics—Calvin's Institutes*

Our pastor then turned to some of the writings of the Reformers. With some care he read the first book of Calvin's *Institutes.* Certain very obvious features at once struck him about Calvin's position.

A.   *The Clarity of Revelation*

He noted that Calvin, following Paul, insists on the *clarity* of natural (or general) revelation.

The final goal of the blessed life, moreover, rests in the knowledge of God (cf. John 17:3). Lest anyone, then, be excluded from access to happiness, he not only sowed in men's minds that seed of religion of which we have spoken but revealed himself and daily discloses himself in the whole workmanship of the universe. As a consequence, men cannot open their eyes without being compelled to see him. Indeed, his essence is incomprehensible; hence, his divineness far escapes all human perception. But upon his individual works he has engraved unmistakable marks of his glory, so clear and so prominent that even unlettered and stupid folk cannot plead the excuse of ignorance (Bk. I, Chapter 5, Section 1).[1]

In other words, what Scripture emphasizes is that even apart from special revelation, men *ought* to see that God is the Creator of the world.

Even the curse of God, resting upon creation because of the sin of man, does not subtract from the clarity of his revelation in nature. If the wicked are not forthwith punished for their sin and if the righteous suffer, men ought not to conclude that God cannot be known or that his revelation is obscure. They ought rather to conclude both that the final judgment day will even out the "irregularities" of history and that the longsuffering of God should not be counted as slackness.

In short, our pastor noted that Calvin, with Augustine, would think of God as one thinks of the sun. All other lights in this world are derived from the sun. One does not first think of other lights as though they shone in their own power, in order after that to investigate open-mindedly *whether* the sun exists. So one cannot *first* think of the facts of the universe, and especially of the mind of man, as though they were possibly not God-dependent but self-sufficient as so many self-powered light bulbs, in order then to inquire whether God exists. One just does not look at light bulbs to find the sun. Knowledge of the sun must precede, and be the foundation of, light bulbs. So one does not look at creation to find a Creator, but rather the latter is the foundation of the former. Therefore true knowledge of creation demands a true knowledge of the Creator.

All the facts of the universe are of necessity God-created, God-dependent facts. Therefore men *ought* to see that God is man's Creator and his Judge. "For the invisible things of him from the creation of the world are clearly seen, being understood by the things that are made, even his eternal power and Godhead; so that they are without excuse" (Rom. 1:20).

Of special importance in this connection is Calvin's view of the *sensus deitatis*. Says Calvin:

> There is within the human mind, and indeed by natural instinct, an awareness of divinity. This we take to be beyond controversy. To prevent anyone from taking refuge in the pretense of ignorance, God himself has implanted in all men a certain understanding of his divine majesty. Ever renewing its memory, he repeatedly sheds fresh drops. Since, therefore, men one and all perceive that there is a God and that he is their Maker, they are condemned by their own testimony because they have failed to honor him and to consecrate their lives to his will (I. 3, 1).

> Indeed, even idolatry is ample proof of this conception. We know how man does not willingly humble himself so as to place other creatures over himself. Since, then, he prefers to worship wood and stone rather than to be thought of as having no God, clearly this is a most vivid impression of a divine being. So impossible is it to blot this from man's mind that natural disposition would be more easily altered, as altered indeed it is when man voluntarily sinks from his natural haughtiness to the very depths in order to honor God! (I. 3,1).

> I confess, indeed, that in order to hold men's minds in greater subjection, clever men have devised very many things in religion by which to inspire the common folk with reverence and to strike them with terror. But they would never have achieved this if men's minds had not already been imbued with a firm conviction about God, from which the inclination toward religion springs as from a seed. . . . If, indeed, there were some in the past, and today not a few appear, who deny that God exists, yet willy-nilly they from time to time feel an inkling of what they desire not to believe. . . . Indeed, they seek out every subterfuge to hide themselves from the Lord's presence, and to efface it again from their minds. But in spite of themselves they are always entrapped. Although it may sometimes seem to vanish for a moment, it returns at once and rushes in with new force (I. 3, 2).

Men of sound judgment will always be sure that a sense of divinity which can never be effaced is engraved upon men's minds. Indeed, the perversity of the impious, who though they struggle furiously are unable to extricate themselves from the fear of God, is abundant testimony that this conviction, namely, that there is some God, is naturally inborn in all, and is fixed deep within, as it were in the very marrow . . . the world (something will have to be said of this a little later) tries as far as it is able to cast away all knowledge of God, and by every means to corrupt the worship of him. I only say that though the stupid harshness in their minds, which the impious eagerly conjure up to reject God, wastes away, yet the sense of divinity, which they greatly wished to have extinguished, thrives and presently burgeons (I. 3, 3).

Experience teaches that the seed of religion has been divinely planted in all men. But barely one man in a hundred can be found who nourishes in his own heart what he has conceived; and not even one in whom it matures, much less bears fruit in its season [cf. Ps. 1.3]. Now some lose themselves in their own superstition, while others of their own evil intention revolt from God, yet all fall away from true knowledge of him. . . . Indeed, vanity joined with pride can be detected in the fact that, in seeking God, miserable men do not rise above themselves as they should, but measure him by the yardstick of their own carnal stupidity, and neglect sound investigation; thus out of curiosity they fly off into empty speculations. They do not therefore apprehend God as he offers himself, but imagine him as they have fashioned him in their own presumption. . . . Indeed, whatever they afterward attempt by way of worship or service of God, they cannot bring as tribute to him, for they are worshiping not God but a figment and a dream of their own heart. Paul eloquently notes this wickedness; "Striving to be wise, they make fools of themselves" [Rom. 1:22 p.] He had said before that that "they became futile in their thinking" (Rom. 1:21). In order, however, that no one might excuse their guilt, he adds that they are justly blinded. For not content with sobriety but claiming for themselves more than is right, they wantonly bring darkness upon themselves—in fact, they become fools in their empty and perverse haughtiness. From this it follows that their stupidity is not excusable, since it is caused not only by vain curiosity but by an inordinate desire to know more than is fitting, joined with a false confidence (I. 4, 1).

This sense of deity and seed of religion is God making himself known to man directly in his own constitution. Man is, and always remains, God's self-conscious creature. It was in the activity of the mind of man that God's revelation in the created universe originally found its consummation. Hence, in the very activity of his own personality, man is confronted with the clearest manifestation of the truth concerning himself outside of redemptive revelation.

B. *The Place of Scripture*

The second very obvious feature of Calvin's *Institutes* noted by our pastor is the place assigned to Scripture. On the basis of present general revelation alone, no one actually knows God truly as Creator. Hence the need of Scripture.

> Now, in order that true religion may shine upon us, we ought to hold that it must take its beginning from heavenly doctrine and that no one can get even the slightest taste of right and sound doctrine unless he be a pupil of Scripture. Hence, there also emerges the beginning of true understanding when we reverently embrace what it pleases God there to witness of himself (I. 6, 2).

Even the world of natural and historical fact with which science deals cannot be truly interpreted by anyone who is not a Christian.

Combining these two points, the clear revelation of God is the universe, both in man's environment and in man himself, and God's revelation in Scripture produces a remarkable result. According to the first point, which is based on Paul's letter to the Romans, every man knows God. No one can help but know God. Self-consciousness immediately involves *God*-consciousness. According to the second point, no one knows God except through Scripture. No one even knows any fact of nature for what it is, as created, directed, and controlled by God, except through Scripture. No one knows how to combine "logic" and "fact" aright in the universe except through revelation.

Both points set Calvin's position over against that of Aquinas. The first does so by stressing the fact that wherever he looks man is naturally and unavoidably confronted with the face of God. It is only by suppressing the truth that man can be said "not to know" the truth. Man cannot be a sinner against God unless he knows God in the sense of Romans 1. On the other hand, man cannot be rescued from sin, i.e., unless he knows God in a saving sense through the death and resurrection of Christ applied to him by the regeneration of the Holy Spirit.

According to Aquinas, the creation of man in the image of God does *not* mean that man unavoidably knows God. The revelation of God round about and within man is *not* so clear as to make it impossible for man not to know God, and himself as the creature of God. Man does full justice to the evidence within and about him if he merely concludes that God *probably* exists. Aquinas argued that man's knowledge begins with sensation. There is in this knowledge of God derived from sensation an inherent uncertainty. We can only be certain of what God *is not.* Any positive statement about God on the basis of natural revelation must, in the nature of the case, be a subjective projection and as such must be uncertain. Finite man cannot be expected to have, through natural revelation, any certain knowledge about God. Ignorance of God is not blameworthy. Why should man be accountable for knowing God and God's requirement for man, if God has not clearly revealed himself to man?

Calvin's point concerning the absolute necessity of Scripture also sets off his position from that of Aquinas. Since man's ignorance of God is blameworthy, this ignorance can be removed by nothing else than the redeeming work of Christ. Only Scripture as the word of Christ reports God's work of redemption in Christ. Only through the mirror of Scripture, therefore, can general revelation be seen for what it is.

For Aquinas, on the other hand, Scripture occupies no such important place. It is not indispensable for the right interpretation of nature. Ignorance of God is not necessarily, at least not exclusively, the result of a misinterpretation of nature. Ignorance of God is inherent in human nature as finite. Hence this ignorance is not exclusively culpable ignorance. The Bible as the message of redemption is not necessary for man's proper interpretation of natural revelation.

C. *The Necessity of the Testimony of the Holy Spirit*

The third obvious feature about Calvin's *Institutes* noted by our pastor is its stress on the necessity of the testimony of the Holy Spirit in the heart of man if he is to receive the Scripture as the Word of God.

> Special revelation, or Scripture in its documented form, provides in point of fact in the view of Calvin, only the objective side of the cure he finds has been provided by God. The subjective side is provided by the *testimonium Spirit Sancti*. The spectacles are provided by the Scriptures: the eyes are opened that they may see even through these specatcles, only by the witness of the Spirit in the heart.[2]

It is not that the Scriptures, in Calvin's view, do not clearly manifest themselves to be the Word of God. On the contrary, "Scripture exhibits fully as clear evidence of its own truth as white and black things do of their color, or sweet and bitter things do of their taste" (I. 7, 2; cf. I. 7, 5). The heavenly nature of its doctrine, the consent of its parts, the majesty of its style, the antiquity of its teaching, the sincerity of its narrative, its miraculous accompaniment, circumstantially confirmed, its continuous use through many ages, its sealing by martyrs' blood, clearly indicate the divinity of Scripture. Even so the words of Scripture "will not find acceptance in men's hearts before it is sealed by the inward testimony of the Spirit. The same Spirit, therefore, who has spoken through the mouths of the prophets must penetrate into our hearts to persuade us that they faithfully proclaimed what had been divinely commanded" (I. 7, 4).

> Some good folk are annoyed that a clear proof is not ready at hand when the impious, unpunished, murmur against God's Word. As if the Spirit were not called both "seal" and "guarantee" [II Cor. 1:22] for confirming the faith of the godly; because until he illumines their minds, they ever waver among many doubts! (I. 7, 4).

> Let this point therefore stand: that those whom the Holy Spirit has inwardly taught truly rest upon Scripture, and that Scripture indeed is self-authenticated; hence, it is not right to subject it to proof and reasoning. And the certainty it deserves with us, it attains by the testimony of the Spirit. For even if it wins reverence for itself by its own majesty, it seriously affects us only when it is sealed upon our hearts through the Spirit. Therefore,

illumined by his power, we believe neither by our own nor by anyone else's judgment that Scripture is from God; but above human judgment we affirm with utter certainty (just as if we were gazing upon the majesty of God himself) that it has flowed to us from the very mouth of God by the ministry of men. We seek no proofs, no marks of genuineness upon which our judgment may lean; but we subject our judgment and wit to it as to a thing far beyond any guesswork! (I. 7, 5).

If now this third point be added to the first two, the following result is obtained: Natural revelation is perfectly clear. Men *ought* from it to know God and ought through it to see all other things as dependent on God. But only he who looks at nature through the mirror of Scripture *does* understand natural revelation for what it is. Furthermore, no one can see Scripture for what it is unless he is given the ability to do so by the regenerating power of the Holy Spirit. Only those who are taught of God see the Scriptures for what they are and therefore see the revelation of God in nature for what it is. To be taught of God is a "singular privilege" which God bestows only on his "elect whom he distinguishes from the human race as a whole." As taught of God, the elect both understand the Bible as the Word of God, and interpret natural revelation through the Bible. The rest of mankind, not taking Scripture as the Word of God, in consequence also misinterpret the natural revelation of God.

If God has willed this treasure of understanding to be hidden from his children, it is no wonder or absurdity that the multitude of men are so ignorant and stupid! Among the "multitude" I include even certain distinguished folk, until they become engrafted into the body of the church. Besides, Isaiah, warning that the prophetic teaching would be beyond belief, not only to foreigners but also to the Jews who wanted to be reckoned as members of the Lord's household, at the same time adds the reason: "The arm of God will not be revealed" to all [Isa. 53:1 p.] Whenever, then, the fewness of believers disturbs us, let the converse come to mind, that only to those to whom it is given can comprehend the mysteries of God [cf. Matt. 13:11] (I. 7, 5).

By this time our pastor has become aware of a radical difference between the approach of Calvin and that of Aquinas!

In the first place there is a basic difference concerning the nature of revelation. For Calvin, revelation is always and everywhere clear. The facts of natural revelation, both within and about man, are so clearly revelatory of God that he who runs may read. The *indicia divinitatis* (marks of divinity) of Scripture are equally clear. In fact, the revelation of God to man is so clear that no man can help but know God. Thus man is *from the beginning* in contact with the truth. Moreover, he cannot separate the *existence* of God from the *character* of God. The intelligibility of anything, for man, presupposes the existence of God—the God whose nature and character are delineated in God's revelation, found both in nature and in Scripture. It is this God—the only God—whom all men, of necessity "know."

Over against this idea of revelation, as clearly and exclusively based upon, and expressive of, the idea of the Creator-creature distinction, stands that of Aquinas. According to Aquinas the revelation of God to man is not inherently clear. As finite man lives on the verge of non-being;[3] and as such a mixture, man's knowledge is derived from the senses. Man is also, therefore, enmeshed in an environment which is not *exclusively* determined by the plan of God, but rather a combination of the forces of God and of chaos.[4] Accordingly, Aquinas thinks that man can intelligently discuss the question of the existence of God without at the same time presupposing the nature of God as revealed in Scripture. Thus the attitude of doubt with respect to the existence of God is assumed to be legitimate. Ignorance is not basically culpable.

Involved in this original separation of the existence and the nature of God is the idea that for man, the nature of God is not exclusively determined by the revelation of God. The nature of God is, in part, determined by man himself.

It is thus that the scholastic notion of natural theology is born. If man, without special revelation, partly determines the nature of God, then this nature of God is, to an extent, defined by the supposed demands of logic and fact, as man knows these independently of the revelation of God. Thus the distinction between the revelation of God *to* man and the interpretation of this revelation *by* man is obscured. *Natural revelation* then tends to be identified with *natural theology.* This idea of natural theology assumes that without Scripture and the testimony of the Spirit men generally can have a measure of morally and spiritually acceptable knowledge of God. It assumes that there can be an interpretation of the natural revelation of God with which both believers and unbelievers are in basic agreement.

The difference between the knowledge of the Christian and the knowledge of the non-Christian consists, then, primarily by the former being more comprehensive than the latter. The Christian *adds* to his knowledge of facts obtained by his own empirical research without reference to Scripture, the information about these facts that he gets from supernatural revelation. On the Thomistic basis the difference between the knowledge of the Christian and the knowledge of the non-Christian is primarily quantitative. To be sure, according to Thomas, sin has *wounded* the natural capacities of man. Accordingly the supernatural must, to some extent, be *remedial* as well as supplementative. This fact, however, does not change the fact that for Thomas supernatural revelation is *primarily* supplementative.

Aquinas thinks of the position of Calvin as being *rationalistic* because he holds that man unavoidably, by virtue of his innate knowledge of God, is in contact with the truth. If all men do of necessity know God, Aquinas would reason, then how could they be responsible for seeking out God in the world? How could they be responsible creatures in the sight of God? Aquinas therefore insists that man is only *potentially,* and not necessarily, in contact with the truth about God.

On the other hand, Aquinas thinks of Calvin's position as being *irrationalistic* because he says that none but the elect, after the entrance of sin, can be said to have any morally or spiritually acceptable knowledge of God. Aquinas would say that *all* men have this truth potentially, but not all realize the full development of this knowledge. Aquinas is concerned, therefore, about *cultivation,* while Calvin is concerned about *implantation* of the grace and knowledge of God, and only after that about its implementation.

Calvin thinks of the position of Aquinas as being *irrationalistic,* because it is not clearly and exclusively from the outset based upon the distinction between God as Creator and man as creature. Any position that is clearly based upon this distinction, Calvin would say, must regard the image of God in man as implying the idea of inherent knowledge of God. It is only this inherent and unavoidable content of human knowledge that makes it possible to avoid scepticism and to hold man responsible for sin. Without this idea of the unavoidability of the knowledge of God on the part of man, it is always possible for man to make an excuse for not knowing God. Herein is the irrationalism of Aquinas.

Secondly, Calvin thinks of Aquinas' position as being *rationalistic* because it assigns to the mind of man the ability to determine to some extent the nature of God apart from the contents of divine revelation. If the knowledge of *God's* nature is not from the outset given with the knowledge of *man's* nature as the creation of God, then it is up to man to determine the nature of both God and man for himself apart from revelation. Man is therefore left to his own devices and determines a "way which seems right unto man."

In the third place, man is also responsible, to some extent, for determining the nature of sin. Thus sin cannot, on Aquinas' position, be "want of conformity to, or transgression of, the law of God" which God has, on the basis of his nature, given to man, but is rather the transgression of that which is "right in his own eyes." The only revelation of himself and his laws which God may give man, therefore, must be in terms of what man has by his own logic and experience already said about God, religion, and morality. God must listen to man before man listens to God.

To be sure, Aquinas does not carry out this point of view with such consistency. But, since he assigns to the mind of man, some measure of ability to determine the nature of both God and man, apart from being taught of God through Scripture and the testimony of the Spirit, God is no longer the sovereign God of mankind.

D. *Common Grace*

The fourth point taken note of by our pastor from the general teaching of Calvin's *Institutes* is the doctrine of "common grace." When he had analyzed the first three points, our pastor expected that Calvin would deny that those not taught of God by the Scriptures and the testimony of the Holy Spirit could know *anything* about God. But then he reminded himself of the fact that Calvin started out with a discussion of natural revelation before he touched on the doctrine of Scripture. In particular, he recalled the fact that Calvin insisted that *all men naturally know God and cannot efface this knowledge of God*. But how, then, account for the categorical statements of Calvin about the universality of the spiritual ignorance of God in all mankind? Does he not say of mankind in general that in the place of the idea of God they have substituted figments of their imagination? Does he not say that men have not a *particle* of knowledge unless they are taught of Scripture?

Does Calvin then teach that all men know, and, at the same time and in the same sense, do not know God? Our pastor soon discovered that Calvin does not thus flatly contradict himself. When Calvin says that only the elect know God, he defines his knowledge by saying:

> Now, the knowledge of God, as I understand it, is that by which we not only conceive that there is a God but also grasp what befits us and is proper to his glory, in fine, what is to our advantage to know of him. Indeed, we shall not say that, properly speaking, God is known where there is no religion or piety.

It is this kind of knowledge that man would have had if Adam had remained upright. But since Adam did not remain upright, no man has such knowledge "until Christ the Mediator comes forward" to make his peace (I. 2, 1).

What then of the generality of men that are not taught of God through Christ and his Spirit? Must it be said, since they have not this "saving knowledge" of God which comes through Christ, that they have no knowledge of God at all? Must it first be shown to them, in terms of a theory of knowledge and reality which they have devised without this knowledge of God, that it is *possible* for them, according to their own principles, to come to the knowledge of God? If so, then why must men be taught by the Christ who has revealed God? Must it be shown to them that in terms of their own principles it is possible for them to learn about the Christ? If so, then must not men *first* teach the Christ of God and the world before the Christ can teach them? Must they be told that in terms of their own principles they can see the need for the regenerating power of the Spirit as a prerequisite to understanding the Scriptures, knowing the Christ and thus coming to God? If so, then why is the Holy Spirit necessary to convict men of sin, of righteousness, and of judgment?

All these questions must, therefore, be answered in the negative. For to answer them in the affirmative would mean that though man as a finite being is not in contact with the truth, that though he be floating in an infinity of Chance, yet he *might* find the truth. If on this basis he would find the truth, it would be because he, by accident, had "hit upon it." When thus hitting upon it, he would "hit upon" a god who is himself afloat in the bottomless ocean of Chance. It would not be the God of the Scriptures at all.

Accordingly Calvin argues that though mankind generally does not have the knowledge that comes from being "taught of God," men do have a knowledge that is created within them and inherited from Adam. It is the knowledge which they have as image bearers of God. Men generally seek to suppress this knowledge of God. They would gladly live where the searchlight of God's revelation does not constantly expose them to themselves. But there is no such place. This searchlight never ceases to shine. It shines particularly *within them*. There is no hiding from it. The knowledge of God is infixed in their being. Hence,

> If for these there is any respite from anxiety of conscience, it is not much different from the sleep of drunken or frenzied persons, who do not rest peacefully even while sleeping because they are continually troubled with dire and dreadful dreams. The impious themselves therefore exemplify the fact that some conception of God is ever alive in all men's minds (I. 3, 2).

> Although Diagoras and his like may jest at whatever has been believed in every age concerning religion, and Dionysius may mock the heavenly judgment, this is sardonic laughter, for the worm of conscience, sharper than any cauterizing iron, gnaws away within (I. 3, 3).

Men in general are, therefore, truth *suppressors*. They are not those who are first of all *without* knowledge of the truth. They are indeed such, if one thinks of the knowledge that must come from

Scripture. But they are first of all truth *possessors,* or truth-knowers, who have, by sinning, become truth *suppressors.* Having taken to themselves the right to define the nature of God and of themselves, they have mingled the idea of their new god with that of the God they know by virtue of their creation. In their natural theology, that is, in what, as sinful men, they set forth as their view about God, they never state the truth without adulteration. They do not completely succeed in suppressing the truth, but they never assert the truth without an overwhelming admixture of error. The god of the philosophers is *never* their Creator and the Creator of the universe. He is always of necessity bound up with his creation. Hence sinful unregenerate men never worship the true God as they ought. In practice they do not know him because when they think of him they, of necessity, think falsely of him; they always degrade him to the level of the creature.

But now, says Calvin, God does not allow this process of degradation to go on to its full expression. The Holy Spirit continues to appeal to men to return to God. And though God may, in punishment for their sin, allow men to fall into ever deeper sin, he never utterly ignores them. He keeps calling men back to himself. "Accordingly, the knowledge of ourselves not only arouses us to seek God, but also, as it were, leads us by the hand to find him" (I. 1, 1). God does not allow men wholly to suppress "that which nature itself permits no one to forget, although many strive with every nerve to this end" (I. 3, 3). God sees to it that it is more difficult to obliterate his impression from the mind of man than to alter our "natural disposition" (I. 3, 1). Though the world "tries as far as it is able to cast away all knowledge of God" and though of all things they most wish to extinguish the sense of deity within them, they never fully succeed in doing so (I. 3, 3).

This maintenance of the sense of deity within men in spite of their most desperate acts of suppression is coupled with the idea that they continue to receive from God his boutiful gifts. God is not man's Creator without as such also being his bountiful benefactor:

> Let us rememember, whenever each of us contemplates his own nature, that there is one God who so governs all natures that he

would have us look unto him, direct our faith to him, and worship and call upon him. For nothing is more preposterous than to enjoy the very remarkable gifts that attest the divine nature within us, yet to overlook the Author who gives them to us at our asking. With what clear manifestations his might draws us to contemplate him! (I. 5, 6).

. . . the prophet shows that what are thought to be chance occurrences are just so many proofs of heavenly providence, especially of fatherly kindness (I. 5, 8).

Consequently, we know the most perfect way of seeking God, and the most suitable order, is not for us to attempt with bold curiosity to penetrate to the investigation of his essence, which we ought more to adore than meticulously to search out, but for us to contemplate him in his works whereby he renders himself near and familiar to us, and in some manner communicates himself. The apostle was referring to this when he said that we need not seek him far away, seeing that he dwells by his very present power in each of us [Acts 17:27-28]. For this reason, David, having first confessed his unspeakable greatness [Ps. 145:3], afterward proceeds to mention his works and professes that he will declare his greatness [Ps. 145:5-6; cf. Ps. 40:5]. It is also fitting, therefore, for us to pursue this particular search for God, which may so hold our mental powers suspended in wonderment as at the same time to stir us deeply. And as Augustine teaches elsewhere, because, disheartened by his greatness, we cannot grasp him, we ought to gaze upon his works, that we may be restored by his goodness (I. 5, 9).

For with regard to the most beautiful structure and order of the universe, how many of us are there who, when we lift up our eyes to heaven or cast them about through the various regions of earth, recall our minds to a remembrance of the Creator, and do not rather, disregarding their Author, sit idly in contemplation of his works? In fact, with regard to those events which daily take place outside the ordinary course of nature, how many of us do not reckon that men are whirled and twisted about by blindly indiscriminate fortune, rather than governed by God's providence? Sometimes we are driven by the leading and direction of these things to contemplate God; this of necessity happens to all men. Yet after we rashly grasp a conception of some sort of divinity, straightway we fall back into the ravings or evil imaginings of our flesh, and corrupt by our vanity the pure truth of God.

In one respect we are indeed unalike, because each one of us privately forges his own particular error; yet we are very much alike in that, one and all, we forsake the one true God for prodigious trifles. Not only the common folk and dull-witted men, but also the most excellent and those otherwise endowed with keen discernment, are infected with this disease (I. 5. 11).

It is therefore in vain that so many burning lamps shine for us in the workmanship of the universe to show forth the glory of its Author. Although they bathe us wholly in their radiance, yet they can of themselves in no way lead us into the right path. . . . For this reason, the apostle, in that very passage where he calls the worlds the images of things invisible, adds that through faith we understand that they have been fashioned by God's word [Heb. 11:3]. He means by this that the invisible divinity is made manifest in such spectacles, but that we have not the eyes to see this unless they be illumined by the inner revelation of God through faith. . . . Therefore, although the Lord does not want for testimony while he sweetly attracts men to the knowledge of himself with many and varied kindnesses, they do not cease on this account to follow their own ways, that is, their fatal errors (I. 5, 14).

In particular Calvin notes that those perfections which are frequently ascribed to God in Scripture are also manifested as "shining in heaven."

Now we hear the same powers enumerated there that we have noted as shining in heaven and earth: kindness, goodness, mercy, justice, judgment, and truth. For power and might are contained under the title *Elohim*.

By the same epithets also the prophets designate him when they wish to display his holy name to the full. That we may not be compelled to assemble many instances, at present let one psalm [Ps. 145] suffice for us, in which the sum of all his powers is so precisely reckoned up that nothing would seem to have been omitted [esp. Ps. 145:5]. And yet nothing is set down there that cannot be beheld in his creatures. Indeed, with experience as our teacher we find God just as he declares himself in his Word (I. 10, 2).

Now, those not "taught of Christ," sometimes in spite of themselves, speak "from a real feeling of nature, as if content with a single God (I. 10, 3). When they thus speak, they "simply use the name god as if they had thought one God sufficient." It is not their "natural theology"—the interpretations usually given by men of the revelation of God—which has in it any particle of truth.

> But all the heathen, to a man, by their own vanity either were dragged or slipped back into false inventions, and thus their perceptions so vanished that whatever they had naturally sensed concerning the sole God had no value beyond making them inexcusable.... As we have already said elsewhere, all the evasions the philosophers have skillfully contrived do not refute the charge of defection; rather, the truth of God has been corrupted by them all. For this reason, Habakkuk, when he condemned all idols, bade men seek God "in his temple" [Hab. 2:20] lest believers admit someone other than him who revealed himself by his Word (I. 10, 3).

The "light of nature," and the "law of their being," speak to men of God, as the bountiful benefactor of mankind calling them back to himself. In the face of this inescapable wooing of God to forsake their rebellion against God,

> man's mind, full as it is of pride and boldness, dares to imagine a god according to its own capacity; as it sluggishly plods, indeed is overwhelmed with the crassest ignorance, it conceives an unreality and an empty appearance as God (I. 11, 8).

Naturally then, Calvin could not do what Aquinas had done with respect to the knowledge of unbelievers. He could not think of taking the Aristotelian view of the analogy of being[5] as an essentially true interpretation of reality. The philosophy of Aristotle, like the philosophy of any of those not "taught by Christ," offers no concepts that are essentially sound. All the concepts of such a philosophy are based upon the assumption that God and the cosmos are aspects of one reality subject to the same laws. The god of Aristotle as well as the god of Plato, in fact, the god of any non-Christian philosopher, is a god constructed by the rebellious mind of man in the interest of suppressing the truth.

This does not mean that no use whatsoever can be made of the interpretations given by non-Christian men of the facts of God's revelation to them. Although not according to their innate principle of rebellion against God but *in spite of it,* when the "light of nature," the revelation of God, shines through to them in spite of themselves, they have been able to speak much truth.

The "idea that God is the soul of the world" is "the most tolerable that philosophers have suggested" (I. 14, 1). However, such a basic interpretation of the world given by fallen man is immanentistic.

In spite of this fact we may freely learn from "secular writers" about many things (I. 15, 2). Though what remains in man of the image of God after his fall into sin is a "frightful deformity" (I. 15, 4), "though nothing remains after the ruin except what is confused, mutilated, and disease ridden" (I. 15, 4), though philosophers, since they do not distinguish between man as he was before, and as he is after, the fall, "mistakenly confuse two very diverse states of man" (I. 15, 7); we may profitably listen to them, especially when they turn their "attention to things below" (II. 2, 13). For all men are under the power of God "whether their minds are to be conciliated, or their malice to be restrained that it may not do harm" (I. 17, 7).

> . . . soundness of mind and uprightness of heart were withdrawn at the same time. This is the corruption of the natural gifts. For even though something of understanding and judgment remains as a residue along with the will, yet we shall not call a mind whole and sound that is both weak and plunged into deep darkness. And depravity of the will is all too well known.

> Since reason, therefore, by which man distinguishes between good and evil, and by which he understands and judges, is a natural gift, it could not be completely wiped out; but it was partly weakened and partly corrupted, so that its misshapen ruins appear. . . .

> Similarly the will, because it is inseparable from man's nature, did not perish, but was so bound to wicked desires that it cannot strive after the right. This is, indeed, a complete definition, but one needing a fuller explanation.

> . . . When we so condemn human understanding for its perpetual blindness as to leave it no perception of any object whatever, we not only go against God's Word, but also run counter to the experience of common sense. For we see implanted in human

nature some sort of desire to search out the truth to which man would not at all aspire if he had not already savored it. Human understanding then possesses some power of perception, since it is by nature captivated by love of truth. . . . Yet this longing for truth, such as it is, languishes before it enters upon its race because it soon falls into vanity. Indeed, man's mind, because of its dullness, cannot hold to the right path, but wanders through various errors and stumbles repeatedly, as if it were groping in darkness, until it strays away and finally disappears. Thus it betrays how incapable it is of seeking and finding truth (II. 2, 12).

. . . This, then, is the distinction: that there is one kind of understanding of earthly things; another of heavenly. I call "earthly things" those which do not pertain to God or his Kingdom, to true justice, or to the blessedness of the future life; but which have their significance and relationship with regard to the present life and are, in a sense, confined within its bounds. I call "heavenly things" the pure knowledge of God, the nature of true righteousness, and the mysteries of the Heavenly Kingdom. The first class includes government, household management, all mechanical skills, and the liberal arts. In the second are the knowledge of God and of his will, and the rule by which we conform our lives to it.

Of the first class the following ought to be said: since man is by nature a social animal, he tends through natural instinct to foster and preserve society. Consequently, we observe that there exist in all men's minds universal impressions of a certain civic fair dealing and order. Hence no man is to be found who does not understand that every sort of human organization must be regulated by laws, and who does not comprehend the principles of those laws. Hence arises that unvarying consent of all nations and of individual mortals with regard to laws. For their seeds have, without teacher or lawgiver, been implanted in all men.

I do not dwell upon the dissension and conflicts that immediately spring up. . . . For, while men dispute among themselves about individual sections of the law, they agree on the general conception of equity. In this respect the frailty of the human mind is surely proved: even when it seems to follow the way, it limps and staggers. Yet the fact remains that some seed of political order has been implanted in all men. And this is ample proof that in the arrangement of this life no man is without the light of reason (II. 2, 13).

Whenever we come upon these matters in secular writers, let

that admirable light of truth shining in them teach us that the mind of man, though fallen and perverted from its wholeness, is nevertheless clothed and ornamented with God's excellent gifts. If we regard the Spirit of God as the sole fountain of truth, we shall neither reject the truth itself, nor despise it wherever it shall appear, unless we wish to dishonor the Spirit of God. . . . shall we count anything praiseworthy or noble without recognizing at the same time that it comes from God? Let us be ashamed of such ingratitude, into which not even the pagan poets fell, for they confessed that the gods had invented philosophy, laws, and all useful arts. Those men whom Scripture [I Cor. 2:14] calls "natural men" were, indeed, sharp and penetrating in their investigation of inferior things. Let us, accordingly, learn by their example how many gifts the Lord left to human nature even after it was despoiled of its true good (II. 2, 15).

Meanwhile, we ought not to forget those most excellent benefits of the divine Spirit, which he distributes to whomever he wills, for the common good of mankind. . . . It is no wonder, then, that the knowledge of all that is most excellent in human life is said to be communicated to us through the Spirit of God. Nor is there reason for anyone to ask, What have the impious, who are utterly estranged from God, to do with his Spirit? We ought to understand the statement that the Spirit of God dwells only in believers [Rom. 8:9] as referring to the Spirit of sanctification through whom we are consecrated as temples to God [I Cor. 3:16]. Nonetheless he fills, moves, and quickens all things by the power of the same Spirit, and does so according to the character that he bestowed upon each kind by the law of creation. But if the Lord has willed that we be helped in physics, dialectic, mathematics, and other like disciplines, by the work and ministry of the ungodly, let us use this assistance. For if we neglect God's gift freely offered in these arts, we ought to suffer just punishment for our sloths. But lest anyone think a man truly blessed when he is credited with possessing great power to comprehend truth under the elements of this world [cf. Col. 2:8], we should at once add that all this capacity to understand, with the understanding that follows upon it, is an unstable and transitory thing in God's sight, when a solid foundation of truth does not underlie it. For with the greatest truth Augustine teaches that as the free gifts were withdrawn from man after the Fall, so the natural ones remaining were corrupted (II. 2, 16).

To sum up: We see among all mankind that reason is proper to our nature; it distinguishes us from brute beasts, just as they by possessing feeling differ from inanimate things. Now, because some are born fools or stupid, that defect does not obscure the general grace of God. . . . For why is one person more excellent than another? Is it not to display in common nature God's special grace, which, in passing many by, declares itself bound to none? . . . Still, we see in this diversity some remaining traces of the image of God, which distinguish the entire human race from other creatures (II. 2, 17).

E. *Implications of Calvinism for Apologetics*

From the four points which our pastor saw clearly in Calvin's *Institutes,* it is apparent that:

1. Calvin makes a sharp distinction between the revelation of God to man and man's response to that revelation. This implies the rejection of a natural theology such as Aquinas taught.

2. He makes a sharp distinction between the responses to God's revelation made by:

(a) man in his original condition, i.e., Adam before the Fall;

(b) mankind, whose "understanding is subjected to blindness and the heart to depravity" (II. 1, 9);

(c) those that are "taught of Christ" through Scripture and whose eyes have been opened by the Holy Spirit.

3. These points together indicate an approach to apologetics on the part of Calvin distinct from that of Aquinas. From Calvin's point of view the Romanist position does not do justice to the Christian doctrine of creation.

(a) This indicates, as noted, first: a measure of irrationalism in Romanist thought.

(1) Romanism does not place all the facts of man's environment exclusively under the categories of creation and providence. This implies sympathy for the idea of "brute facts," facts that are not now, or are not yet, interpreted by God. In toning down the biblical doctrines of creation and providence by seeking to combine them with the Aristotelian notion of the analogy of being (that the world is both somehow participant in Being, and participant in non-

Being), Romanism takes away from the clarity of the revelation of God so far as this revelation surrounds man.

(2) Romanism does not think of the image of God in man exclusively in terms of creation and providence and redemption through Christ. It thinks of man, in part at least, in terms of Aristotle's notion of the analogy of being. Accordingly, man is thought of as having an inherent weakness—a bias towards sin. Man, as created, lives on the verge of non-being. On an Aristotelian basis, non-being is evil. Thus the biblical idea of sin, as exclusively ethical in its import, is confused, to some extent, with the idea of sin as inherent in man because of his finitude.

(b) This indicates, secondly, a measure of rationalism in Romanist thought.

(1) In not interpreting man's environment exclusively in terms of creation and providence, Romanism tends to think of the facts of this environment as part of a chain of being which includes God as well as the universe. As the Aristotelian notion of the analogy of being tends on the one hand to the idea of brute fact and therefore to irrationalism, so this same notion tends on the other hand to conceive the difference between eternal and temporal being as merely a gradational one. This again indicates the presence of a measure of rationalism in Romanist thought.

(2) In Romanist thinking, the image of God in man is partly based upon the idea of man's participation in the being of God. Thus man's own constitution is not exclusively revelational of God on a created plane. The idea of participation in the nature of God in part cancels out the idea of God's revealing himself to man within man.

In consequence, too, man's ideal of knowledge would not exclusively be that of re-interpreting God's revelation within and about man. His ideal of knowledge would become, in part, a joint enterprise with God of interpreting Reality. Thus revelation and response to revelation tend to merge into one process of rational inquiry. Thus rationalism appears in the apologetic of Thomas.

Turning these things over in his mind, our pastor realized in a general way that his sympathies lay with Calvin. He began to realize that the difference between Roman Catholic theology and the Reformed faith is an all-pervasive one. He began to realize too that this all-pervasive difference in theology implies a difference in the method of defending Christianity. He sensed in particular that on the Romanist basis he would still be the victim of the battle between experts. There would be no finished revelation available to him. The revelation he would deal with would not be fully clear. And such would be true even for the experts themselves. The Pope himself, though the vicar of Christ, would still be facing the same impenetrable mystery that is inherent in Reality which he, a pastor, faces. The revelation of God would tend to merge with the theology of man. Man would have to shift for himself; he would have no *absolute* authority speaking to him. The Pope, though the vicar of Christ, would tend to be no more than a wiser man than other men.

In particular it appeared to our pastor that on the Romanist position man cannot be thought of as a *covenant* being. Since man is not directly and exclusively dependent upon God in all his knowledge and action, his sin would not be essentially sin against God. Sin would not be the self-conscious breaking of the law of God. It would be in part a failure to live up to the law of his being which participates in the law of the being of God.

There could, on this basis, be no genuine *responsibility* on the part of man in the course of history. Even the plan of God is, on the Romanist view, not all-determinative of the course of history. This plan of God is not all-determinative, because man participates in the being of God. The will of man participates in the nature of the will of God. Hence God could not and did not confront the will of man in Adam with a choice that would bring all men under the condemnation of God. The condemnation of men by God could not depend upon an act of the human will, because the human will is not exclusively a creation of the will of God, and the will of God is not in a position to issue an absolute command to man. Man's will is, on this view, not *exclusively* the will of a creature of God, and therefore it is not, at the beginning of history, a perfect will. Its finitude implies a measure of imperfection.

Furthermore, on the Romanist view, when Adam fell into sin his *intellect* did not become blinded, and his *will* did not become wholly perverse in its intent. Being *already* partly blind by virtue of its finitude, man's fall could not result in intellectual blinding. So also, being partly immersed in non-being, the will could not be wholly perverted by the fall. On the other hand, being partly participant in the *intellect* of God, the *intellect* of man could not lose its inherent measure of divinity. So also the *will* of man, being participant in the *will* of God, could not lose this inherent measure of divinity. In short, to the extent that Romanist thought is patterned after the idea of the analogy of being, man was originally *never* placed high enough to fall very low and *never* fell low enough to need the reaching down of the grace of God for his restoration before he could think or will that which is true and right.

Our pastor could now see that on the view of Calvin the difference between believer and unbeliever as they confront one another may be summarized as follows.

F. *Christian and Non-Christian Views*

1. *Reality*

Both Christians and non-Christians make presuppositions about the *nature of reality*.

a. The Christian presupposes the self-contained God and his plan for the universe as back of all things and therewith the absolute distinction between Creator and creation.

b. The non-Christian presupposes "Chaos and Old Night," or the self-existence of matter in some sense.

2. *Epistemology*

Neither Christian nor non-Christian can, as finite beings, by means of logic, legislate what reality *should* be.

a. Knowing this, the Christian observes facts and arranges them logically in self-conscious subjection to the plan of God revealed in Scripture, i.e., he listens to God's explanation of his relation to the world and man, both in Adam and in Christ, before he "listens" to, and during his observation of, the "facts." He knows that the

fear of the Lord is the *beginning* of wisdom. Assuming the plan of
of God, the Christian knows that the facts have a divine order. The
Christian's task in science is to uncover the God-ordained structure
of the world. For the Christian, man and the world are made for
one another so that the rational abilities of man are applicable to
the world as man seeks to "subdue the earth."

b. Knowing this, the non-Christian, nonetheless, constantly
attempts the impossible by demanding a coherence that originates
with himself.

(1) Negatively, he must assume that reality is not divinely
created and controlled in accordance with God's plan at all, and that
the Christian story therefore cannot be true. The world of "facts"
springs from "Chaos and Old Night"—ultimate Chance.

(2) Positively, he must assume that reality is after all
rationally constituted and answers exhaustively to his logical manipu-
lations. If the world were not rational or "uniform," then there could
be no science. Any "cosmic mind," or God, must therefore be able
to be manipulated by man-made categories. Any God not reducible
to logical or empirical categories, and therefore completely understandable, is a false God.

3. *Facts*

Both Christian and non-Christian claim that their position is "in
accord with the facts of experience."

a. The Christian claims this because he interprets the facts
and his experience of them in terms of his presupposition. The
"uniformity of nature" and his knowledge of that uniformity both
rest for him upon the plan of God. The coherence which he sees in
his experience he takes to be analogical to, and indeed, the result of,
the absolute coherence of God.

b. The non-Christian also interprets the facts in terms of
his presuppositions. On the one hand is the presupposition of ultimate non-rationality. On such a basis, any fact would be different in
all respects from all other facts. There could be no "uniformity," the
foundation of all science. Here is "Chaos and Old Night" with a
vengeance. On the other hand is the presupposition that all reality

is rational in terms of the reach of logic as manipulated by man. On such a basis the nature of any fact would be identical with the nature of every other fact, or, in short, only one big universal fact. There then could be no experience, because there could be no change. All would be a static unity. The non-Christian tries somehow to balance these *contradictions*. While in the first place he tells us he can never as much as discover *any* fact, or know anything of its nature, he in the second place after he *has discovered* what he *cannot discover*, turns around and tells us everything about it. On his principles he knows everything if he knows anything, though at the same time he *cannot* know anything; but he does know *some*thing, which means he knows *every*thing.

4. *Logic*

Each claims that his position is "in accord with the demands of logic."

a. The Christian claims this because he interprets the reach of logic as manipulated by man, in terms of God's revelation of the relation of man to the world and therefore in terms of his presupposition of God. Genesis tells him that nature is made subject to man, and both are subject to God and his purpose. Thus his logic is in gear with reality, but it does not claim to control God himself and therewith all possibility.

b. The non-Christian claims that his position is logical but cannot put any intelligible meaning into the claim. If he works according to his presupposition about the ultimate non-rationality of facts, then all logic operates in a void. It has no contact with the world. If he works according to his presupposition of the ultimacy of all facts, then all facts are reduced to logic and thereby destroyed because they lose their individuality; logic has a validity that is, therefore, purely formal. It could only be a logic of identity, merely saying *A* is *A*, for all would be one.

5. *Evil*

Each claims that with respect to the problem of evil his position is in accord with conscience.

a. The Christian claims this because he interprets his moral consciousness, an aspect of his total experience, in terms of his presupposition. He knows that the judge of the whole earth must do right. All the facts and problems of evil and sin take their meaning from, and find their solution in, terms of the plan of God according to Scripture. The approvals and disapprovals of his conscience take their meaning from the Word of God and from it alone.

b. The non-Christian claims this because he takes his conscience to be its own ultimate point of reference. Evil has not come into the world because of man's disobedience; it is metaphysically ultimate, i.e., it just is! Evil cannot, ultimately, be distinguished from good; what is, ought to be. Even assuming that good could be distinguished from evil, there is no right to expect that the one will ever be victorious over the other. If those who think they are good succeed in making what they think is "good" prevail upon earth, it can be only by the suppression of the "good" of others who also think they are "good." Thus power politics will forever replace all ethical distinctions.

Our Reformed pastor saw, therefore, that for Calvin the Christian lives above all by the authority of the Scripture message. If then a non-Christian should urge our pastor to take off his "rose-colored glasses" and look at the cosmos "with the naked eye of reason," or should appeal to conscience to refute the interpretation of human experience as given in Scripture, our pastor knows that to do so would be to take the ground from under his own feet. Reason would then be truly "naked" or formal; its assertions would be as meaningless as the gyrations of a propeller of an airplane engine without the airplane. If facts could be said to exist at all, they would be utterly interchangeable with one another. The appeal to a man's conscience would be as useless and hopeless as it was in the case of Charles Strickland in W. Somerset Maugham's story of *The Moon and Sixpence*.

Our pastor now sees that it is only in Reformed theology that we have a method of apologetics that meets the requirements of the hour. It alone challenges the natural man in the very citadel of his being. It alone is able to show how he who will not accept God's interpretation of life has no coherence in his experience.

IV. *Arminian Apologetics*

Having contemplated these matters, our pastor realized that he could not engage in the propagation and defense of Christian faith conjointly with those who are committed to the Roman Catholic point of view. The reason for this now appeared to be obvious to him. One's theology and one's apologetics go together. A Roman Catholic theologian will, naturally, also be a Roman Catholic apologist, and will, therefore, encourage the non-Christian to hold onto his covenant-breaking viewpoint. The Roman Catholic apologist is unable to challenge the wisdom of the world.

But how about the differences among Protestants? The basic difference in historic Protestantism is that of Arminianism and Calvinism.

What about Arminian evangelicals? Perhaps they can offer our pastor an apologetic less drastic and therefore more acceptable to the natural man than that of Calvin. But can one, who has seen with Benjamin Breckinridge Warfield that Calvinism is Christianity come to its own, cooperate with Arminian Christians in an effort to defend the faith?

Arminianism holds, as Warfield says, to a defective theology. Arminianism is inconsistent Protestantism. In its view of the "freedom" of the will of man, Arminianism resembles Romanism. Like the Romanist theologian, though to a lesser extent, the Arminian theologian holds to some measure of self-salvation. Warfield therefore says that "Calvinism is just Christianity." Must we then not also say that Reformed apologetics is just Christian apologetics?

If this should be the case then we must, perhaps, speak of a Romanist-Arminian method and, in contrast with it, of a Reformed method of apologetics.

Suppose now that our young pastor meets his close friend, the young minister from the "evangelical"[6] church down the street. Certainly on more than one occasion they have agreed that they together have far more in common than they do with the Roman Catholic priest. This Arminian evangelical gives our pastor a copy of Bishop Butler's *Analogy*. Surely it will indicate a truly *Protestant* method of defending Christianity. Let us look with him into this work and see what we find.

We soon find that the Butler type of argument also assumes that there is an area of "fact" on the interpretation of which Christians and non-Christians agree. It assumes a non-rational principle of individuation, which means that a "fact" may be discovered, analyzed, and "known" in isolation from all other facts. It therefore concedes to the unbeliever that since historical facts are "unique" nothing certain can be said of them by way of significance or meaning. But this assumption, always untrue, has never appeared so clearly false as in our own day.

To be sure, there is a sense in which it must be said that all men have all facts "in common." Saint and sinner alike are face to face with God and the universe of God. But the sinner is like the man with colored glasses on his nose. The Scriptures tell us that the facts speak plainly of God (Rom. 1:20; 2:14, 15). But all is yellow to the jaundiced eye. As the sinner speaks of the facts, he reports them to himself and others as "yellow." There are no exceptions to this. It is the facts as reported to himself by himself, as distorted by his own subjective condition, which he assumes to be *the facts as they really are.*

Failing to keep these things in mind, Butler appealed to the sinner as though there were in his repertoire of "facts" some that he did not see as "yellow," such as the life, death, and resurrection of Christ, or miracles in general. Butler actually placed himself on a common position with his opponents on certain "questions of fact," i.e., "Did Christ rise from the dead?"

The compromising character of this position is obvious. It is compromising, in the first place, with respect to the *objective clarity* of the evidence for the truth of Christian theism. The psalmist does not say that the heavens *probably* declare the glory of God; they infallibly and clearly do. Probability is not, or at least should not be, the guide of life. Men ought, says Calvin following Paul, to believe in God, for each one is surrounded with a superabundance of evidence with respect to him. The whole universe is lit up by God. Scripture requires men to accept its interpretation of history as true without doubt. Doubt of this is as unreasonable as doubt with respect to the primacy of the light of the sun in relation to the light bulbs in our homes. It is as unreasonable as a child asking whether he has parents and, after looking at the evidence, concluding that he *probably* has!

But according to Butler, men have done full justice by the evidence if they conclude that God *probably* exists. Worse than that, according to this position, men are assumed to have done full justice by the evidence if they conclude that *a* God exists. But *a* god is a *finite* god, which is *no* god, but an idol. How can they then identify this *probable* God with the God of the Bible on whom all things depend for their existence?

In presupposing a non-Christian philosophy of fact, the Butler type of argument naturally also presupposes a non-Christian principle of coherence, or rationality. The two go hand in hand. The law of non-contradiction employed positively or negatively by man assuming his own ultimacy,[7] is made the standard of what is possible or impossible, both for men and for whatever "gods" may be. But on this basis the Bible cannot speak to man of any God whose revelation and whose very nature is not essentially penetrable to the natural intellect of man.

In the second place, the Butler type of argument is compromising on the *subjective* side. It allows that the natural man has the plenary ability to interpret certain facts correctly even though he wears the colored spectacles of the covenant-breaker. As though covenant-breakers had no axe to grind! As though they were not anxious to avoid seeing the facts for what they really are!

The traditional argument of Butler is, moreover, not only compromising but also self-destructive. Today, more than ever before, men frankly assert that facts are *taken* as much as *given*. Thus they admit that they wear glasses. But these glasses are said to *help* rather than to hinder vision. Modern man assumes that, seeing facts through the glasses of his own ultimacy, he can really see these facts for what they are. For him it is the orthodox believer who wears the colored glasses of prejudice. Thus the Christian walks in the valley of those who more than ever before, identify their false *interpretations* about themselves and about the facts, with the facts themselves.

However, the argument of Butler does not challenge men to repentance for their sin of misrepresentation. It virtually grants that
they are right. But then, if men are virtually told that they are right
in thus identifying their false interpretations of the facts, with the
facts themselves, in certain instances, why should such men accept the
Christian interpretation of other facts? Are not all facts within one
universe? If men are virtually told that they are quite right in interpreting certain facts without God, they have every *logical right*
to continue their interpretation of all other facts without God.

From the side of the believer in the infallible Word of God, the
claim should be made that there are not, because there cannot be,
other facts than God-interpreted facts, i.e., facts which are what they
are because of their place in the plan of God. In practice, this means
that since sin has come into the world, God's interpretation of the
facts must come in finished, written form and be comprehensive in
character. God continues to reveal himself in the facts of the created
world, but the sinner needs to interpret every one of them in the
clearer light of Scripture. Every thought on every subject must become obedient to the requirement of God as he speaks in his Word,
every thought must be brought into subjection to Christ. The Butler
argument fails to make this requirement and thus fatally compromises
the claims of Scripture.

It has frequently been argued that this view of Scripture is *im-
practicable*. Christians differ among themselves, after all, in their
interpretation of Scripture.

This objection, however, is not to the point. No one denies a subjective element in a *restricted* sense. The real issue is whether God
exists as self-contained, whether therefore the world runs according
to his plan, and whether God has confronted those who would frus-
trate the realization of that plan, with a self-contained interpretation
of that plan (the Bible). The fact that Christians individually and
collectively can never do more than restate the given self-contained
interpretation of that plan *approximately* neither implies the *non-
existence* of that plan itself nor the *impossibility* of the self-revelation
of that plan given by Christ in the Scriptures.

The self-contained circle of the ontological trinity (the trinity considered apart from economic relations) is not broken up by the fact that there is an *economical* relation of this triune God to man. No more is the self-contained character of Scripture broken up by the fact that there is a diversity of transmission and acceptance of that word of God. Such at least is, or ought to be, the contention of Christians if they would really challenge the modern principle. The Christian principle must present the full force and breadth of its claim. It is compelled to engage in an all-out war against the misinterpretation of the universe by the natural man.

In contrast, therefore, with both Catholic and Arminian types of apologetics, the Reformed apologist insists that the natural man is quite mistaken in starting from his own sense of freedom as an ultimate *given* of experience. It is this which both Catholic and Arminian apologetics cannot do. They allow the natural man to continue to assume the ultimate freedom of himself and the facts about himself. In defending Christianity, our Reformed pastor then realized that he must challenge the non-Christian to see himself in the light that Christ gives to men in Scripture. Our pastor knew, to be sure, that even this the natural man cannot do, for he cannot, himself, remove his colored glasses. He needs, therefore, the operation of the Holy Spirit to regenerate him, to open his eyes so that he may see. He must be born again.

The natural man, says Warfield, needs new light—the Bible, and new power of sight—regeneration.

When the sinner has by God's grace in Christ received this new light and this new power of sight then he sees all things in their proper relationships. Formerly he stood on his head while now he stands on his feet. Formerly he referred all things to himself as the final point of reference. Now he refers all things to God his Creator, and to Christ his redeemer as the final point of reference. His conversion was a Copernican revolution. It was not accomplished by steps or stages. It was an about-face. Before his conversion he looked away from the God and the Christ of Scripture. *After* his conversion he can't see a fact in the world that he does not wish to deal with to the glory of God. The words of Paul, "Whether ye eat, or drink, or do *anything* else, do all to the glory of God," are now his motto. Deeply conscious of his continued sinfulness he is, none the less, now, in the core of his being, a lover instead of a hater of God.

With great urgency he now seeks to go back to his erstwhile partners whose goal continues to be to glorify *man* in all that they do.

We have now, with our young pastor, looked into the various methods of defending Christianity. Our young pastor has seen that cooperative efforts in presenting and defending Christianity are impossible for there is only one consistent Christianity and only one consistent defense of it. He has also noted the radical difference which exists between the world-views of Christians and non-Christians. In the following section, we shall attempt to illustrate these points in the form of a dialogue among two Christians—one Reformed and the other Arminian—and a non-Christian.

V.   *A Dialogue—Mr. Black, Mr. White, Mr. Grey*

We have first the non-Christian, who worships the creature rather than the Creator. We shall call him Mr. Black. Mr. Black may be a very "decent" sort of man. By God's common grace he may do much that is "good." Even so he is, as long as he remains in his unconverted state, black in the sight of God.

On the other hand we have a representative of those who have, by the grace of God, become worshipers of the Creator-Redeemer, called Mr. White. Mr. White is far from what, judging him by his name, we should expect him to be. But he is washed in the blood of the Lamb. *In Christ* he is whiter than snow. Mr. White is the Reformed Christian.

But, strangely enough, there is a third party, an Arminian, called Mr. Grey. Of course, *in Christ* Mr. Grey is as white as is Mr. White. Mr. Grey thinks that Mr. White is too severe in his evaluation of Mr. Black. Mr. Black is not all *that black*. It is not pedagogically wise to require of Mr. Black that he make a complete about-face. Surely no such complete revolution is necessary in the field of science and in the field of philosophy. Many of Mr. Black's followers have valiantly defended the existence of God against materialism, atheism, and positivism. Even in theology many of these disciples of Mr.

Black have sprung to the defense of God when he was attacked by the God-is-dead theologians. Mr. Grey, therefore typifies the Aquinas-Butler method of defending Christianity.

Let us now note the difference between the way Mr. White and the way Mr. Grey approach the unbeliever, Mr. Black, with the gospel of Christ.

Let us say that Mr. Black has a toothache. Both Mr. White and Mr. Grey are dentists. Mr. White believes in a radical methodology. He believes that Mr. Black should have all the decayed matter removed from his tooth before the filling is put in. Mr. Grey is a very kind-hearted man. He does not want to hurt Mr. Black. Accordingly, he does not want to drill too deeply. He will, therefore, take only a part of the decayed matter out of the tooth and then fill it.

Naturally Mr. Black thinks this is marvelous. Unfortunately, Mr. Black's tooth soon begins to decay again. He goes back to Mr. Grey. But Mr. Grey can never bring himself to do anything radical. As a consequence he is never able to resolve Mr. Black's toothache problem.

Let us now suppose that instead of coming to Mr. Grey, Mr. Black had gone to the office of Mr. White. Mr. White is radical, very radical. He uses the X-ray machine to diagnose Mr. Black's condition. He drills deeply. All of the tooth decay is removed. The tooth is filled. Mr. Black never need return. This simple illustration points out a basic truth.

The Bible says that man is spiritually dead in sin. The Reformed creeds speak of man's total depravity. The only cure for this spiritual deadness is his regeneration by the Holy Spirit on the basis of the atoning death of Christ. It is therefore by means of the light that Scripture sheds on the natural man's condition that Mr. White examines all his patients. Mr. White may also, to be sure, turn on the light of experience, but he always insists that this light of experience derives, in the first place, from the light of Scripture. So he may appeal to reason or to history, but, again, only as they are to be seen in the light of the Bible. He does not even look for *corroboration* of the teachings of Scripture in experience, reason, or history, except insofar as these are themselves first seen in the light of the Bible. For him, the Bible, and therefore the God of the Bible, is like the sun from which the light that is given by oil lamps, gas lamps, and electric lights is derived.*

Quite different is the attitude of the Arminian. Mr. Grey uses the Bible, experience, reason, or logic as equally independent sources of information about his own and therefore about Mr. Black's predicament. I did not say that for Mr. Grey the Bible, experience, and reason *are equally* important. Indeed they are not. He knows that the Bible is by far the most important. But he none the less constantly appeals to "the facts of experience" and to "logic" without first dealing with the very idea of fact and with the idea of logic in terms of the Scripture.

The difference is basic. When Mr. White diagnoses Mr. Black's case he takes as his X-ray machine, the Bible only. When Mr. Grey diagnoses Mr. Black's case he first takes the X-ray machine of experience, then the X-ray machine of logic, and finally his biggest X-ray machine, the Bible. In fact, he may take these in any order. Each of them is, for him, an independent source of information.

Let us first look briefly at a typical procedure generally followed in evangelical circles today. Let us, in other words, note how Mr. Grey proceeds with an analysis of Mr. Black, and at the same time see how Mr. Grey would win Mr. Black to an acceptance of Christianity. We take for this purpose a series of articles which appeared in the January, February, and March, 1950, issues of *Moody Monthly,* published by the Moody Bible Institute in Chicago. The late Edward John Carnell, author of *An Introduction to Christian Apologetics* and Professor of Apologetics at Fuller Theological Seminary, was the writer of this series. Carnell's writings were among the best that appeared in evangelical circles. In fact, in his book on apologetics Carnell frequently argues as we would expect a Reformed apologist to argue. By and large, however, he represents the Arminian rather than the Reformed method in apologetics.

---

*The following material is taken, with slight alteration, from the present writer's *The Defense of the Faith* (Presbyterian and Reformed Publishing Company, 1955), pp. 320-353.

When Carnell instructs his readers "How Every Christian Can Defend His Faith," he first appeals to facts and to logic as independent sources of information about the truth of Christianity. Of course, he must bring in the Bible even at this point. But the Bible is brought in only as a book of information about the fact of what has historically been called Christianity. It is not from the beginning brought in as God's Word. It must be shown to Mr. Black that it is the Word of God by means of "facts" and "logic." Carnell would thus avoid at all costs the charge of reasoning in a circle. He does not want Mr. Black to point the finger at him and say: "You prove that the Bible is true by an appeal to the Bible itself. That is circular reasoning. How can any person with any respect for logic accept such a method of proof?"

Carnell would escape such a charge by showing that the facts of experience, such as all men recognize, and logic, such as all men must use, point to the truth of Scripture. This is what he says: "If you are of a philosophic turn, you can point to the remarkable way in which Christianity fits in with the moral sense inherent in every human being, or the influence of Christ on our ethics, customs, literature, art, and music. Finally, you can draw upon your own experience in speaking of the reality of answered prayer and the witness of the Spirit in your own heart. . . . If the person is impressed with this evidence, turn at once to the gospel. Read crucial passages and permit the Spirit to work on the inner recesses of his heart. Remember that apologetics is merely a preparation. After the ground has been broken, proceed immediately with sowing and watering."[8]

It is assumed in this argument that Mr. Black agrees with the evangelical, Mr. Grey, on the character of the "moral sense" of man. This may be true, but then it is true because Mr. Grey has himself not taken his information about the "moral sense" of man exclusively from Scripture. If, with Mr. White, Mr. Grey had taken his conception of the moral nature of man from the Bible, then he would hold that Mr. Black will, as totally depraved, misinterpret his own moral nature. True, Christianity is in accord with the moral nature of man. But this is so only because the moral nature of man is first in accord with what the Bible says it is, i.e., originally created perfect, it is now wholly corrupted in its desires through the fall of man.

If you are reasoning with a naturalist, Carnell advises his readers, ask him why, when a child throws a rock through his window, he chases the child and not the rock. Presumably even a naturalist knows that the child, not the rock, is free and therefore responsible. "A bottle of water cannot ought; it must. When once the free spirit of man is proved, the moral argument—the existence of a God who imposes moral obligations—can form the bridge from man to God."[9]

Here the fundamental difference between Mr. Grey's and Mr. White's aproaches to Mr. Black appears. The difference lies, as before noted, in the different notions of the free will of man. Or, it may be said, the difference is with respect to the nature of man as man. Mr. White would define man, and therefore his freedom, in terms of Scripture alone. He would therefore begin with the fact that man is the creature of God. This implies that man's freedom is a derivative freedom. It is a freedom that is not and cannot be wholly ultimate, that is, self-dependent. Mr. White knows that Mr. Black would not agree with him in this analysis of man and of his freedom. He knows that Mr. Black would not agree with him on this any more than he would agree on the biblical idea of total depravity.

Mr. Grey, on the other hand, must at all costs have "a point of contact" in the system of thought of Mr. Black, who is typical of the natural man. Just as Mr. Grey is afraid of being charged with circular reasoning, so he is also afraid of being charged with talking about something that is "outside of experience." So he is driven to talk in general about the "free spirit of man." Of course, Mr. Black need have no objections from his point of view in allowing for the "free spirit of man." That is at bottom what he holds even when he is a naturalist. His whole position is based upon the idea of man as a free spirit, that is, a spirit that is not subject to the law of his Creator God. Carnell does not distinguish between the biblical doctrine of freedom as based upon and involved in the fact of man's creation, and the doctrine of freedom, in the sense of autonomy, which makes man a law unto himself.

Of course, Mr. Black will be greatly impressed with such an argument as Mr. Grey has presented to him for the truth of Christianity. In fact, if Christianity is thus shown to be in accord with the moral nature of man, as Mr. Black himself sees that moral nature, then Mr. Black does not need to be *radically* converted to accept Christianity. He only needs to accept something *additional* to what he has always believed. He has been shown how nice, even how important, it would be to have a second story built on top of the house which he has already built according to his own plans.

To be sure, the evangelical intends no such thing. Least of all does Carnell intend such a thing. But why then does the "evangelical" not see that by presenting the non-Christian with Arminianism rather than with the Reformed faith he compromises the Christian religion? Why does Carnell not see that in doing what he does, the non-Christian is not really challenged either by fact or by logic? For facts and logic which are not themselves first seen in the light of Christianity have, in the nature of the case, no power in them to challenge the unbeliever to change his position. Facts and logic, not based upon the creation doctrine and not placed in the context of the doctrine of God's all-embracing Providence, which culminates in the redemption through Christ, are without *significant* relation to one another and therefore wholly meaningless.

It is this truth which must be shown to Mr. Black. The folly of holding to any view of life except that which is frankly based upon the Bible as the absolute authority for man must be pointed out to him. Only then are we doing what Paul did when he said: "Where is the wise? where is the scribe? where is the disputer of this world? hath not God made foolish the wisdom of the world?" (I Cor. 1:20).

As a Reformed Christian, Mr. White therefore cannot cooperate with Mr. Grey in his analysis of Mr. Black. This fact may appear more clearly if we turn to see how Mr. Black appears when he is analyzed by Mr. White in terms of the Bible alone.

According to Mr. White's analysis, Mr. Black is not a murderer. He is not a drunkard or a dope addict. He lives in one of the suburbs. He is every whit a gentleman. He gives to the Red Cross and to the United Fund campaigns. He was a Boy Scout; he is a member of a lodge; he is very civic minded; now and then his name is mentioned in the papers as an asset to the community. But he is spiritually dead. He is filled with the spirit of error. Perhaps he is a member of a "fine church" in the community, but nevertheless he is one of those "people that do err in their heart" (Ps. 95:10). He lives in a stupor (Rom. 11:8). To him the wisdom of God is foolishness. The truth about God, and about himself in relation to God, is obnoxious to him. He does not want to hear of it. He seeks to close his eyes and ears to those who give witness to the truth. He is, in short, utterly self-deceived.

On the other hand, Mr. Black is certain that he looks at life in the only proper way. Even if he has doubts as to the truth of what he believes, he does not see how any sensible or rational man could believe or do otherwise. If he has doubts, it is because no one can be fully sure of himself. If he has fears, it is because fear is to be expected in the hazardous and ambiguous situation in which modern man lives. If he sees men's minds break down, he thinks this is to be expected under current conditions of stress and strain. If he sees grown men act like children, he says that they once were beasts. Everything, including the "abnormal," is to him "normal."

In all this, Mr. Black has obviously taken for granted that what the Bible says about the world and himself is not true. He has *taken this for granted*. He may never have argued the point. He has cemented yellow spectacles to his own eyes. He cannot remove them because he will not remove them. He is blind and loves to be blind.

But do not think that Mr. Black has an easy time of it. He is the man who always "kicks against the pricks." His conscience troubles him all the time. Deep down in his heart he knows that what the Bible says about him and about the world is true. Even if he has never heard of the Bible, he knows that he is a creature of God and that he has broken the law of God (Rom. 1:19, 20; 2:14, 15). When the prodigal son left his father's house he could not immediately efface from his memory the look and voice of his father. That look and that voice came back to him even when he was at the swine trough! How hard he had tried to live as though the money with which he so freely entertained his "friends" had not come from his father! When asked where he came from he would answer that he came "from the other side." He did not want to be reminded of his past. Yet he could not forget it. It required a constant act of suppression to forget his past. But that very act of suppression itself keeps alive the memory of the past.

Mr. Black daily changes the truth of God into a lie. He daily holds the truth in unrighteousness (Rom. 1:18). But what a time he has with himself! He may try to sear his conscience as with a hot iron. He may seek to escape the influence of all those who witness to the truth. But he can never escape *himself* as witness bearer to the truth.

His conscience keeps telling him: "Mr. Black, you are a fugitive from justice. You have run away from home, from your father's bountiful love. You are an ingrate, a sneak, a rascal! You shall not escape meeting justice at last. The father still feeds you. Yet you despise the riches of his goodness and forbearance and longsuffering; not recognizing that the goodness of God is calculated to lead you to repentance (Rom. 2:4). Why do you kick against the pricks? Why do you stifle the voice of your conscience? Why do you use the wonderful intellect that God has given you as a tool for the suppression of the voice of God which speaks to you through yourself and your environment? Why do you build your house on sand instead of on rock? Can you be sure that no storm is ever coming? Are you omniscient? Are you omnipotent? You say that nobody knows whether God exists or whether Christianity is true. You say that nobody knows this because man is finite. Yet you assume that God *cannot* exist and that Christianity *cannot* be true. You assume that no judgment will ever come. You must be omniscient to know that. Yet you have just said that all man declares about 'the beyond' must be based upon his brief span of existence in this world of time and chance. How, then, if you have taken for granted that chance is one of the basic ingredients of all human experience, can you at the same time say what *can* or *cannot* be in all time to come? You certainly have made a fool of yourself, Mr. Black," says Mr. Black to himself. "You reject the claims of truth which you know to be the truth, and you do that in terms of the lie which really you know to be the lie. It is you, not Mr. White, who engages in circular reasoning.

It is you, not Mr. White, who refuses to face the facts as they are. It is you, not Mr. White, who crucifies logic."

It is not always that Mr. Black is thus aware of the fact that he lives like the prodigal who would have eaten of the things the swine did eat, but who knew he could not because he was a human being. Mr. Black is not always thus aware of his folly. This is, in part at least, because of the failure of evangelicals and particularly of Reformed Christians to stir him up to a realization of this basic depth of his folly. The Reformed Christian should, on his basis, want to stir up Mr. Black to an appreciation of the folly of his ways.

However, when the Reformed Christian, Mr. White, is to any extent aware of the richness of his own position and actually has the courage to challenge Mr. Black by presenting to him the picture of himself as taken through the X-ray machine called the Bible, he faces the charge of "circular reasoning" and of finding no "point of contact" with experience. He will also be subject to the criticism of the Arminian for speaking as if Christianity were irrational and for failing to reach the man in the street.

Thus we seem to be in a bad predicament. There is a basic difference of policy between Mr. White and Mr. Grey as to how to deal with Mr. Black. Mr. Grey thinks that Mr. Black is not really such a bad fellow. It is possible, he thinks, to live with Mr. Black in the same world. Mr. Black is pretty strong. It is best to make a compromise peace with him. That seems to be the way of the wise and practical politician. On the other hand, Mr. White thinks that it is impossible to live permanently in the same world with Mr. Black. Mr. Black, he says, must therefore be placed before the requirement of absolute and unconditional surrender to Christ. Surely it would be out of the question for Mr. White first to make a compromise peace with Mr. Black and then, after all, to require unconditional surrender to Christ! But what, then, about the charge of circular reasoning and about the charge of having no point of contact with the unbeliever?

A. *A Consistent Witness*

The *one* main question to which we are to address ourselves now is whether Christians holding to the Reformed Faith must also hold to *a specifically Reformed method of reasoning* when they are engaged in the defense of the faith.

This broad question does not pertain merely to the "five points of Calvinism." When Arminians attack these great doctrines (total depravity, unconditional election, limited atonement, irresistible grace, perseverance of the saints) we, as Calvinists, are quick to defend them. We believe that these five points are directly drawn from Scripture. But the question now under discussion is whether, in the defense of *any* Christian doctrine, Reformed Christians should use a method *all* their own.

People easily give a negative reply to this question. Do we not have many doctrines in common with all evangelicals? Do not all orthodox Protestants hold to the substitutionary atonement of Christ? More particularly, what about the simple statements of fact recorded in Scripture? How could anyone, if he believes such statements at all, take them otherwise than as simple statements of fact? How could anyone have a specifically Reformed doctrine of such a fact as the resurrection of Christ? If together with evangelicals we accept certain simple truths and facts of Scripture at face value, how then can we be said to have a separate method of defense of such doctrines?

Yet it can readily be shown that a negative answer to these questions cannot be maintained. Take, for example, the doctrine of the atonement. The Arminian doctrine of the atonement is not the same as the Reformed doctrine of the atonement. Both the Arminian and the Calvinist assert that they believe in the substitutionary atonement. But the Arminian conception of the substitutionary atonement is colored, and as Calvinists we believe discolored, by the view of "free will." According to the Arminian view, man has absolute or ultimate power to accept or to reject the salvation offered him. This implies that the salvation offered to man is merely the *possibility* of salvation.

To illustrate: suppose I deposit one million dollars to your account in your bank. It is still altogether up to you to believe that such wealth is yours, and to use it to cover the floor of your house with Persian rugs in place of the old threadbare rugs now there. Thus, in the Arminian scheme, the very possibility of things no longer depends exclusively upon God, but, in some areas at least, upon man. What Christ did *for* us is made to depend for its effectiveness upon what is done *by* us. It is no longer right to say that with God *all* things are possible.

It is obvious, therefore, that Arminians have taken into their Protestantism a good bit of the leaven of Roman Catholicism. Arminianism is less radical, less consistent in its Protestantism than it should be.

Now Mr. Grey, the evangelical, seems to have a relatively easy time of it when he seeks to win Mr. Black, the unbeliever, to an acceptance of "the substitutionary atonement." He can stand on "common ground" with Mr. Black on this matter of what is possible and what is impossible. Listen to Mr. Grey as he talks with Mr. Black.

"Mr. Black, have you accepted Christ as your personal Savior? Do you believe that he died on the cross as your substitute? If you do not, you will surely be lost forever."

"Well now," replies Mr. Black, "I've just had a visit from Mr. White on the same subject. You two seem to have a 'common witness' on this matter. Both of you believe that God exists, that he has created the world, that the first man, Adam, sinned, and that we are all to be sent to hell because of what that first man did, and so forth. All this is too fatalistic for me. If I am a creature, as you say I am, then I have no ultimate power of my own and therefore am not free. And if I am not free, then I am not responsible. So, if I am going to hell, it will be simply because your 'God' has determined that I should. You orthodox Christians kill morality and all humanitarian progress. I will have none of it. Good-by!"

"But wait a second," says Mr. Grey, in great haste. "I do not have a common witness at this point with the Calvinist. I have a common witness with you against the Calvinist when it come to all that determinism that you mention. Of course you are free. You are absolutely free to accept or to reject the atonement that is offered to you. I offer the atonement through Christ only as a possibility. You yourself must make it an actuality for yourself. I agree with you over against the Calvinist in saying that 'possibility' is wider than the will of God. I would not for a moment say with the Calvinist that God's counsel determines 'whatsoever comes to pass.'

"Besides, even less extreme Calvinists like Dr. J. Oliver Buswell, Jr., virtually agree with both of us. Listen to what Buswell says: 'Nevertheless, our moral choices are choices in which we are ourselves ultimate causes.' Dr. Buswell himself wants to go beyond the 'merely arbitrary answer' in Romans 9:20, 21, which speaks of the potter and the clay, to the 'much more profound analysis of God's plan of redemption' in Romans 9:22-24, in which Paul pictures Pharaoh as '. . . one who, according to the foreknowledge of God, would rebel against God.' "[10]

"I understand then," replies Mr. Black, "that you Arminians and more moderate Calvinists are opposed to the determinism of the regular, old-style Calvinists of the historic Reformed Confessions? I am glad to hear that. To say that all things have been fixed from all eternity by God is terrible! It makes me shudder! What would happen to all morality and decency if all men believed such teaching? But now you Arminians have joined us in holding that 'possibility' is independent of the will of God. You have thus with all good people and with all liberal and neo-orthodox theologians, like Barth, made possible the salvation of all men.

"That means, of course, that salvation is also possible for those too who have never heard of Jesus of Nazareth. Salvation is therefore possible without an acceptance of your substitutionary atonement through this Jesus of whom you speak. You certainly would not want to say with the Calvinists that God has determined the bounds of all nations and individuals and has thus, after all, determined that some men, millions of them, in fact, should never hear this gospel.

"Besides, if possibility is independent of God, as you evangelicals and moderate Calvinists teach, then I need not be afraid of hell. It is then quite possible that there is no hell. Hell, you will then agree, is that torture of a man's conscience which he experiences when he fails to live up to his own moral ideals. So I do not think that I shall bother just yet about accepting Christ as my personal Savior. There is plenty of time."

Poor Mr. Grey. He really wanted to say something about having a common testimony with the Calvinists after all. At the bottom of his heart he knew that Mr. White, the Calvinist, and not Mr. Black, the unbeliever, was his real friend. But he had made a common witness with Mr. Black against the supposed determinism of Mr. White, the Calvinist, so it was difficult for him, after that, to turn about face and also make a common testimony with Mr. White against Mr. Black. He had nothing intelligible to say. His method of defending his faith had forced him to admit that Mr. Black was basically right. He had not given Mr. Black an opportunity of knowing what he was supposed to accept, but his testimony had confirmed Mr. Black in his belief that there was no need of his accepting Christ at all.

It is true, of course, that in practice Mr. Grey is much better in his theology and in his method of representing the gospel than he is here said to be. But that is because in practice every evangelical who really loves his Lord is a Calvinist at heart. *How could he really pray to God for help if he believed that there was a possibility that God could not help?* In their hearts all true Christians believe that that God controls "whatsoever comes to pass." But the Calvinist cannot have a common witness for the substitutionary atonement with Arminians who first make a common witness with the unbeliever against him on the all-important question whether God controls all things that happen.

It must always be remembered that the first requirement for effective witnessing is that the position defended be intelligible. Arminianism, when consistently carried out, destroys this intelligibility.

The second requirement for effective witnessing is that he to whom the witness is given must be *shown why* he should forsake his own position and accept that which is offered him. Arminianism, when consistently carried out, destroys the reason why the unbeliever should accept the gospel. Why should the unbeliever change his position if he is not shown that it is wrong? Why should he exchange his position for that of Christianity if the one who asks him to change is actually encouraging him in thinking that he is right? The Calvinist will need to have a better method of defending the doctrine of the atonement therefore than that of the Arminian.

We have dealt with the doctrine of the atonement. That led us into the involved question whether God is the source of possibility, or whether possibility is the source of God. It has been shown that the Arminian holds to a position which requires him to make both of these contradictory assertions at once. But how about the realm of fact? Do you also hold, I am asked, that we need to seek for a specifically Reformed method of defending the "facts" of Christianity? Take the resurrection of Christ as an example—why can there be no common witness on the part of the Arminian and the Calvinist to such a fact as that?

Once more Mr. Grey, the Arminian, pushes the doorbell at Mr. Black's home. Mr. Black answers and admits him.

"I am here again, Mr. Black," begins Grey, "because I am still anxious to have you accept Christ as your personal Savior. When I spoke to you the other time about the atonement you got me into deep water. We got all tangled up on the question of 'possibility.'

"But now I have something far simpler. I want to deal with simple facts. I want to show you that the resurrection of Jesus from the dead is as truly a fact as any fact that you can mention. To use the words of Dr. Wilbur Smith, himself a 'moderate' Calvinist but opposed to the idea of a distinctively Reformed method for the defense of the faith: 'The *meaning* of the resurrection is a theological matter, but the fact of the resurrection is a historical matter; the nature of the resurrection body of Jesus may be a mystery, but the fact that the body disappeared from the tomb is a matter to be decided upon by historical evidence.' [11] The historical evidence for the resurrection is the kind of evidence that you as a scientist would desire.

"Smith writes in the same book: 'About a year ago, after studying over a long period of time this entire problem of our Lord's resurrection, and having written some hundreds of pages upon it at different times, I was suddenly arrested by the thought that the very kind of evidence which modern science, and even psychologists, are so insistent upon for determining the reality of any object under consideration is the kind of evidence that we have presented to us in the gospels regarding the resurrection of the Lord Jesus, namely, the things that are seen with the human eye, touched with the human hand, and heard by the human ear. This is what we call empirical evidence. It would almost seem as if parts of the gospel records of the resurrection were actually written for such a day as ours when empiricism so dominates our thinking.' [12]

"Now I think that Smith is quite right in thus distinguishing sharply between the *fact* and the *meaning* of the resurrection. I am now only asking you to accept the fact of the resurrection. There is the clearest possible empirical evidence for this fact. The living Jesus was touched with human hands and seen with human eyes of sensible men after he had been crucified and put into the tomb. Surely you ought to believe in the resurrection of Christ as a historical fact. And to believe in the resurrected Christ is to be saved."

"But hold on a second," says Mr. Black. "Your friend the Calvinist, Mr. White, has been ahead of you again. He was here last night and spoke of the same thing that you are now speaking about. However, he did not thus distinguish between the fact and the meaning of the resurrection. At least, he did not for a moment want to separate the fact of the resurrection from the system of Christianity in terms of which it gets its meaning. He spoke of Jesus Christ, the Son of God, as rising from the dead. He spoke of the Son of God through whom the world was made and through whom the world is sustained, as having risen from the dead. When I asked him how this God could die and rise again from the dead, he said that God did not die and rise from the dead but that the second person of the Trinity had taken to himself a human nature, and that it was in this human nature that he died and rose again. In short, in accepting the fact of the resurrection he wanted me also to accept all this abracadabra about the trinitarian God. I have a suspicion that you are secretly trying to have me do something similar."

"No, no," replies Mr. Grey. "I am in complete agreement with you here against the Calvinist. I have a common witness with you against him. I, too, would separate fact from system. Did I not agree with you against the Calvinist, in holding that possibility is independent of God? Well then, by the same token I hold that all kinds of facts happen apart from the plan of God. We Arminians are in a position, as the Calvinists are not, of speaking with you on neutral ground. With you, we would simply talk about the "facts" of Christianity without immediately bringing into the picture anything about the meaning or the significance of those facts.

"It makes me smile," continues Mr. Grey, "when I think of Mr. White coming over here trying to convert you. That poor fellow is always reasoning in circles! I suppose that such reasoning in circles goes with his determinism. He is always talking about his self-contained God. He says that all facts are what they are because of the plan of God. Then each fact would of necessity, to be a fact at all, prove the truth of the Christian system of things and, in turn, would be proved as existing by virtue of this self-same Christian system of things. I realize full well that you, as a modern scientist and philosopher, can have no truck with such horrible, circular reasoning as that.

"It is for this reason that, as Arminian evangelicals, we have now separated sharply between the resurrection as a historical *fact* and the *meaning* of the resurrection. I'm merely asking you to accept the *fact* of the resurrection. I am not asking you to do anything that you cannot do in full consistency with your freedom and with the 'scientific method.' "

"Well, this is delightful," replies Mr. Black. "I always felt that the Calvinists were our real foes. But I read something in the paper the other day to the effect that some Calvinist churches or individuals were proposing to make a common witness with Arminian evangelicals for the gospel. Now I was under the impression that the gospel had something to do with being saved from hell and going to heaven. I knew that the modernists and the 'new modernists,' like Barth, do not believe in tying up the facts of history with such wild speculations. It was my opinion that 'fundamentalists' did tie up belief in historical facts, such as the death and resurrection of Jesus, with going to heaven or to hell. So I am delighted that you, though a fundamentalist, are willing to join with the liberal and the neo-liberal in separating historical facts from such a rationalistic system as I thought Christianity was.

"Now as for accepting the resurrection of Jesus," continued Mr. Black, "as thus properly separated from the traditional system of theology, I do not in the least mind doing that. To tell you the truth, I have accepted the resurrection as a fact now for some time. The evidence for it is overwhelming. This is a strange universe. All kinds of 'miracles' happen in it. The universe is 'open.' So why should there not be some resurrections here and there? The resurrection of Jesus would be a fine item for Ripley's *Believe It or Not*. Why not send it in?"

Mr. Grey wanted to continue at this point. He wanted to speak of the common witness that he had, after all, with the Calvinist for the gospel. But it was too late. He had no "common" witness left of any sort. He had again tried to gallop off in opposite directions at the same time. He had again taken away all credibility from the witness that he meant to bring. He had again established Mr. Black in thinking that his own unbelieving reason was right. For it was as clear as crystal to Mr. Black, as it should have been to Mr. Grey, that belief in the fact of the resurrection, apart from the system of Christianity, amounts to belief that the Christian system is not true, to believe in the universe as run by Chance, and to believe that it was not *Jesus Christ, the Son of God*, who rose from the dead.

To be sure, in practice the Arminian is much better in his witness for the resurrection of Christ than he has been presented here. But that is, as noted already, because every evangelical, as a sincere Christian, is *at heart* a Calvinist. But witnessing is a matter of the head as well as of the heart. If the world is to hear a consistent testimony for the Christian faith, it is the Calvinist who must give it. If there is not a distinctively Reformed method for the defense of every article of the Christian faith, then there is no way of clearly telling an unbeliever just how Christianity differs from his own position and why he should accept the Lord Jesus Christ as his personal Savior. We are happy and thankful, of course, for the work of witnessing done by Arminians. We are happy because of the fact that, in spite of their inconsistency in presenting the Christian testimony, something, often much, of the truth of the gospel shines through unto men, and they are saved.

B. *The Authority of Scripture*

"But how can anyone know anything about the 'beyond'?" asks Mr. Black.

"Well, of course," replies Mr. Grey, "if you want absolute certainty, such as one gets in geometry, Christianity does not offer it. We offer you only 'rational probability.' 'Christianity,' as I said in effect a moment ago when I spoke of the death of Christ, 'is founded on historical facts, which, by their very nature, cannot be demonstrated with geometric certainty. All judgments of historical particulars are at the mercy of the complexity of the time-space universe. . . . If the scientist cannot rise above rational probability in his empirical investigation, why should the Christian claim more?' And what is true of the death of Christ," adds Mr. Grey, "is, of course, also true of his resurrection. But this only shows that 'the Christian is in possession of a world-view which is making a sincere effort to come to grips with actual history.' " [13]

By speaking thus, Mr. Grey again seeks for a neutral point of contact with Mr. Black. For Mr. Black, history is something that floats on an infinitely extended and bottomless ocean of Chance. Therefore he can say that *anything* may happen. Who knows but the death and resurrection of Jesus as the Son of God might issue from this womb of Chance? Such events would have an equal chance of happening with "snarks, boojums, splinth, and gobble-de-gook." God himself may live in this realm of Chance. He is then "wholly other" than ourselves, and his revelation in history would then be wholly unique.

The Arminian does not challenge this underlying philosophy of Chance as it controls the unbeliever's conception of history. He is so anxious to have the unbeliever accept the *possibility* of God's existence and the *fact* of the resurrection of Christ that, if necessary, he will exchange his own philosophy of the facts for that of the unbeliever. Anxious to be genuinely "empirical" like the unbeliever, he will throw all the facts of Christianity into the bottomless pit of Chance. Or, rather, he will throw all these facts at the unbeliever, and the unbeliever throws them over his back into the bottomless pit of Chance.

Of course, this is the last thing that such men as Wilbur Smith, Edward J. Carnell, and J. Oliver Buswell, Jr., want to do. But in failing to challenge the philosophy of Chance that underlies the unbeliever's notion of "fact," they are, in effect, doing it.

This approach of Mr. Grey's is unavoidable if one hold to an Arminian theology. The Arminian view of man's free will implies that "possibility" is above God. But a "possibility" that is above God is the same thing as Chance. A God surrounded by Chance cannot speak with authority. He would be speaking into a vacuum. His voice could not be heard. If God were surrounded by Chance, then human beings would be too. They would live in a vacuum, unable to hear either their own voices or those of others. Thus the whole of history, including all of its facts, would be without meaning.

It is this that the Reformed Christian, Mr. White, would tell Mr. Black. In the very act of presenting the resurrection of Christ or in the very act of presenting any other fact of historic Christianity, Mr. White would be presenting it as authoritatively interpreted in the Bible. He would argue that unless Mr. Black is willing to set the facts of history in the framework of the meaning authoritatively ascribed to them in the Bible, he will make "gobble-de-gook" of history.

If history were what Mr. Black assumes that it is, then *anything* might happen, and then *nobody* would know what may happen. No one thing would then be more likely to happen than any other thing. David Hume, the great skeptic, has effectively argued that, if you allow any room for Chance in your thought, then you no longer have the right to speak of probabilities. Whirl would then be king. No hypothesis would then have any more relevance to facts than any other hypothesis. Did God raise Christ from the dead? Perchance he did. Did Jupiter do it? Perchance he did. What is Truth? Nobody knows. Such would be the picture of the universe if Mr. Black were right.

No comfort can be taken from the assurance of the Arminian that, since Christianity makes no higher claim than that of rational probability, "the system of Christianity can be refuted only by probability. Perhaps our loss is gain." How could one ever argue that there is a greater probability for the truth of Christianity than for the truth of its opposite, if the very meaning of the word "probability" rests upon the idea of Chance? On this basis, nature and history would be no more than a series of pointer readings pointing into the blank.

In assuming his philosophy of Chance and thus virtually saying that *nobody knows* what is back of the common objects of daily observation, Mr. Black *also* virtually says that the Christian view of things is *wrong*.

If I assert that there is a black cat in the closet, and you assert that nobody knows what is in the closet, you have virtually told me that I am wrong in my hypothesis. So when I tell Mr. Black that God exists, and he responds very graciously by saying that perhaps I am right since nobody knows what is in the "Beyond," he is virtually saying that I am wrong in my hypothesis. He is obviously thinking of such a god as could comfortably live in a closet. But the God of Scripture cannot live in a closet.

When confronted with the claims of God and his Christ, Mr. Black's response is essentially this: *Nobody knows*—nevertheless your hypothesis is certainly *wrong* and mine is certainly *right!* Nobody knows whether God exists, but God certainly does not exist and Chance certainly does exist.

When Mr. Black thus virtually makes his universal negative assertion, saying in effect that God *cannot* possibly exist and that Christianity *cannot* possibly be true, he must surely be standing on something very solid. Is it on solid rock that he stands? No, he stands on water! He stands on his own "experience." But this experience, by his own assumption, rests again on Chance. Thus standing on Chance, he swings the "logician's postulate" and modestly asserts what cannot be in the "Beyond," of which he said before that nothing can be said.

Of course, what Mr. Black is doing appears very reasonable to himself. "Surely," he says, if questioned at all on the subject, "a rational man must have systematic coherence in his experience. Therefore he cannot accept as true anything that is not in accord with the law of non-contradiction. So long as you leave your God in the realm of the 'Beyond,' in the realm of the indeterminate, you may worship him by yourself alone. But as soon as you claim that your God has revealed himself in creation, in providence, or in your Scripture, at once I shall put that revelation to a test by the principle of rational coherence.

"And by that test none of your doctrines are acceptable. All of them are contradictory. No rational man can accept any of them. If your God is eternal, then he falls outside of my experience and lives in the realm of the 'Beyond,' of the unknowable. But if he is to have anything to do with the world, then he must himself be wholly within the world. I must understand your God throughout if I am to speak intelligently of any relationship that he sustains to my world and to myself. Your idea that God is both eternal and unchangeable and yet sustains such relationships to the world as are involved in your doctrine of creation and providence, is flatly contradictory.

"For me to accept your God," continues Mr. Black, "you must do to him what Karl Barth has done to him, namely, strip him of all the attributes that orthodox theology has assigned to him, and thus enable him to turn into the opposite of himself. With that sort of God I have a principle of unity that brings all my experience into harmony. And that God is wholly within the universe. If you offer me such a God and offer him as the simplest hypothesis with which I may seek to order my experience as it comes to me from the womb of Chance, then the law of non-contradiction will be satisfied. As a rational man I can settle for nothing less."

All this amounts to saying that Mr. Black, the lover of a Chance philosophy, the indeterminist, is at the same time an out-and-out determinist or fatalist. It is to say that Mr. Black, the irrationalist, who says that nobody knows what is in the "Beyond," is at the same time a flaming rationalist. For him only that *can be*, which he thinks he can exhaustively determine by logic *must be*. He may at first grant that anything may exist, but when he says this, he at the same time says, in effect, that nothing can exist and have meaning for man but that which man himself can exhaustively know. Therefore, for Mr. Black, the God of Christianity *cannot* exist. For him the doctrine of creation *cannot* be true. There *can* be no revelation of God to man through nature and history. There *can* be no such thing as the resurrection of Christ.

Strangely enough, when Mr. Black thus says, in effect, that God *cannot* exist and that the resurrection of Christ *cannot* be a fact, and when he also says that God may very well exist and that the resurrection of Christ may very well be a fact, he is not inconsistent with himself. For he must, to be true to his method, contradict himself in every statement that he makes about any fact whatsoever. If he does not, then he would deny either his philosophy of Chance or his philosophy of Fate. According to him, every fact that he meets has in it the two ingredients: that of Chance and that of Fate, that of the wholly unknown and that of the wholly known. Thus man turns the tools of thought, which the Creator has given him in order therewith to think God's thoughts after him on a created level, into the means by which he makes sure that God *cannot* exist, and therefore certainly *cannot* reveal himself.

When Mr. White meets Mr. Black he will make this issue plain. He will tell Mr. Black that his methodology cannot make any fact or any group of facts intelligible to himself. Hear him as he speaks to the unbeliever:

"On your basis, Mr. Black, no fact can be identified by distinguishing it from any other fact. For all facts would be changing into their opposites all the time. All would be 'gobble-de-gook.' At the same time, nothing could change at all. Hath not God made foolish the wisdom of this world? He clearly has. I know you cannot see this even though it is perfectly clear. I know that you have taken out your own eyes. Hence your inability to see is at the same time unwillingness to see. Pray God for forgiveness and repent."

But what will be the approach of the Arminian, Mr. Grey, on this question of logic? He will do the same sort of thing that we saw him do with respect to the question of facts. Mr. Gray will again try to please Mr. Black by saying that, of course, he will justify his appeal to the authority of the Bible by showing that the very idea of such an appeal, as well as the content of the Bible, are fully in accord with the demands of logic. Listen to him as he speaks to the unbeliever.

"You are quite right in holding that nothing meaningful can be said without presupposing the validity of the law of non-contradiction," says Mr. Gray.[14] " 'The conservative ardently defends a system of authority.'[15] But 'without reason to canvass the evidence of a given authority, how can one segregate a right authority from a wrong one? . . . Without systematic consistency to aid us, it appears that all we can do is to draw straws, count noses, flip coins to choose an authority. Once we *do* apply the law of contradiction, we are no longer appealing to *ipse dixit* authority, but to coherent truth.'[16] 'The Scriptures tell us to *test* the spirits (I John 4:1). This can be done only by applying the canons of truth. God cannot lie. His authority, therefore, and coherent truth are coincident at every point. Truth, not blind authority, saves us from being blind followers of the blind.'[17]

" 'Bring on your revelations!' " continues Mr. Grey. " 'Let them make peace with the law of contradiction and the facts of history, and they will deserve a rational man's assent.'[18] 'Any theology which rejects Aristotle's fourth book of the *Metaphysics* is big with the elements of its own destruction.'[19] 'If Paul were teaching that the crucified Christ were objectively foolish, in the sense that he cannot be rationally categorized, then he would have pointed to the insane and the demented as incarnations of truth.' "[20]

"Well," says Mr. Black, "this is great news indeed. I knew that the modernists were willing with us to start from human experience as the final reference point in all research. I knew that they were willing with us to start from Chance as the source of facts, in order then to manufacture such facts of nature and of history as the law of non-contradiction, based on Chance, will allow. I also knew that the famous neo-orthodox theologian, Karl Barth, is willing to re-make the God of historic Christianity so that he can change into the opposite of himself, in order that thus he may satisfy both our irrationalist philosophy of Chance and our rationalist philosophy of logic. But I did not know that there were any orthodox people who were willing to do such a thing. But you have surprised me before. You were willing to throw your resurrection into the realm of Chance in order to have me accept it. So I really should have expected that you would also be willing to make the law of non-contradiction rest upon man himself instead of upon God.

"I am extremely happy, too, that not only Arminian fundamentalists but also less extreme or moderate Calvinists, like Buswell, Carnell, and Smith, are now willing to test revelation by a principle that is wholly independent of that revelation. It is now only a matter of time until they will see that they have to come over on our side altogether.

"I do no like the regular Calvinists. But they are certainly quite right from their own point of view. Mr. White claims that I am a creature of God. He says that all facts are made by God and controlled by the providence of God. He says that all men have sinned against God in Adam their representative. He adds that therefore I am spiritually blind and morally perverse. He says all this and more on the basis of the absolute authority of Scripture. He would interpret me, my facts, and my logic in terms of the authority of that Scripture. He says I need this authority. He says I need nothing but this authority. His Scripture, he claims, is sufficient and final. The whole thing, he claims, is clear in the light of Scripture.

"Now all this looks like plain historic Protestantism to me. I can intellectually understand the Calvinist on this matter of authority. I cannot understand you. You seem to me to want to have your cake and eat it. If you believe in scriptural authority, then why not explain all things, man, fact, and logic, in terms of it? If you want with us to live by your own authority, by the experience of the human race, then why not have done with the Bible as absolute authority? It, at best, gives you the authority of the expert.

"In your idea of the rational man who tests all things by the facts of history and by the law of non-contradiction, you have certainly made a point of contact with us. If you carry this through, you will indeed succeed in achieving complete coincidence between your ideas and ours. With us, you will have achieved complete coincidence between the ideas of man and the ideas of God. The reason for this coincidence of your ideas with ours, and for the coincidence of man's ideas with God's, is that you, like we, then have a God and a Christ who are virtually identical with man.

"Do you not think, Mr. Grey, that this is too great a price for you to pay? I am sure that you do not thus mean to drag down your God into the universe. I am sure that you do not thus mean to crucify your Christ afresh. But why then halt between two opinions? I do not believe Christianity, but, if I did, I would stand with Mr. White."

C. *Proofs for the Existence of God*

When Mr. Black objects against Mr. White that unconditional surrender to the authority of Scripture is irrational, then Mr. Grey nods approval and says that, of course, the "rational man" has a perfect right to test the credibility of Scripture by logic. When the Bible speaks of God's sovereign election of some men to salvation this must mean something that fits in with his "rational nature." When Mr. Black objects to Mr. White that unconditional surrender to Scripture is rationalistic, then Mr. Grey again nods approval and says that, of course, genuine human personality has a perfect right to test the content of Scripture by experience. When the Bible speaks of God controlling by his counsel whatsoever comes to pass, this must mean something that fits in with man's "freedom." God created man and gave man a share in his own freedom; men therefore participate in his being.

But what of natural or general revelation? Here surely there can be no difference, you say, between the requirements of Mr. White and Mr. Grey. Here there is no law and no promise; here there are only the facts of nature. How can you speak of any requirement at all with respect to them? Here surely Mr. White can forget his "five points of Calvinism" and join Mr. Grey in taking Mr. Black through the picture gallery of this world, pointing out its beauties to him so that with them he will spontaneously exclaim, "The whole chorus of nature raises one hymn to the praise of its Creator."

Let us think of Mr. White as trying hard to forget his "five points." "Surely," he says to himself, "there can be nothing wrong with joining Mr. Grey in showing Mr. Black the wonders of God's creation. We believe in the same God, do we not? Both of us want to show Mr. Black the facts of creation so that he, too, will believe in God. When Mr. Black says, 'I see no meaning in all I have seen, and I continue, just as I was, confused and dismayed,' Mr. Grey and I can together take him to the Mt. Wilson observatory so he may see the starry heavens above. Surely the source of knowledge for the natural sciences is the Book of Nature which is given to everyone. Do not the Scriptures themselves teach that there is a light in nature which cannot be, and is not, transmitted through the spectacles of the Word? If this were not so, how could the Scriptures say of those who have only the light of nature that they are without excuse?"

So the three men, Mr. White, Mr. Grey, and Mr. Black, go here and there and everywhere. Mr. White and Mr. Grey agree to share the expense. Mr. Black is their guest.

They go first to the Mt. Wilson observatory to see the starry skies above. "How wonderful, how grand!" exclaims Mr. Grey. Then to the marvels of the telescope they add those of the microscope. They circle the globe to see "the wonders of the world." They listen to the astronauts speaking down to the earth from the vicinity of the moon. There is no end to the "exhibits" and Mr. Black shows signs of weariness. So they sit down on the beach. Will not Mr. Black now sign on the dotted line?

As they wait for the answer, Mr. Grey spies a watch someone has lost. Holding it in his hand he says to Mr. Black: "Look around the world: contemplate the whole and every part of it: you will find it to be nothing but one great machine, subdivided into an infinite number of lesser machines, which again admit of subdivisions, to a degree beyond that which human senses and faculties can trace and explain. All these various machines, and even their minute parts, are adjusted to each other with an accuracy which forces admiration from all men who have ever contemplated them. The curious adapting of means to ends, throughout all nature, resembles exactly, though it much exceeds, the productions of human contrivance, of human designs, thought, wisdom, and intelligence. Since, therefore, the effects resemble each other, we are led to infer, by all the rules of analogy, that the causes also resemble one another. The Author of Nature is somewhat similar to the mind of man, though possessed of much larger faculties, proportioned to the grandeur of the work, which he has executed.

"Now, Mr. Black, I don't want to put undue pressure on you. You know your own needs in your own business. But I think that as a rational being you owe it to yourself to join the theistic party. Isn't it highly probable that there is a God?

"I'm not now asking you to become a Christian. We take things one step at a time. I'm only speaking of the Book of Nature. Of course, if there is a God and if this God should have a Son, and if this Son should also reveal himself, it is not likely to be more difficult for you to believe in him than it is now to believe in the Father. But just now I am only asking you to admit that there is a great accumulation of evidence of the sort that any scientist or philosopher must admit to be valid for the existence of a God back of and above this world. You see this watch. Isn't it highly probable that a power higher than itself has made it? You know the purpose of a watch. Isn't it highly probable that the wonderful contrivances of nature serve the purpose of a god? Looking back we are naturally led to a god who is the cause of this world; looking forward we think of a god who has a purpose with this world. So far as we can observe the course and constitution of the universe there is, I think, no difficulty on your own adopted principles, against belief in a god. Why not become a theist? You do want to be on the winning side, don't you? Well, the Gallup poll of the universe indicates a tendency toward the final victory of theism."

When Mr. Grey had finished his obviously serious and eloquent plea, Mr. Black looked very thoughtful. He was clearly a gentleman. He disliked disappointing his two friends after all the generosity they had shown him. But he could not honestly see any basic difference between his own position and theirs. So he declined politely but resolutely to sign on the dotted line. He refused to be "converted" to theism. In substance he spoke as follows: "You speak of evidence of rationality and purpose in the universe. You would trace this rationality or purpose back to a rational being who is back of the universe who, you think, is likely to have a purpose with the universe. But who is back of your God to explain him in turn? By your own definition your God is not absolute or self-sufficient. You say that he *probably* exists; which means that you admit that he may not exist.

Probability rests upon possibility. I think that any scientific person should come with an open mind to the observation of the facts of the universe. He ought to begin by assuming that *any* sort of fact may exist. I was glad to observe that on this all-important point you agree with me. Hence the only kind of god that either of us can believe in is one who may or may not exist. In other words, *neither* of us does or can believe in a *God who cannot not exist*. It was just this sort of God, a God who is self-sufficient, and as such *necessarily* existent, that I thought you Christian theists believed in."

By this time Mr. White was beginning to squirm. He was beginning to realize that he had sold out the God of his theology, the sovereign God of Scripture, by his silent consent to the argument of Mr. Grey. Mr. Black was right, he felt at once. Either one presupposes God back of the ideas of possibility or one presupposes that the idea of possibility is back of God. Either one says with historic Reformed theology on the basis of Scripture that what God determines and only what God determines is possible, or one says with all non-Christian forms of thought that possibility surrounds God. But for the moment Mr. White was stupefied. He could say nothing. So Mr. Black simply drew the conclusion from what he had said in the following words:

"Since, in your effort to please me, you have accepted my basic assumption with respect to possibility and probability, it follows that your God, granted he exists, is of no use whatsoever in explaining the universe. He himself needs in turn to be explained. Let us remember the story of the Indian philosopher and his elephant. It was never more applicable than to the present subject. If the material world rests upon a similar ideal world, this ideal world must rest upon some other; and so on, without end. It were better, therefore, never to look beyond the present material world. In short, gentlemen, much as I dislike not to please you, what you offer is nothing better that what I already possess. Your God is himself surrounded by pure possibility or Chance; in what way can he help me? How could I be responsible to him? For you, as for me, all things ultimately end in the irrational."

At this point Mr. Grey grew pale. In desperation he searched his arsenal for another argument that might convince Mr. Black. There was one that he had not used for some time. The arguments for God that he had so far used, he had labeled *a posteriori* arguments. They ought, he had thought, to appeal to the "empirical" temper of the times. They started from human experience with causation and purpose and by analogy argued to the idea of a cause of and a purpose with the world as a whole. But Mr. Black had pointed out that if you start with the ideas of cause and purpose as intelligible to man *without* God, when these concepts apply to relations *within* the universe, then you *cannot* consistently say that you need God for the idea of cause or purpose when these concepts apply to the universe *as a whole.* So now Mr. Grey drew out the drawer marked *a priori* argument. In public he called this the argument from finite to absolute being. "As finite creatures," he said to Mr. Black, "we have the idea of absolute being. The idea of a finite being involves of necessity the idea of an absolute being. We have the notion of an absolute being; surely there must be a reality corresponding to our idea of such a being; if not, all our ideas may be false. Surely we must hold that reality is ultimately rational and coherent and that our ideas participate in this rationality. If not, how would science be possible?"

When Mr. Grey had thus delivered himself of this appeal to logic rather than to fact, then Mr. White for a moment seemed to take courage. Was not this at least to get away from the idea of a God who probably exists? Surely the "incommunicable attributes of God," of which he had been taught in his catechism classes, were all based upon, and expressive of, the idea of God as necessarily existing. But Mr. Black soon disillusioned him for the second time. Said he in answer to the argument from Mr. Grey, "Again I cannot see any basic difference between your position and mine. Of course, we must believe that reality is ultimately rational. And of course, we must hold that our minds participate in this rationaliy. But when you speak thus you thereby virtually assert that we must not believe in a God whose existence is independent of our human existence. A God whom we are to know must, with us, be a part of a rational system that is mutually accessible to, and expressive of, both. If

God is necessary to you, then you are also necessary to God. That is the only sort of God that is involved in your argument."

"But Mr. Black, this is terrible, this is unbearable! We do want you to believe in God. I bear witness to his existence. I will give you a Bible. Please read it! It tells you of Jesus Christ and how you may be saved by his blood. I am born again and you can be born again too if you will only believe. Please do believe in God and be saved!"

Meanwhile, Mr. White took new courage. He realized that he had so far made a great mistake in keeping silent during the time that Mr. Grey had presented his arguments. The arguments for the existence of God taken from the ideas of cause and purpose as set forth by Mr. Grey had led to pure irrationalism and Chance. The argument about an absolute being as set forth by Mr. Grey had led to pure rationalism and determinism. In both cases, Mr. Black had been quite right in saying that a God whose existence is problematic, or a God who exists by the same necessity as does the universe, is still an aspect of, or simply the whole of, the universe. But now he felt that perhaps Mr. Grey was right in simply witnessing to the existence of God. He thought that, if the arguments used are not logically coercive, they may at least be used as a means with which to *witness* to unbelievers. And surely witnessing to God's existence was always in order. But poor Mr. White was to be disillusioned again. For the witness-bearing done by Mr. Grey was based on the assumption that the belief in God is a purely non-rational or even irrational matter.

Mr. Black's reply to the words of Mr. Grey indicated this fact all too clearly. Said Mr. Black to Mr. Grey: "I greatly appreciate your evident concern for my 'eternal welfare.' But there are two or three questions that I would like to have you answer. In the first place, I would ask whether in thus simply *witnessing* to me of God's existence you thereby admit that the *arguments* for the existence of God have no validity? Or rather do you not thereby admit that these arguments, if they prove anything, prove that God is finite and correlative to man and therefore that your position is not basically different from mine?"

Mr. Grey did not answer because he could not answer this question otherwise than by agreeing with Mr. Black.

"In the second place," said Mr. Black, "you are now witnessing to Christ as well as to God, to Christianity as well as to theism. I suppose your argument for Christianity would be similar in nature to your argument for theism, would it not? You would argue that the Jesus of the New Testament is probably the Son of God and that he quite probably died for the sins of men. But now you witness to me about your Christ. And by witnessing *instead* of reasoning you seem to admit that there is no objective claim for the truth of what you hold with respect to Christ. Am I right in all this?"

Again Mr. Grey made no answer. The only answer he could consistently have given would be to agree with Mr. Black.

"In the third place," said Mr. Black, "you are now witnessing not only to God the Father, to Jesus Christ the Son, but also to the Holy Spirit. You say you are born again, that you know you are saved and that at present I am lost. Now, if you have had a special experience of some sort, it would be unscientific for me to deny it. But, if you want to witness to me *about* your experience, you must make plain to me the *nature* of that experience. To do that you must do so in terms of principles that I understand. Such principles must needs be accessible to all. Now if you make plain your experience to me in terms of principles that are plain to me as unregenerate, then how is your regeneration unique? On the other hand, if you still maintain that your experience of regeneration is unique, then can you say anything about it to me so that I may understand? Does not then your witness-bearing appear to be wholly unintelligible and devoid of meaning? Thus again you cannot make any claim to the objective truth of your position.

"Summing up the whole matter, I would say in the first place, that your arguments for the existence of God have rightfully established me in my unbelief. They have shown that nothing can be said for the existence of a God who is actually the Creator and controller of the world. I would say in the second place that using such arguments as you have used for the existence of God commits you to using similar arguments for the truth of Christianity with similar fatal results for your position. In both cases you first use intellectual argument upon principles that presuppose the justice of my unbelieving position. Then, when it is pointed out to you that such is the case, you turn to witnessing. But then your witnessing is in the nature of the case an activity that you yourself have virtually admitted to be wholly irrational and unintelligible."

When Mr. Black had finished, Mr. White was in great distress. But it was through this very distress that he at last saw the richness of his own faith. He made no pretense to having greater intellectual power than Mr. Grey. He greatly admired the real faith and courage of Mr. Grey. But he dared keep silence no longer. His silence had been sin, he now realized. Mr. Black had completely discomforted Mr. Grey, so that he had not another word to say. Mr. Black was about to leave them establishd rather than challenged in his unbelief. And all of that in spite of the best intentions and efforts of Mr. Gray, speaking for both of them. A sense of urgent responsibility to make known the claims of the sovereign God pressed upon him. He now saw clearly, first, that the arguments for the existence of God, as conducted by Mr. Grey, are based on the assumption that the unbeliever is right with respect to the principles in terms of which he explains all things. These principles are: (a) that man is not a creature of God but rather is ultimate and as such must properly consider himself instead of God the final reference point in explaining all things; (b) that all other things beside himself are non-created but controlled by Chance; and (c) that the power of logic that he possesses is the means by which he must determine what is possible or impossible in the universe of Chance.

At last it dawned upon Mr. White that first to admit that the principles of Mr. Black, the unbeliever, are right and then to seek to win him to the acceptance of the existence of God the Creator and judge of all men is like first admitting that the United States had historically been a province of the Soviet Union but ought at the same time to be recognized as an independent and all-controlling political power.

In the second place, Mr. White now saw clearly that a false type of reasoning for the truth of God's existence and for the truth of

Christianity involves a false kind of witnessing for the existence of God and for the truth of Christianity. If one reasons for the existence of God and for the truth of Christianity, on the assumption that Mr. Black's principles of explanation are valid, then one must witness on the same assumption. One must then make plain to Mr. Black, in terms of principles which Mr. Black accepts, what it means to be born again. Mr. Black will then apply the principles of modern psychology of religion to Mr. Grey's "testimony" with respect to his regeneration and show that it is something that naturally comes in the period of adolescence.

In the third place, Mr. White now saw clearly that it was quite "proper," for Mr. Grey, to use a method of reasoning and a method of witness-bearing that is based upon the truth of anti-Christian and anti-theistic assumptions. Mr. Grey's theology is not Reformed. It is therefore based upon the idea that God is not wholly sovereign over man. It assumes that man's responsibility implies a measure of autonomy of the sort that is the essence and foundation of the whole of Mr. Black's thinking. It is therefore to be expected that Mr. Grey will assume that Mr. Black needs not to be challenged on his basic assumption with respect to his own assumed ultimacy or autonomy.

From now on Mr. White decided that, much as he enjoyed the company of Mr. Grey and much as he admired his evident sincerity and basic devotion to the truth of God, yet he must go his own way in apologetics as he had, since the Reformation, gone his own way in theology. He tried to make an appointment with Mr. Black then to see him soon. Meanwhile he expressed to Mr. Grey his great love for him as a fellow believer, his great admiration for his fearless and persistent efforts to win men to an acceptance of truth as it is in Jesus. Then he confessed to Mr. Grey that his conscience had troubled him during the entire time of their travels with Mr. Black. He had started in good faith, thinking that Mr. Grey's efforts at argument and witnessing might win Mr. Black. He had therefore been quite willing, especially since Mr. Grey was through his constant study much more conversant with such things than he himself was, to be represented by Mr. Grey. But now he had at last come to realize that not only had the effort been utterly fruitless and self-frustrating but, more than that, it had been terribly dishonoring to God. How could the eternal I AM be pleased with being presented as being *a* god and as *probably* existing, as probably necessary for the explanation of *some* things but not of all things, as one who will be glad to recognize the ultimacy of his own creatures? Would the God who had in paradise required of men implicit obedience now be satisfied with a claims-and-counter-claims arrangement with his creatures?

From the dialogue given above, the reader can for himself discern why we have advocated what seems to us to be a Reformed as over against the traditional method of apologetics. The traditional method, the method practiced by various Christians for centuries, was constructed by Roman Catholics and Arminians. It was, so to speak, derived from Romanist or Arminian theology. Just as Roman Catholic and Arminian theology compromises the Christian doctrines of Scripture, of God, of man, of sin, and of redemption, so the traditional method of apologetics compromises Christianity in order to win men to an acceptance of it.

The traditional method compromises the biblical doctrine of *God* in not clearly distinguishing his self-existence from his relation to the world. The traditional method compromises the biblical doctrine of God and his relation to his revelation to man by not clearly insisting that man, as a creature and as a sinner, must not seek to determine the nature of God, otherwise than from his revelation.

The traditional method compromises the biblical doctrine of the *counsel* of God by not taking it as the only all-inclusive ultimate "cause" of whatsoever comes to pass.

The traditional method therefore compromises the *clarity* of God's revelation to man, whether this revelation comes through general or through special revelation. Created facts are not taken to be clearly revelational of God; all the facts of nature and of man are said to indicate no more than that *a* god *probably* exists.

The traditional method compromises the *necessity* of supernatural revelation in relation to natural revelation. It does so in failing to do justice to the fact that even in paradise man had to interpret natural revelation in the light of the covenantal obligations placed upon him by God through supernatural communication. In consequence, the traditional method fails to recognize the necessity of redemptive supernatural, as concomitant to natural, revelation after the fall of man.

The traditional method compromises the *sufficiency* of redemptive supernatural revelation in Scripture inasmuch as it allows for wholly new facts to appear in Reality, new for God as well as for man.

The traditional method compromises the *authority* of Scripture by not taking it as self-attesting in the full sense of the term.

The traditional method compromises the biblical doctrine of man's *creation* in the image of God by thinking of him as being "free" or ultimate rather than as analogical.

The traditional method compromises the biblical doctrine of the *covenant* by not making Adam's representative action determinative for the future.

The traditional method compromises the biblical doctrine of *sin,* in not thinking of it as an ethical break with God which is complete in principle even though not in practice.

In spite of these things, this traditional method has been employed by Reformed theologians, and this fact has stood in the way of the development of a distinctly Reformed apologetic.

VI.   *Conclusion*

It has become even more apparent now that our Reformed pastor cannot, as he defends the Christian faith, cooperate with the Arminian any more than he could cooperate with the Roman Catholic.

The Arminian as well as the Roman Catholic fails to present to the believer a challenge to the effect that he needs a radical conversion. Neither the Arminian nor the Roman Catholic so much as gives the unbeliever the opportunity of seeing what the gospel really is. They do not direct the all-revealing searchlight of the Scripture toward him. They do not even show him the face of the Great Physician lest this Great Physician should say that the heart of the natural man is desperately wicked and that no man knows the depth of that wickedness except the Great Physician, who would heal all his diseases.

Of course we are speaking primarily of systems rather than men.

Many Roman Catholics, and especially many Arminians are much more biblical than are their systems. Therein must all rejoice. But the Reformed Christian must be true to his Lord. He must love sinners with a deep compassion. But he must not love sinners more than he loves Christ. The more truly he loves sinners the more uncomprisingly will he require of them that they must be saved on God's terms, not their own. It is Christ, through his Word in Scripture, who must diagnose their disease even as it is Christ who heals only those who confess that their disease is what the Great Physician says it is.

NOTES

1. All references to Calvin's *Institutes of the Christian Religion* are from the translation by Ford Lewis Battles, edited by John T. McNeill, in "The Library of Christian Classics" (Philadelphia: The Westminster Press; London: S.C.M. Press, Ltd., 1965).

2. B. B. Warfield, *Calvin and Calvinism* (New York: Oxford, 1931), pp. 69-70.

3. Man is a mixture of form (Being) and matter (non-Being). Except for his participation in God (Being), a participation which God himself sustains, man would be wholly absorbed into matter or pure Chaos (non-Being), which is the polar opposite of God and therefore evil. It is, however, *equally ultimate* with God. (By "equally ultimate" we mean that neither in any way is dependent on the other for existence.)

4. Since both man and nature are in some sense *combinations* of the finite (Chaos) and infinite (Rationality), the witness of both man and nature is *unclear*. Therefore the existence of God, for Aquinas, is a matter of *question* and can be answered only in terms of rational and empirical argumentation. Of course, Aquinas thought that his arguments for the existence of God were completely valid. Many modern orthodox apologists, however, recognizing the inadequacies of the "theistic proofs," generally maintain that, when all of the arguments are taken together, God's existence is seen to be highly probable. However, they still hold to Aquinas' belief in (1) the lack of clarity in God's revelation; and (2) the ability of man's intellect to reason about God correctly prior to, and independently of, the revelation of God.

5. The concept of the "analogy of being" entails the idea that in so far as objects participate in Being, in that degree properties of Being (God) will be in them. Thus a "natural theology" is possible because, in so far as man is able to locate properties which could not be characteristics of non-

72 THE REFORMED PASTOR AND MODERN THOUGHT

Being (matter-evil), e.g., changlessness, man is able to speak of God (Being).

6. For the sake of simplicity we use this as a synonym for non-Reformed.
7. To hold to the ultimacy of man means to proceed on the basic fundamental supposition that man is the supreme authority in deciding any question. In other words, man is autonomous, rather than dependent.
8. *Moody Monthly* (January, 1950), p. 313.
9. *Ibid.*, p. 343.
10. J. O. Buswell, Jr., *What Is God?* (Grand Rapids: Zondervan, 1937), pp. 50, 53, 54.
11. Wilbur M. Smith, *Therefore Stand* (Boston: Wilde, 1945), p. 386.
12. *Ibid.*, pp. 389, 390.
13. E. J. Carnell, *An Introduction to Christian Apologetics* (Grand Rapids: Eerdmans, 1949), p. 113.
14. *Ibid.*, p. 114.
15. Cf. *ibid.*, p. 57.
16. *Ibid.*, p. 71.
17. *Ibid.*, p. 72.
18. *Ibid.*, p. 73.
19. *Ibid.*, p. 178.
20. *Ibid.*, pp. 77, 78.

Chapter II

THE REFORMED PASTOR AND
TRADITIONAL ROMAN CATHOLICISM

I. *Introduction*

Traditional Roman Catholic theology and philosophy is of interest to the Reformed pastor, for the foundations of the Papacy in the twentieth century remain those constructed by Aquinas in the twelfth. It is against Roman Catholic theology as a background that the reformers, especially Calvin, developed what we now call the Reformed Faith. The Reformed pastor must therefore understand the philosophy and theology of Thomas Aquinas if he is to truly appreciate his Calvinistic heritage.

The purpose of this chapter is twofold: (1) to give the pastor a deeper understanding of his own faith, and (2) to enable him to set his faith clearly over against the faith proposed and developed by traditional Catholicism. There seems to be no better way of doing this than to contrast the positions of Thomas Aquinas and John Calvin, paying special attention to the philosophical assumptions which governed the theology of Thomas Aquinas. However, the final purpose is primarily apologetical. The argument is that inasmuch as traditional Roman Catholicism does not hold to the gospel in its purity, it cannot challenge the modern unbeliever to see that both in his thinking and his living he is bankrupt.

In introducing the subject of the relationship of Thomas Aquinas to Calvin, a few introductory remarks are in order.

In this chapter we are concerned primarily with philosophy, not with theology. Yet it will not be possible to avoid dealing with what is ordinarily thought of as narrowly theological. We have a frankly religious interest in our discussion. It will be our aim to demonstrate that one who holds to the philosophical principles of Thomas Aquinas cannot consistently hold to the Reformed Faith as it has been worked out by Calvin. Roman Catholic philosophy and Roman Catholic theology are complementary to one another.

The claim is constantly made in Reformed circles, and made truly, that it is the Reformed Faith alone that is able to meet the challenge of modern thought. The reason for this claim lies near at hand. All thinking, whether it be in the philosophical or in the theological field, is, in the last analysis, bound to start from some final reference point. This reference point must be taken as *self-contained*, or ultimate, that is, as self-sufficient and self-interpretative; in the nature of the case it cannot be impersonal. Every appeal to law, no matter how that law be conceived, involves, in the last analysis, an appeal either to God or to man as the ultimate arbiter in both moral and intellectual matters.

When sin entered into the world, man made himself instead of God the final reference point of all interpretative endeavor. But it was not till modern times, and notably since Kant, that the fact of man's ultimacy or independence from all authority other than his own rational and moral consciousness (i.e., man's autonomy) has come to the foreground with unmistakable clarity. Even now, this fact is obscured by those modern theologians and philosophers who continue to speak of God as the "highest" or "final reference point" while in reality this "God" is for them no more than an enlarged image of man constructed by man himself and projected into the realm of the unknown.

It is therefore more apparent in modern times than it has ever been before that there is no real theism that is not at the same time *Christian* theism. Every use of the word "God" in one's system of thought that is not mediated through the Word, through Christ, is an illegitimate, a blank, undefined "X." But then the word "Christ" can be misused as well as the word "God." And such misuse has characterized modern theology. Modern theology in its varieties of immanentism (whereby God and man are identified with one another)[1] and in its varieties of transcendence (whereby God and man are so separate that contact between them is impossible)[2] has, to be sure, mediated "God" to man by means of "Christ"—but has falsified the meaning of the word "Christ," by making it once again a projection of the ideals of the self-sufficient man.

It follows, then, that both the words "God" and "Christ" must come to us *as infallibly interpreted to us* by God and Christ, or else they will mean only what we *want* them to mean. Without a written revelation from God wherein he reveals both himself and his Christ, as well as man and his world, man would be left to his own devices in locating some sort of redemptive plan for himself. Modern man has rejected this revelation and has chosen to go it alone. However, truly Christian thinking of any sort, whether in theology or in philosophy, will presuppose the infallible authority of Scripture in what it says about God, Christ, man, and the world around man, for we know that only by presupposing this, will we see all things as God sees them, rather than as man sees them with sin-blinded eyes.

It is, therefore, the historic Protestant and, more particularly, the historic Reformed Faith that must be set over against Romanism. We have a cleavage between Protestantism and Romanism that cannot be avoided at any point. It is of the essence of Romanism that the authority of the living church interprets to the individual believer the meaning of the word "God" and the word "Christ." What the Bible says to the individual is *mediated through* the declarative activity of the church which is assumed to be infallible. Although Thomas Aquinas stresses the fact that philosophy must work by its own method and hold for true that which it has discovered to be true independently of all authority of the church, he also maintains that this same philosophy must not discover anything that is out of accord with the pronouncements of the church given by "infallible authority."

The two points of view, each admittedly differing on essential questions pertaining to the relation of God to man, and each involving in its position a relation to an infallible authority, stand over against one another. If it be said that this difference is limited to points of theology, and therefore does not involve the question of philosophical interpretation, we reply that the theology of each party does in fact make pronouncements about the whole of reality. More particularly, the two theologies differ on the question of the ultimate reference point. The theology of Roman Catholicism and the theology of the Reformed Confessions admittedly are opposed to one another on the question of man's free will in relation to God. Even taking into account the differences of interpretation that prevail in Romanist theology on the question of human will, it remains true that even the most Augustinian of Romanists still are not Calvinists; for the Council of Trent rejects the Reformed conception of predestination as destructive of the created freedom of man. And this really amounts to a difference on all doctrines of the Christian faith as well, for it implies a totally different view of God and his relation to the world and a different view of the relation of man's reason to both God and the world.

In view of this dramatic cleavage between Protestantism and Romanism, it might be maintained that Protestants should join in forming a common philosophical approach as they are said already to have a common Reformation theology. We have been told that the Protestant churches have in common such doctrines as the sub-stitutionary atonement. Nothing could be further from the truth. Moreover, whatever may be said to be the distinguishing mark of the Reformed Faith as over against non-Reformed evangelical Protestant-ism, it cannot be said to be most basically the "Five Points of Cal-vinism." There is, of course, an element of truth in saying that only Calvinism holds to election. But then it is also true that other Protestants hold to "election" or did hold to election. Even Romanism holds to "election." The whole question is what is *meant* by the word "election." Each group defines it, ultimately, in terms of its final or basic personal reference point. For Calvinism this reference point is the triune God of Scripture.

In the Reformed point of view, every doctrine is colored by the consistency with which it makes God and his revelation through Christ in the Scriptures *primary* in its thought. And it is only in the Reformed Confessions that one sees a consistent application of this basic doctrine of the self-contained ontological trinity to all the doc-trines of Scripture, i.e., only in Reformed theology does one find an attempt to take the fundamental motif of Scripture, the self-contained ontological trinity, and understand all the teachings of Scripture in terms of that motif. It is because of this unique conception of God that the doctrines of Scripture such as creation, fall, covenant, redemption, etc., take on their particular Reformed structure which speaks first and always of the glory of God.

Two consequences are immediately apparent. The first is that it is only in the Reformed view that one has a position that is squarely set over against modern theology, modern philosophy, and modern science. All other forms of theology compromise to some extent with the very idea of human freedom and self-sufficiency (autonomy) which is the root heresy of all false theology and philosophy.

Secondly, the Romanist is unable to meet and challenge modern thought such as has been developed by Kant and his successors because in their own approach to philosophy they share the idea of autonomy with that of modern thought.

*   *   *   *   *

As a corollary of these points, the necessity of setting out the difference between the scholastic or traditional Roman Catholic approach to philosophy and the Calvinistic approach should be apparent. The history of Reformed theology shows that the tendency to make common cause with the scholastics against "unbelief" is ever in our midst. When Voetius called on a Roman Catholic priest to help him in answering the false philosophical approach of Descartes, he set a bad example that is still being followed in our day. If as followers of Calvin we see our responsibility of challenging the world today with the full Christian gospel, the whole counsel of God, then we must make sure that there is no admixture of scholasticism in our approach at any point.

II. *Analogy*

We shall now deal in detail with subjects more explicitly philosophical: epistemology, metaphysics, and, briefly, ethics. In each case our discussion will center largely on the word *analogy*. It is our conviction that in the Roman doctrine of *analogia entis* (analogy of being) is concentrated all the heresy that is Romanism, and that in the Reformed conception of *analogia fidei* (analogy of faith) is concentrated all that is biblical. Karl Barth was *formally* quite correct when he set the *analogia fidei* over against the *analogia entis* as defended by the Roman Catholic, Przywara. We shall argue, however, that the *analogia fidei* of Barth and the *analogia entis* of Rome are both of the same species after all. The two have in common the assumption of man's autonomy.

Why, first of all, is the question of *analogy* so important? What is involved in the question of analogy. It is the question of the relation of God to man. It is the question, more specifically, as to the *priority* of these two. There are those who worship and serve the creature rather than the Creator. There are also those, having been saved by grace, who worship and serve the Creator rather than the creature. It would be a happy day if orthodox Christians would give up their "block-house" mode of thinking, by which they divide philosophies into pantheism, deism, and theism, as if the last of these three were somehow a happy medium between the former two; it is unfortunate that many feel that such concepts as "immanence" and "transcendence" can be arranged and rearranged as so many bricks, until some satisfying structures are reached, and that people are only in need of a "shot" of transcendence or immanence to correct their one-sided condition and thereby make them balanced, and therefore Christian.

There are only *two* kinds of people in the world, covenant-breakers and covenant-keepers. Covenant-breakers are such in all that they do, and covenant-keepers are such in all that they do.[3] Covenant-breakers make God in man's image, and covenant-keepers make man in God's image. This distinction, thus baldly stated, indicates the antithesis between the believer and the unbeliever *in principle*. Of course, this principle does not come to full expression in this life. Any doctrine of common grace or general grace that we hold will surely need to be consistent with this basic point.

But, if things are as simple as that, you may say, how is it that philosophers have not always frankly asserted that they are doing without God altogether? Some philosophers have been frank in making man the center of all things. Modern existentialism as represented by Heidegger, and Jean Paul Sartré could hardly go much further in this direction. With them, the prodigal stands at the swine trough and refuses to return to the father's house. But, as a rule, the prodigal is still some distance from the position where he openly and finally declares his utter self-sufficiency. He is actually under the pressure of God's revelation at all times. Deep down in his being he knows that he is a creature of God and that he will be called upon to meet his Creator in the judgment day for his breaking of the covenant made with him through Adam. Every man is confronted with the revelation of God not only within him but also round about him. Everywhere and all the time the face of God confronts him. Every fact of the universe speaks to him of his responsibility to be a covenant-keeper and therefore at the same time of his sin of actually being a covenant-breaker.

What will the sinner do about all this? He will try to make himself believe that he can explain to himself the nature of the world and himself without God. Taking to himself the place ascribed to God in a true Christian theology, he assumes that reality must be of such a nature as he says it is. Using the gift of logical manipulation given to him for the purpose of thinking God's thoughts after him on a created scale (in order thus to form an analogical system that in some measure reflects the plan of God), he absolutizes himself and compels the nature of reality to be equal to the reach of his logical thought. *This is his principle of continuity.* By using this principle consistently, the Greeks, especially Parmenides, came to the conclusion that there is no creation out of nothing. There *cannot* be such a thing, he said. Involved in this position, therefore, is the idea that man himself cannot be a creature of God. It is inconsistent with the honor that he owes to himself as a thinking or rational man that he should be a creature of God.

III. *Greek Foundations*

A. *Parmenides*

Using this principle by itself, man would thus seem able to make short shrift of his own creaturehood and of his own responsibility to his Creator. But the trouble was that in disproving his creaturehood he also virtually disproved his selfhood as an individual. He had proved too much. Logic required him to find *absolute unity,* he said. But to find absolute unity one must be able to prove that there *can be no change of any sort.* The only change that can be thought of on a non-Christian basis is such a change as is independent of reason. *So Parmenides denied the possibility of all change.* If things seemed to change, this was but appearance and not reality. Yet human thinking itself takes place in the realm of change. Man is not conscious of thought unless he is at the same time conscious of change. So Parmenides virtually had to deny self-consciousness with the denial of change. The testimony of Scripture, on the other hand, is that a man cannot be conscious of himself without thinking of himself as a creature of *God*.

B. *Anaximander*

There was, therefore, for anyone who wished to retain man's consciousness of himself and the world, no escape from the necessity of positing some sort of principle of *discontinuity* (change) alongside of the principle of continuity. Anaximander had introduced the principle of discontinuity by speaking of the *"apeiron"* ("indeterminate"). There has been much discussion in the histories of philosophy as to the meaning of this *apeiron.* But this much is clear: it had to be *unlike* any one of the elements that were "known" to man and yet not so unlike as to be *wholly* unlike. It had to be unlike earth or air or fire or water, or it could not serve as the common source of supply of all of them. On the other hand, if it were wholly unlike all of them, it would no longer be rationally related to man and his experiences.

This *apeiron* of Anaximander may, for convenience, help us to understand the ingredients that went into the Greek concept of analogy as it was later developed by Aristotle. There are three ingredients that go into the makeup of this concept. The first is the *autonomy* of man as the ultimate reference point. The second is a *principle of continuity* or *logical relationship*, which would, if carried out consistently and to the end, lead to the denial of time, change, and human individuality. The third is a *principle of discontinuity* or chance. This third principle is as irrational as the principle of continuity is basically rational. The difference among various philosophers is the result of the various degrees of emphasis that they have given either to the *rationalist principle of continuity* or to the *irrationalist principle of discontinuity.* The philosophy of Aristotle was characterized by the niceness of balance between these two principles.

C. *Plato*

In his doctrine of reminiscence as well as in his doctrine of ideal identification of man with God through intuition, Plato laid great emphasis upon the principle of *changeless unity.* Man had himself to be participant in this principle in order to have unity in his experience. Accordingly, he tended to deny either the existence, or at least the real significance, of change. The world of "becoming" had only a quasi-existence and knowledge of it was only a quasi-knowledge. In man, however, there was a rational soul which was not part of this quasi-existent world of chance, but was participant in the divine.

Plato spoke much of the reality of that which is above man in the way of eternal truth. In order for man to exist and to know at all, he had to be essentially divine; that is, in his intellectual soul man had to be participant in the very being of the ideal world. The world of temporal reality was not, for Plato, the revelation of the self-contained God. If, therefore, he could prove that his world-view could make intelligible the nature of reality, thereby making the world understandable without reference to the Creator-Redeemer, he would have justified to himself and to his followers his covenant-breaking attitude.

D. *The Sophists*

Plato sought in his philosophy to answer the Sophists, who stressed the *irrational* principle of discontinuity. They argued that there could be no knowledge of God since there is no ascertainable character in any fact. From Heraclitus they had learned that all opposites change wholly into each other. All knowledge was relative to man, and man had justified his covenant-breaking attitude.

E. *Aristotle*

Aristotle's course lay midway between that of the Sophist and Plato. Aristotle rightly saw that it was no virtue to speak of an ideal world if that world was after all so similar to ours that the same problems that face us here will again face us there. If there were *ideas* of mud and hair and filth, then mud and hair and filth would be eternal and ineradicable. The God of Plato, for all his supposed transcendence, was in reality not transcendent enough. On the other hand, the God of Plato was not a God that was immanent in the world and present in it. Plato's principle of continuity was too detached from the facts of the temporal world. To make contact with the world, the *ideas* had to be unified internally and made to be immanent in the space-time world from the start. Aristotle did not put his criticism of Plato in quite this fashion, yet such was the essential nature of his reason for distinguishing his position from that of his teacher.

If it seems contradictory to say that the God of Plato was both not sufficiently transcendent and at the same time too transcendent to suit Aristotle, the solution lies in the idea that Aristotle tried to make the two principles, those of continuity and discontinuity, more correlative to one another than Plato had done. By making the two correlative to one another he *formalized* the principle of continuity and raised the principle of discontinuity from the position of virtual non-being, or nothingness, to that of *otherness*. (By "formalized" and "otherness," we merely wish to indicate that Aristotle altered the principles of continuity and discontinuity to such an extent that each would be more easily made correlative to the other.)

By formalizing the principle of continuity he made it more flexible. It was now like a string that could be used for stringing the beads of pure plurality instead of like a rod that would insist on its stability and therefore would not cooperate with pure contingency. In other words, to the extent that the principle of continuity was formalized, to that extent that it was supposed to be able to adapt itself to the irrational principle of discontinuity. And on the other hand, to the extent that the principle of discontinuity was turned into the idea of *otherness* instead of that of *non-being*, to that extent it would admit of being rationalized. The whole was neatly expressed in the relation of potentiality to actuality.

Thus, in contradistinction from Parmenides, Aristotle holds that being is not all of one kind; it is inherently various and hierarchical. At the bottom of the ladder is pure matter or potentiality. At the top of the ladder is pure form. But we never meet with either pure form or pure matter in actual experience. *Reality as we see it is always composite.* The matter in it contributes the individuating, and the form in it, the universalizing, element. Thus Aristotle thinks that he can do justice to individuality and universality alike.

The relation of Aristotle to his predecessors is therefore very similar to that of Kant to the empiricist, Hume, and the rationalist, Leibniz. Aristotle's position may, we think, not unfairly be said to be a sort of pre-phenomenalist phenomenalism.[4] Of course Aristotle's position is not modern; it is realistic, not critical. Our contention is that he takes the first important step in the direction of modern phenomenalism, and that there was nowhere else that anyone, who wanted to maintain the non-Christian concept of the autonomy, of man, could go. The autonomous man must on the one hand seek to explain reality exhaustively; he must hold that unless he does so, he has not explained it at all. By definition, he has no Creator-Redeemer Mind back of his own mind. On the other hand, the autonomous man must hold that any diversity that exists is independent of God.

As Kant's philosophy seemed to many to leave room for faith or even to require faith as a supplement to science, so the philosophy of Aristotle seemed to do justice to the requirements of reason and at the same time to allow for supernatural revelation. Or so it seemed to Thomas Aquinas in the thirteenth century.

IV. *Thomas Aquinas*

It must be admitted that there was in the days of Thomas Aquinas no system of theology or philosophy that had adequately solved the problem of the relation of faith to reason. For the Augustinian tradition then prevalent, philosophy was largely patterned after Plato or Plotinus. (This tradition, of course, is not to be identified with the theology of Augustine himself.) What happened to the doctrines of Christianity if they were interpreted in accord with Platonic-Plotinic principles, is patent from the work of Scotus Erigena. For Scotus the primary relation of man to God is negative. The positive affirmations about God are merely metaphorical. We can only know *that* God is but not *what* he is. The assumption is that unless man knows comprehensively, he does not really know at all. If man cannot penetrate the essence of God, he can really say nothing about it. Neither does God know what he is. "If He did know what He is, He would have defined Himself, and how is it possible to limit the infinite by definition?"[5] On the other hand, all things in the universe are necessarily related to God and God is necessarily related to them. With God, to be and to will and to act are all the same thing. Thus the philosophy of the "Augustinian tradition" killed the theology of Christianity when it had the opportunity of doing so. On the other hand, the primacy of faith over reason, as it was maintained in this same tradition, seemed to kill all true philosophy. If the ideas of Plato were reduced to exemplars in the mind of the God of Christianity and men were expected to see reflections of the trinity in all the world about them, what then was there left for free inquiry?

Thomas had the vision of saving both philosophy and theology by the use of Aristotle rather than Plato. In using Aristotle's method of philosophy he would be able to present Christianity to its cultured despisers just as Schleiermacher and many others tried to do later. A true theology, a true philosophy, and a true apologetic: all three seemed to be in his mind; it was well worth the effort of the great mind that God had given him. And the great synthesis that resulted was approved by Christ himself, it is said.

The theology in which Aquinas believed in his early life was that of semi-pelagianism.[6] If in his later works he approached what seemed to be an Augustinian conception of election, such was not true of his early work on the *Sentences of Lombard*. From a Reformed point of view such a theology would be criticized among other things for its relative stress on human autonomy, its rationalism in rejecting such doctrines as election, and its irrationalism in holding to free will.

If any Christian theology could be made to fit into the philosophy of Aristotle, it would be such a theology as that produced by Thomas.

But let us note the results as they appeared in the great synthesis that is Roman Catholicism. Naturally we can do this only on certain main points. We shall note in each instance how the great synthesis which resulted is, on the one hand, so rationalistic and deterministic that, if carried through consistently, it would destroy historical Christianity, and, on the other hand, so irrationalistic that if it were carried through consistently it would destroy the whole unity of the plan of God, indeed, make any such thing as the plan of God impossible.

A. *Epistemology*

1. *The Subject of Knowledge*

It is not necessary here to go into the details as to the difference between the Platonic and the Aristotelian concepts of the human soul. In both cases it is the intellect of man that is virtually said or assumed to be *eternal* and of the *essence of deity*. In the case of Plato this was true immediately, with the result that the immortality of the soul was proved by its deiformity.[7] In the case of Aristotle this was less obviously, but no less truly, so. In accordance with his general principle of the correlativity of form and matter, Aristotle was able to make a greater distinction between the human and the divine intellect than was Plato. Aristotle spoke of the passive intellect and of the active intellect. The passive intellect was for him the *capacity* in man for intellection. It fitted in with the general idea that human knowledge derives from the senses and that man must therefore, to begin with at least, be passive in the reception of that which comes to it from without. Aristotelianism has, therefore, frequently been presented as though it were an essentially empiricistic approach to the learning process over against the Platonic, which was essentially *a priori*. Edward Carnell in his well-known *Introduction to Christian Apologetics* thinks of Romanism in this fashion and seeks to refute it in the way that a modern idealist would refute the arguments of scepticism, i.e., by pointing out the necessity of thinking of a mental activity of judgment as already involved in every act of observation.

But, if Romanism could be refuted in this way, then Romanism might be said to have refuted itself. Nothing is further from the truth than to say that Aristotelianism is really empiricism unless one points out also that even in empiricism there are non-Christian *a priori* assumptions.

It should be noted that Aristotle himself never separated sharply between the passive and the active intellect in man. He was indeed anxious to develop realism, the reality of facts and their true existence apart from the activity of the human mind with respect to them. Similarly, Romanist apologists today are very zealous to point out that it is on a scholastic basis of realism alone that one can be saved from Cartesian or Kantian subjectivism. If such were really the case, we should be thankful to them. But it would be strange indeed if a system that carried out the idea of human ultimacy and autonomy consistently could be refuted by a system that also starts in large measure from human autonomy. The fact of the matter is that the "passive intellect" of Aristotle is but a correlative to his "active intellect." In Aristotelianism *God is pure active intellect. He is pure act.* Man's mentality *shares* in the nature of the divine activity. It is only on the basis of this *sharing in the divine activity* that abstraction from the sensible world, or the making of generalizations, so essential to the Aristotelian scheme, can be effected. The intellect of man abstracts the intelligible species that that are said to be found in the facts that surround him. All *certain knowledge* is exclusively of universals. The intellect cannot deal with sensible facts otherwise than in terms of *concepts*. But facts *are* not concepts; they are *individuations of concepts*. Matter as such, pure matter as opposed to pure ACT, is non-rational and cannot be the object of intellectual knowledge. It is the *species* that exist in the facts of sense that are said to be discovered by the intellect, and this discovery is not merely a passive something. True, it is not conceived of actively in the way that Kantianism thinks of it. The categories are not said to be subjective. On the contrary, the species are assumed to be in the things and may in a sense be said to impress themselves upon the mind of man. But no non-Christian can finally escape the virtual identification of the human mind with the divine mind. So Aristotle, in thinking of the human mind as discovering the intelligible species in the things, is virtually attributing the same powers to the human mind that he attributes to the divine mind. The active mind of man is ideally identical with the active mind which is God.

Thus there is no essential difference between the activity of the subject and the object of knowledge, in modern idealistic or scholastic thought. Speaking of the mind and its work, Aristotle says:

Mind in this sense of it is separable, impassible, unmixed, since it is in its essential nature activity (for always the active is superior to the passive factor, the originating force to the matter which it forms). Actual knowledge is identical with its object: in the individual, potential knowledge is in time prior to actual knowledge, but in the universe as a whole it is not prior even in time. When mind is set free from its present conditions it appears as just what it is and nothing more: this alone is immortal and eternal (we do not, however, remember its former activity because, while mind in this sense is impassible, mind as passive is destructible) and without it nothing thinks.[8]

For Aristotle the *intelligible* in act is the same as the *intellect* in act. That is to say, to be a realist in Aristotle's sense of the word means in effect that one must assume that man is potentially divine. Man cannot know the object till he is, as it were, identified with it. This position is the exact opposite of that of Calvin. For Thomas there can be no such thing as a revelation of God *to* man in the penetralia of his consciousness. To the extent that man knows God from knowing himself he must also *be* God. All knowledge about anything, in particular about the human self, is knowledge to the extent that the Creator-creature distinction—what was left of it in Aristotle's positing of the difference between the divine as entirely active and the human as partly passive intellect—is virtually wiped out.

2. *The Law of Contradiction*

That such is actually the case may be seen from the Thomistic attitude toward the law of identity and contradiction. When Thomas develops his arguments for the existence of God, he begins by showing that in any process of reasoning that is not to go round in circles, one must take for granted as ultimate the laws of identity and of non-contradiction. These, he says, are self-evident principles. Now in a sense that is true. It is impossible for any human being to reason discursively at all except by means of these laws. But by their being self-evident, Thomas meant that by using them man can get at what is the changeless essence of things. By reason, says Thomas, man knows the essence of a stone exhaustively. True, Thomas also asserts that we cannot prove the existence of God by doing it in the way that Anselm did it. Even if Anselm was forced to admit that according to Christian theology God is a being higher and greater than can be formulated, his main point was that the existence of God was as self-evident as were the first principles of reasoning. Against this Aquinas holds that only the first principles of reasoning are self-evident and that God is wholly other than man, and that, in consequence, we can only know what he is not. What this position really amounts to, is that man can by these self-evident principles interpret reality correctly without taking God into consideration from the outset.

This position is, to be sure, not the same as that of Parmenides, or even of Plato. For convenience we may say that whereas Parmenides wanted to use the law of contradiction positively, Aristotle wanted to use it more in the way modern philosophy uses it—negatively. We do not say that he was doing what Kant did when he formalized and subjectivized universality entirely. Aristotle was still a realist and not critical in the modern Kantian sense of the term. But he was working in the direction of Criticism. He was frankly allowing that there was a reality beyond that which can be conceptualized by man. But he was also saying that for any such reality to be known by man, it had to lose its uniqueness and be subjected to the classification of formal logic.

The essential point, then, about the human mind as active, in the way Aristotle conceived of it, is that it is virtually *taken out of its temporal conditions*. The intellect of man is absolutized. Its ultimately legislative character is taken for granted. When it is compelled to admit that there is anything in reality that is beyond its control, it assumes that this something can have no determinative significance for the knowledge that man has.

When Thomas took over the Aristotelian concept of the mind of man he was faced with the problem of relating it to the fact of man's creation in the image of God. Here his own semi-pelagian theology came in conveniently to make the juncture. It is only a theology that holds to a measure of human autonomy that can make peace with a philosophy that is built on human autonomy, indeed, on the essential divinity of the intellect. A theology that rejects the specific

Christian teaching about the all-inclusive particularistic control of God over all things, because it is not in accord with the law of contradiction, does not have any great difficulty in making friends with a philosophy that is based on the idea of the law of contradiction as the tool by which man can legislate for the nature of reality.

The question here is that of the nature of the *a priori*, that is, the assumed. The consistently Christian conception of the *a priori* is that which presupposes the Creator-creature distinction and makes the covenant inclusive of all the activities of man. Thus there is involved in every act of interpretation a twofold activity, an activity of God and an activity of man. The two are not opposed to one another. Nor do they work at different times or in different dimensions. No facts can be interpreted without reference to the activity of the human mind. But if scepticism and subjectivism are to be avoided there must be back of the activity of man the activity of God. This must be the case in a totally different sense than is meant by any form of Aristotelian realism. According to the latter, the God that is back of the mind of man is but the limiting concept of man, that is, whatever God there may be has said nothing to man, and even if he did say something, it would be nothing which man could not have said himself. God is merely, therefore, a necessary intellectual concept. And to say this is, in effect, to make more final man's own ideal of complete comprehension in knowledge.

3. *The Object of Knowledge*

Corresponding to the question of the subject of knowledge is the question of the object of knowledge. Dooyeweerd has dealt with this at length in his discussion of "individualiteitstructuren." The Thomistic notion of the mind of man as potentially participating in the mind of God, leads to an impersonal principle that is purely formal, and as such is correlative to brute factual material of a non-rational sort. It follows that it is only by abstraction from individuality that the facts can be *known*. The whole scheme of the philosophy of nature is made into a "Chain of Being"[9] idea, fitted into a pattern of ever-increasing universality. Inasmuch as anything is higher in the scale of being than something else, it is to that extent less individual. All knowledge is of universals. And, as already observed, it is the mind conceived of as ultimate and as correlative to these facts, that has to abstract from particularity in order to know them.

The point we are now most concerned to make here is that the position of Aristotle and Thomas is essentially no more realistic than is any form of modern idealism.[10] The pure intelligible essences of Thomistic philosophy are virtually intellectual constructs. If they did exist, they would be eternal and unchangeable and as such destructive of the Christian teaching about history.

4. *The Subject-Object Relation*

If now we combine these questions about the subject and the object of knowledge, we note at once that Aquinas is bound to reject the biblical notions both of general (or natural) and of special (or supernatural) revelation and is bound to have a false conception of the relation between these two.

In the Thomistic notion of the *subject* of knowledge, the distinction between God and man is one merely of potentiality and actuality. We have already observed how this notion destroys the idea that God should speak to man authoritatively in the penetralia of his consciousness.

Similarly, in the Thomistic notion of the *object* of knowledge there is a non-rational principle of individuation, and thus there is no possibility of God speaking through the individual facts of nature in their historical development. By the time a man learns to *know* the nature of the things by which God might reveal himself to man, this man has destroyed the revelatory character of these facts as facts. When it is the individual thing that speaks, it is, alas, no longer the individual thing that speaks, for man cannot know it in its individuality.

The result is that man can think or not think, act or refrain from acting, without thinking or acting for or against God. He is not a covenant-being that is always confronted with the revelation of God and always bound either to obey or not to obey God. There is in Thomas no room for the true biblical existentialism which Calvin has taught us. Calvin argued that no man can know himself without at the same time knowing himself as a creature of God. No man can observe the facts of nature and history round about him without seeing clearly manifested in them the all-controlling and judging activity of the Creator-Redeemer God. Thomas starts from the abstract concept of *Being* and introduces the Creator-creature distinction *afterwards*. He reduces the Creator-creature distinction to something that is consistent with the idea of God and the cosmos as involved in a chain of being, with varying degrees of intensity. His philosophy and psychology thus make any true Christian theology impossible.

Thomas was also bound to have a mistaken notion of "supernatural" revelation. As given to man in paradise this supernatural revelation was, as Geerhardus Vos calls it, pre-redemptive in character. Supernatural Word-revelation was given to man at the outset of history, even before the entrance of sin, as a supplement to revelation in and about man. Man was told in paradise what would happen to him if he ate of the forbidden fruit. This pre-redemptive supernatural revelation presupposed the complete control of all factual existence in the space-time world by the power of God. But on Thomas' view there is no such complete control. His non-rational principle of individuation implies that God could at best make a shrewd guess at what would happen if man ate of the forbidden tree. Thus the idea of the revelation of God, as absolutely authoritative and final in every way, is undermined in the Thomistic concept of the nature of man and of reality in general.

The total result of such a false view of general and supernatural revelation as entertained by Thomas, involves also a false view of the nature of the fall of man. Catholic theologians are accustomed to saying that in the fall man lost the *donum superadditum* (supernatural gift), and that as a result, man's nature was *wounded*. But it should be noted that according to Romanism, man's essential nature is his rationality, and that this rationality cannot be changed. The *donum superadditum* was only accidentally related to human nature, and when it was lost, man's essential nature was, to all intents and purposes, still intact. Man's metaphysical freedom, that is, the freedom to do what is against even the secret counsel of God, is found in the sinner today as much as it was in Adam before he sinned. And since the revelation of God's will to him, whether through his own consciousness or through the facts of nature, was never clear, the word "guilt" can scarcely be connected with the sin of man. And certainly Adam could not be the representative of all mankind so that through his sin all men became guilty. The forensic relationships, so prominent in Scripture, are all reduced to those of ethics, and ethics in turn is virtually reduced to metaphysics, and the metaphysics held to is essentially that of an all-comprehensive *process*.

How, then, are we to think of the natural man? He is not to be thought of as a covenant-breaker who is under the condemnation of God and who suborns his intellect as well as the other powers of his being in the interests of his selfish God-defying purposes. He is rather to be thought of as one whose nature consists in *rationality,* and free will, in the same way that it did before the fall, but as one who has lost these supernatural additions of a "grace" which is not grace. Man is therefore no more in need of grace after than before the entrance of sin, even though he is in need of *more* "grace." Man has as much right after as before the fall to demand that revelation to him shall not be out of accord with the law of non-contradiction, and that the supernatural grace shall be connected with his nature in such a way that he can see through the relationship—at least to such an extent that the whole thing shall appear reasonable to him. He will retain the same power of free will to accept or reject the plan of salvation by God for man, that he had before the fall.

There can therefore be no such thing as a finished revelation in history. All reality is process, and revelation too is always in process. There can be no incarnation that is finished once for all in the past. The meaning of a finished incarnation as an individual fact in history could never be made reasonable. The incarnation is a process continued in the church, as the whole of human personality is in process of divinization. There could be no one fact at the beginning of history by which all men are influenced to the extent of being guilty as well as polluted; so there could not be one finished fact in history by virtue of which men are made righteous and holy in principle. The distinction between justification and sanctification is practically wiped out; or rather justification is virtually reduced to the process of sanctification, and sanctification is virtually said to be elevation in the scale of being.

It will be apparent now that the debate between Barth the Protestant and Przywara the Catholic was a debate between two men neither of which had made the Creator-creature distinction basic in his thought. The positions of both are largely activistic. Przywara might seem to be nearer to the truth than Barth on the concept of revelation in nature and in man, since he claimed that it is possible for man to know something truly about God by the direct study of the universe as the effect of God's "causative" activity, while Barth claims that man cannot know anything of God at all by way of direct revelation in nature or himself. On the other hand, it might seem that Barth was right as over against Przywara, because he stressed the priority of faith over reason. Yet the views of both are activistic and virtually do away with the concept of revelation *in distinction* from man's reception to it.

Both may be said to be *prematurely* and therefore falsely Christological in their outlook. In Thomas, man needed grace *before* as well as after the fall. But grace cannot be properly attached to anything but the name of the historic Christ. For Thomas, the incarnation and all that pertains to the work of Christ would have been virtually as necessary before as after the fall. No one fact in history, such as the fall of Adam the first man, could make any important changes in human nature or in its needs. The idea of redemption is woven deep into the pattern of metaphysical being. How else can it be made acceptable to the natural man? Similarly for Barth human self-consciousness presupposes or is based upon Christ-consciousness. He *is* not till he is a Christian. The mysteries of the faith are wholly irrational and yet a man cannot even be rational unless he lives by virtue of these irrationalities. The triumph of grace is "built into nature" by both Aquinas and Barth.

B. *Ontology*

The way has now been prepared for a discussion of ontology. Here again there is the correlativity of the principle of continuity that would lead to complete univocism or identity, and the corresponding principle of discontinuity that would lead to complete equivocism or discreteness. The position maintained is constantly that which is midway between univocism and equivocism.

1. *Proof of God's Existence*

A word may first be said about the proof Thomas gives for the existence of God from the fact of *motion* in the universe. The significant point here is that he "proves" the existence of God from motion as something that is neither created, nor an aspect of created reality. In other words, Thomas says that creation cannot be proved by reason; it is an article of faith. The import of this point cannot well be overrated. On his assumptions he was right. The probative force of his argument for a first mover depends entirely upon the assumption that the human mind is at least potentially divine, that is, upon an *a priori* which is found in a universal that comes to expression with equal directness, if not with equal intensity, both in the human and in the divine mind.

This *a priori* is an impersonal abstract principle that, in the nature of the case, has no productive power. It is misleading to speak of it as the first mover. It does not move itself or anything else at all. It does not really even stand as an ideal, except as one uses metaphors and similes.

It follows that according to Thomas, motion must be considered as ultimate in order that God's existence my be proved.

The prime mover as the first cause is for Aquinas, following Aristotle, merely one among other ultimate causes of explanation. And this means in effect that the idea of cause is virtually identical with the idea of a principle of explanation. Besides having the non-rational principle of prime matter, one also needs the idea of a *universal form* in relation to which the individuality that springs from matter receives its unification. Individuation by a non-rational principle would lead to pure indetermination—to an infinite regress. If one had billions of beads without any string, how would one ever have a string of beads? On the other hand, it is equally true that if you had nothing but the string, you still would have no string of beads.

The other argument for God's existence from cause and effect, from gradation, from necessity, and from purpose which Thomas propounds are the same in character as the one which he apparently himself considered the most important of them all.

The probative force of these arguments depends upon the measure of their Parmenidean character. That is true of the probative force of any argument on a non-Christian foundation. Spinoza best expressed this fact when he quite fearlessly asserted that the order and connection of ideas is the same as the order and connection of things, and when, in addition, he said that the human mind is of a piece with the divine. On any non-Christian methodology a thing can be known to exist only if it is categorized in a system of timeless logic. When it is so systematized, it has lost all its temporal character and all its individuality. Thus the argument for a first mover in the Thomistic form is to the effect that God's existence as the first mover is proved only if there be no motion, no time, no history at all.

This pure univocism and fatalism is not immediately seen to be the result of his argument because Thomas, following Aristotle, has inserted the fact of prime matter as the actual principle of individuation. The last thing Aristotle and Thomas want is to arrive at a stark identity philosophy. Yet on their principles the only way to escape this is to assume an ultimate non-rational principle of indivuation. Thomas is quite willing to sacrifice something for this purpose. He is quite willing to say that man cannot by reason prove the *nature* of God; he can only prove his *existence*. But of course he cannot make this distinction absolute. It would make no sense to prove the existence of something about the nature of which you could have no information at all. Yet the nature of his argument really required him to say that he knew all about the nature of God. On his argument he could not at all prove the *existence* of God unless he fully knew the *nature* of God.

He himself faces the question how it is possible that we should be able to say *any*thing about God, if we cannot say *every*thing about him. Is not the essence of the thing the middle part of syllogism? he asks. And his answer is that in this unusual case we cannot take the nature of the thing we are speaking of as being the middle of the syllogism, but that we must take account of the meaning of the word of God. Everybody calls the first cause of reality God. If we have proved the necessity for the idea of a first cause, therefore, we have proved the existence of God. But who, we ask, is "everybody"? It is the whole *massa perditionis,* the millions of covenant-breakers who have suppressed the knowledge of the Creator within themselves. It is they who are subtly making themselves believe that they are doing justice by the revelation of God when talking about a "first cause." They want to be theists if only they do not need to face the Creator and Judge.

We must therefore hold Thomas to his point. He is logically bound to tell us all about the nature of God if we are to accept his proof for the existence of God as valid.

This leads us on to a further consideration. Thomas thought that he could hold onto the creation out of nothing idea as taught to him by faith, at the same time that he could hold onto the probative force of the argument for a first mover. In this he was mistaken. He was not mistaken in holding that one can believe in the sort of God that Thomas himself believed in by faith, while holding to his rational argument for God's existence. But then this only shows that the synthesis he was making was a false synthesis.

We have seen that one of the ingredients in the argument of Thomas is the non-rational principle of individuation. It is by means of it and by it alone that Thomas must seek to escape the nemesis of pure identity. Well then, it is this pure non-rationality that must serve as the sole object of faith, for if reason must reduce everything to blank identity, faith must have the realm of the utterly irrational. If Thomas, the theologian, hears by revelation that God has created the universe out of nothing and he tells this to Thomas, the philosopher, the latter will answer that he cannot know such to be the case, indeed, that he *will never be able* to know such a thing to be so. He must add that the nature of reality *does not allow* for any such thing to be so. For surely faith will never teach anything that is out of accord with right reason, and has not God given reason to man? Thomas maintains that faith takes over where reason cannot go. But what will he do when both "reason" and "faith" make contradictory statements about the nature of reality? In other words, the argument with respect to the first mover is an argument about the nature of the whole of reality that is utterly out of accord with the nature of this reality as it is said to be in the Christian religion.

In all this there is to be found the best of illustrations of the nature of the *analogia entis* idea. It is the means by which the purest fatalism or determinism, and the purest Chance or indeterminism, are kept in constant balance with one another. It is the combination of a philosophy that is controlled by the form-matter scheme, that is, a philosophy that is already in itself a synthesis of pure univocism and pure equivocism, that is made the foundation of a theology that is itself also a mixture of the same ingredients. The only difference between the theology and the philosophy of Thomas is that in his theology there is a larger proportion of equivocism than there is in his philosophy. The grace-nature scheme of Thomas fits in well with the form-matter scheme of Aristotle. The two are equaly destructive of faith and of reason. The face of the covenant God cannot shine through this scheme, or it must shine through *in spite of* it, as it no doubt does to some extent.

However, the face of the covenant God does shine in *Calvin's* doctrine of the *sensus deitatis*. It is based on the idea of man's immediate self-awareness, or awareness of meaning as involving or presupposing the awareness of God, as Creator and Judge. But this is as much as to say that we cannot (1) accept the mind of man as furnishing in any way the *ultimate* reference point for predication; (2) that we cannot take the *principles of identity* and of non-contradiction as a self-evident principle by which the nature of being is to be determined in any ultimate way; (3) that on the other hand we cannot take the idea of an *ultimate irrational principle* of individuation as contributing to the nature of reality, and that therefore (4) we cannot take the meaning of the word "God," as this is held by mankind generally as a substitute for that knowledge of the nature of God revealed in Scripture in anything that we seek to prove.

Valid rational activity cannot be carried on by the mind of man with respect to anything in the universe except upon the basis of, and in conjunction with, the supernatural revelation (by means of positive thought communication) of the nature and purpose of God.

Even in paradise man could not, by reason, without word-revelation, know his place and task as a covenant creature. The things with which he dealt were what they were precisely because of this ultimate plan of God. Thomas' teaching about the *donum superadditum* in the case of Adam was not wrong insofar as it brought in the supernatural *at the outset* of the human race; it was wrong insofar as it did not think of this supernatural aid as positive word communication from God. The same thought carried through concerning man *after the fall* implies that *no valid interpretation of any fact can be carried on except upon the basis of the authoritative thought communication to man of God's final purposes in Scripture, as this Scripture sets forth in final form the redemptive work of Christ. Every fact must be interpreted Christologically.*

It is the mistaken notion of much Protestant apologetics that a reason which does not from the outset subject itself to the Scripures, may be expected, nonetheless, to be open and ready to receive its revelation at a later date. It is not true that faith can carry us "the rest of the way." It is not true that the theistic proofs establish the *probable* existence of God and that faith must bring us certainty. The existence of God must be *presupposed* as the *basis* of all possibility and probability instead of the reverse. It is not true that these proofs may well establish the believer in his faith and be merely witness to unbelievers. What is objectively valid ought to be proof and witness for both unbeliever, and believer, and what is not objectively valid ought to be neither for either. Calvin has taught us not merely to distinguish the Christian principle of continuity from the non-Christian principle of continuity, but also to distinguish the Christian principle of discontinuity from the non-Christian principle of discontinuity. How could either of these things be done unless both were done simultaneously? Calvin has therefore taught us to reject direct fatalism and determinism on the one hand, and direct chance or indeterminism on the other hand, but also the happy or unhappy "solution" in between them called "moderate realism."

2. *The Nature of God*

Following Thomas' discussion of the proofs for the existence of

God is his discussion of the nature of God. By the help of the *analogy* idea, Thomas thinks he has gained the right to say *something* about the nature of God without saying *all* about it.

In God essence and existence are identical, says Thomas. Yet we are said to have proved the existence of God without knowing *anything* of his essence. Thomas should tell us therefore what is existence apart from essence in God so that the former may be proved apart from the latter. This would be flatly contradictory were it not for the fact that the *analogy* concept has given him the right, so he thinks, to hold to God as transcendent *without* being wholly out of reach of the intellectual concepts of man. We have seen how untenable this position is. He loses the probative force of his argument in exact proportion to the extent that he holds to the transcendence of God. And what is even worse, if possible, is that on his view nothing can be said about the transcendent God except by blind faith. If one does not begin with presupposing God in the scriptural meaning of the term, if one does not presuppose the ontological trinity and the idea of the plan of God as the principle of individuation, there is nothing left but either complete scepticism or pure blind faith.

Thomas has no right at all to employ the "way of eminence." He says that every perfection that is found in the creature is found in God in infinite perfection. This is the constant refrain throughout both the *Summa Theologica* and the *Summa Contra Gentiles*.

When, therefore, Thomas says that in God essence and existence are identical, this can mean merely that God is *pure form*. Being, he says, is the most formal of all concepts. Being in God is pure actuality; it is that in which there is no remnant even of potentiality. As such God is infinite; God is perfect; God is immutable and eternal. He is good and one and true.

On the basis of these assertions about what God is in himself Thomas maintains that God's providence is over all things. The causality of God extends to all things, not only to the constituent principles of species but also to the individualizing principles; not only to things incorruptible but also to things corruptible.[11] God's providence goes over high things and low. Being eternally good, God of necessity wanted to express this goodness. But his own infinite being and goodness cannot be expressed fully in the created world. The goodness of God, when expressed in the created world, is therefore expressed or manifested in manifold ways; hence the degrees of reality and goodness. For the completion of the universe, it is necessary that there be these varying degrees of reality. So then, following upon and included in the doctrine of providence is that of election. God determines the number of the elect.

If carried through consistently, this would lead to pure determinism. For causation is nothing but participation in the being of God, and God is the form of all reality. But we should remember that this concept of the form is only half the story. There is the other half represented by the idea of pure matter or indetermination. It is here that both the will of God and the will of man make their appearance. The will of God is, on the one hand, said to be identical with the intellect of God. This is on Thomas' principles sheer monism. But then again the will of God is set over against the intellect of God and is made purely irrational. Lovejoy has signalized this fact in his *Chain of Being*. This will of God stresses the idea of the "otherness" of God. It is virtually the equivalent of the "hiddenness" of God in Barth's theology. On the one hand, in willing himself God wills all things, and his will—following his understanding—also wills all things in understanding all things. "All possibles fall under an infinite understanding, in Spinoza's phrase and indeed belong to its essence; and therefore nothing less than the sum of all genuinely possibles could be the object of the divine will, i.e., of the creative act."[12] And all the possibles are those that can take place in accord with the law of non-contradiction.[13] On the other hand, for Thomas possibility is a matter of concepts and therefore of classes or types. The type of things toward an end is providence.[14] "We must remember that necessary and contingent are consequent upon being as such."[15]

"Accordingly providence does not impose necessity upon all things. Predestination does not refer to anything in the predestined but only in the one who predestines.[16] "Whence it is clear that predestination is a kind of type of ordering of some persons toward eternal salvation, existing in the divine mind."[17] This also makes it possible to understand what is meant by reprobation. "Thus as men are ordained to eternal life through the providence of God it likewise is part of that providence to permit some to fall away from that end; this is called reprobation."[18] Reprobation does not take away anything from the persons affected; that the reprobate cannot obtain grace "must not be understood as implying an absolute impossibility."[19] There is first a general communication of being or goodness to all and then there is, in addition, a special communication of goodness to some, and this is election.[20] We are told that this is not the sort of necessity that Leibniz had in mind in his theodicy. Maritain sets the Romanist position over against that of Leibniz. Perfection of the universe requires that there be some beings that can fall from goodness; and if there are beings that can fall from goodness, the result will be that such defection will in fact sometimes occur in those beings.[21] A free creature naturally impeccable would be a square circle. A creature drawn from nothingness is free from a freedom that is kindred to nothingness.[22] God can no more create a being by nature impeccable than he can cease to exist and to be what he is.[23]

3. *God and Men*

But over against necessity which is involved in the very nature of God (reality) there is the realm of grace. Sin in the creature leads to redemption on the part of God. And sin has come in by the free activity of man. This freedom of man is lack of being. It is not evil in itself. It is merely an absence of the use of the rule of reason. Man may act or not act according to the rule of reason. Says Maritain,

> The lack or defect [of freedom] which we are discussing has as its primary cause freedom itself, which can act or not act and which does not act, does not pay attention to the rule; and this defect comes, I do not mean in time but in the ontological order, before the act of choice. Here we are at the very beginning; impossible to go any further back: a free defect, a defect of which freedom itself is the negative and deficient primary cause;—and it is the will thus in default which, acting with this defect, is the cause—in *quantum deficiens*—or moral evil.[24]

"There is as yet no fault or evil in the mere absence which consists in not actually considering the rule, 'because the soul is not obliged, nor for that matter is it able, constantly to take the rule into consideration, in act.' "[25]

> What is required of the soul is not that it should always look to the rule or to have the rule constantly in mind and but that it should *produce its act* while looking to the rule. Now in the metaphysical moment we are examining here there is as yet no act produced, there is merely an absence of consideration of the rule, and it is only in the act which will be produced, in terms of that absence, that evil will exist. Therein lies an extremely subtle point of doctrine, one of capital importance. Before the moral act, before the *bonum debitum*, the *due good* which makes up the quality of this act and whose absence is a privation and an evil, there is a metaphysical condition of the moral act, which, taken in itself, is not a due good, and the absence of which consequently will be neither a privation nor an evil but a pure and simple *negation* (absence of a good that is *not* due), and that metaphysical condition is a *free* condition.[26]

God then has not created man a moral character, a character who is by nature covenant-keeping; man then is not one who cannot look about or within himself without beholding and acting either in obedience to, or in rebellion against, that covenant. Evil is thus mere negation, non-moral in character, found as it is within the realm of those things that are possibles by the law of logic. It is by making of man a moral amoeba near the bottom of the scale of being that Thomas hopes to escape the charge of determinism. It is by thinking of the will of God as pure identification with abstract rationality, and by making man's will the principle of moral indeterminacy, and then bringing both of these concepts to bear upon the moral acts of man that Thomas hopes to escape both determinism and indeterminism. If, when deciding to act morally, man places before himself the ideal of the vision of deity, he will more and more participate in the being of God. And on his part, God, by spreading abroad his goodness widely but thinly at the bottom of reality and more narrowly and heavily toward the top of reality, opens the way of opportunity for man to approach God himself in intensity of being and goodness, and enables man to do what of himself without such grace he could not do.

In this way Maritain has, he thinks, avoided the charge that would be launched against Calvin's doctrine of an all-determinative providence and an all-compelling predestination. Pighius voiced the typical Romanist objection to Calvin's view when he said that according to Calvin, there can be no real responsibility in man and God is made responsible for sin.

Here the difference between the two concepts of analogy comes out very strikingly. Calvin holds that all things happen by the ultimate will of God, and that in subordination to that ultimate will there is the created will of man. He maintains that we cannot hold to a sound doctrine of the grace of God unless we maintain that even in the case of the reprobate, it is ultimately this decision of God that decides the final destiny of men. There we have the truly Reformed doctrine of analogy, the doctrine whereby everything is ultimately referred to the counsel of God and to his sovereign disposition while *within* this plan the will of man finds its genuine freedom and responsibility. Man always acts for or against God.

Over against this, Thomas maintains that to be free, man's moral action must have no determinative divine moral action back of it. Thomas starts man off neutrally as far as his nature is concerned. True, man never existed in the pure state of nature. When Adam was created he was at once given a supernatural grace. But this grace did not violate his nature and his nature consisted of freedom to act or not to act, i.e., pure moral neutrality. On this neutrality is based the idea that even the natural man who, though he has lost the *donum superadditum*, can nevertheless exist without moral turpitude. When God offers grace he can accept it or reject it as he will; when he has rejected it, he may later accept it; when he has accepted it, he may later reject it. As Maritain says, ". . . the creature slinks, not by an action but a free non-action or disaction,—from the influx of the First Cause,—which influx is loaded with being and goodness—it slinks from it insofar as this influx reaches the free region as such, it renders this influx sterile, it *nihilates* it."[27] What comes from nothing tends to nothingness. "There then is something wherein the creature is the first, the primary cause; there then, is a line in which the creature is the first cause but it is the line of nothingness, and of evil."[28] Without me ye can do nothing.

Looking at the doctrine of the will in man as Thomas develops it, we see at once that real freedom for him is absence of being. On the other hand, nothing but being can be a cause of anything. "But only good can be a cause, because nothing can be a cause unless it is a being, and every being as such, is good."[29] To the extent that man has being he participates in the being of God and as such is good. According to the extent that he has being, man may be said with God to be the giver of the rule, the lawgiver. Here again is the principle that the moment the individual speaks, this individual has lost his individuality. Or if man seeks freedom by living in subordination to the rules, he becomes the rule-giver. The goal is the ideal of becoming his own rule-giver, complete identification with God.

We conclude that the traditional Roman Catholic position in theology and philosophy is not basically Christian and, therefore, cannot be used by the Reformed pastor in order with it to challenge modern thought.

NOTES

1. The theology of Friedrich Schleiermacher and Albert Ritschl.
2. The theology of Karl Barth, Emil Brunner, etc.
3. 1 John 2:3, 4, 5; 3:4, 6, 9, 10, 23, 24.
4. Phenomenalism: "The theory that all we know is a phenomenon, that is, reality present to consciousness, either directly or reflectively; and that phenomena are all that there are to know, there being no thing-in-itself or object out of relation to consciousness" (*Dictionary of Philosophy and Psychology*, ed. James Baldwin, Gloucester: 1960).
5. Henry Bett, *Johannes Scotus Erigena* (Cambridge, 1925), p. 27.
6. Cf. A. D. R. Polman.
7. Cf. A. E. Taylor, *Plato, The Man and His Work* (New York, 1936).
8. *De Anima*, 3, 5, 430a, 17ff.
9. Cf. A. O. Lovejoy's *The Great Chain of Being* (Cambridge, 1942).
10. J. Maritain, a Roman Catholic philosopher, has attempted in his *Degrees of Knowledge* (London, 1959), to establish, unsuccessfully from our point of view, this more "realistic" nature of Thomas' thought.

11. *The 'Summa Theologica' of St. Thomas Aquinas*, trans. by the Fathers of the English Dominican Province, 2nd rev. ed. (London, 1921), Question 22, Article 1.
12. Lovejoy, *op. cit.*, p. 74.
13. *Summa Theologica*, Q. 25, Art. 3.
14. *Ibid.*, Q. 22, Art. 1.
15. *Ibid.*, Q. 22, Art. 4; Reply Obj. 3.
16. *Ibid.*, Q. 22, Art. 1.
17. *Ibid.*, Q. 23, Art. 2; Obj. 4.
18. *Ibid.*, Q. 23, Art. 3; Obj. 3.
19. *Ibid.*, Q. 23, Art. 3; Reply Obj. 3.
20. *Ibid.*, Q. 23, Art. 4.
21. Jacques Maritain, *St. Thomas and the Problem of Evil* (Milwaukee, 1942), p. 6. Maritain quotes Thomas on this point.
22. *Ibid.*, p. 15.
23. *Ibid.*, p. 17.
24. *Ibid.*, pp. 25-26.
25. *Ibid.*
26. *Ibid.*, pp. 26-27.
27. *Ibid.*, p. 34.
28. *Ibid.*, p. 35.
29. *Summa Theologica*, Q. II, 277.

Chapter III

THE REFORMED PASTOR AND
MODERN PROTESTANTISM
(The Philosophy and Religion of Immanuel Kant)

When the Reformed pastor today undertakes to present the sovereign grace of God not only to those *within* but also to those *without* his fold he meets two rivals. One of them is Roman Catholicism, which we have dealt with in its traditional form in the previous chapter, and which we shall deal with in its modern form in a subsequent chapter. In the present chapter and in the one following we deal with Protestantism. It also has a traditional and a modern form. The traditional form of Protestantism finds expression in the historical "evangelical creeds," the creeds of the Lutheran and Reformed churches.

Because of the influence of modern philosophy and modern science, and particularly because of the philosophy of Immanuel Kant and his followers, modern Protestantism rejects traditional Protestantism. Both nineteenth century liberalism and twentieth century neo-orthodoxy reject traditional or historic Protestantism because it is supposed to be metaphysical or dogmatic. But Kant, we are told, has saved science and made room for religion by rejecting every form of metaphysics and dogmatism. Modern science and modern philosophy is, therefore, anti-metaphysical. If modern theology wants to meet modern man, influenced as he is by modern science and modern philosophy, he must re-express the principles of Christianity and, in particular, the principles of Protestantism in anti-metaphysical or "critical" terms.

I. *The Philosophy of Kant*

As a background for an understanding of liberal and neo-orthodox theology, we must look briefly at the nature of nineteenth century thought, which is largely controlled by the philosophy of Immanuel Kant.

Kant's philosophy, says Richard Kroner, involves, in the first place, "ethical dualism."[1] To save science and, at the same time, to make room for religion, Kant set the realm of *freedom* sharply over against the realm of *necessity*. The realm of freedom is the realm of morality and religion. The realm of necessity is the realm of science. The two realms must be thought of as standing *absolutely,* or *wholly,* over against one another. Accordingly, knowledge and faith are also dualistically opposed to one another. Of the world of science we have conceptual *knowledge*. This knowledge is *absolute*, i.e., absolute in the sense that all rational beings *must* agree on it. Rational beings are rational beings just because they cannot help but impress upon the raw stuff of sense-experience such forms or categories as causality and substance. These categories together constitute the source of rationality anywhere in the space-time world.

Correlative to this notion of the categories of rationality as constituting the universality of all knowledge of the space-time world is the notion of the "material" or stuff of knowledge as *purely* contingent. The "facts" of scientific knowledge are not facts which have characteristics of their own prior to their discovery by man. They become "scientific" facts when the universal human consciousness "makes" them so.

A. *Pre-Kantian Modern Philosophy*

If the "facts" of scientific knowledge had, each and all of them, characteristics of their own prior to their being known by man, they would, argues Kant, be forever unknowable.

The rationalists before Kant attempted to know such facts, but in the process of knowing them, reduced their individuality or uniqueness to blank identity. For Spinoza the "facts" simply *had* to be what the intellect of man, using the laws of logic, and especially the law of contradiction, said they must be. Accordingly for Spinoza, the order and connection of things is said to be identical with the order and connection of thought. Similarly Leibniz aimed at finding the individuality of facts by means of complete description.

According to these rationalists, therefore, there was not and there could not be anything new in science.

Yet the very idea of science presupposes that genuinely new facts are discovered and that in being discovered they are not lost in a net of abstract logical relations but really add to a fund of existing knowledge. If the rationalists were right, logic itself would be reduced to an eternal changless principle of identity. All facts would be wholly known by abstract thought thinking itself. Thus not only would there be no facts not wholly known but the idea of the "wholly known" would become an abstract contentless principle. Logic itself would become meaningless. There would be no longer any process of reasoning; such a process would be absorbed in identity.

The empiricist also believed in facts that had characteristics in themselves, prior to their being known in terms of relations between them and in terms of their relation to the one who knows them. Moreover, the empiricists saw what happened to these facts in the hands of angry rationalists. To keep the facts and their individuality from being swallowed up by logic, the empiricist proposed to bring the facts into relation with one another by means of *induction* rather than by *deduction*. To make sure that logic would do no damage to the individuality of space-time facts, John Locke, the father of empiricism, insisted that the mind is a *tabula rasa*. The mind simply *receives* and therefore does not destroy the uniqueness of the facts as it brings them together. The objectivity of knowledge is thus guaranteed, because the mind receives the facts *just as they are*.

However, the troubles of empiricism appeared clearly when its most brilliant exponent, David Hume, insisted that in receiving facts the mind is so passive, that its "concepts" are but faint replicas of its "percepts." This was evidence for Hume of the fact that the mind has no organizing power at all. Even if all the facts were brought into the mind in the forms of concepts they would still be utterly unrelated. It would be as though the human mind, like a modern Noah's ark, had gathered together all facts which the womb of chance has produced in the past and would produce in the future, only to realize that the concept of the ark is itself nothing but the faint replica of a percept. Thus all the facts would still be not partially but *wholly* hidden.

One step more needs to be taken in our analysis of rationalism and empiricism. If the rationalists were not to defeat their own purposes by being wholly successful, i.e., in attaining the realization of their ideal of exhaustive reduction of all space-time factuality, to a Parmenidean notion of abstract identity, then they would have to fall back on the idea of an unknown and unknowable realm of facts, in which each fact differs from all other facts by characteristics *wholly* unknowable. This would apply both to the supposed objects and to the supposed subjects of knowledge. If each of the objects of knowledge were to retain its identity, it would have to be impervious to other objects and to the mind of any knower. Similarly if the mind of the individual knower was not to be absorbed in advance by the Universal Mind, it had to be *wholly* unaffectible by other, equally impervious, individual minds, and wholly inexplicable by any supposed universal mind.

The empiricists must fall back on the notion of the facts as being *wholly* and exhaustively known and reduced to one block of identity. Otherwise they would defeat themselves by being too successful in their attempt to attain absolute objectivity. The mind of the knower, the subject of knowledge, is said to be purely passive instead of creative, and the objects of knowledge are said to exist independently of the subject of knowledge. Without this rationalist notion of a logic that swallows up all facts, the empiricists could not explain how they could identify one fact in distinction from any other fact. The post-Kantian idealist critics of empiricism have pressed this point by saying that there is no possibility of counting without the presupposition of an absolute system of truth.

B. *The Greek Form-Matter Scheme*

It is well to note briefly at this point that in pre-Kantian rationalism and empiricism the motif of Greek philosophy is carried out. The motif of Greek philosophy is (a) that all reality is one; (b) that all space-time differentiation emanates from this one; and (c) that all this space-time factuality is reabsorbed by the one.

Together with all other men, the Greeks were descendants of

Adam. In and with Adam they were, therefore, covenant-breakers. Deep down in their hearts they, together with all men, were aware of the fact that they were creatures of God. Paul says that all men know God in this sense (Rom. 1:19; 2:14-15). But in and with Adam they sought to suppress this increated knowledge of God. They did this by telling themselves that unless there was a common or univocal point of being between God and themselves, they would not even be able to identify, let alone see the reasonableness of, any command of any god. In fact, they virtually insisted that they could not see the reasonableness of any word of authority spoken by any god presumed to be above them, unless they could see that such a command is in accord with reason. Socrates expressed this notion when he said to Euthyphro that he wanted for himself, in view of his participation in reason, i.e., in view of the univocal element that must eternally obtain for himself as a rational being, to know the nature of holiness regardless of what gods and men say about it.

Thus the idea that the mind of man *is not* created in the image of God but is a law unto itself and that the laws of the universe, both the laws of logic and the laws of nature, are not ordained by God but exist in themselves, was the assumption of underlying Greek philosophy.

Dr. Herman Dooyeweerd and his associates speak of Greek philosophy as controlled by the form-matter scheme.

According to this form-matter scheme, man and the world are not created. When Thales said that *All* is water, when Anaximander said that *All* is indeterminate, when Anaximenes said that *All* is air, when Parmenides said that *All* is a changeless One, and when Heraclitus said that *All* is flux, they were assuming that they could intelligently speak of Being in general without, from the outset, introducing the creator-creature distinction. At the same time they assumed that chance instead of the plan of God is the ultimate source of differentiation in the space-time world. For the Greeks there is no revelation of God the creator in "nature" any more than there is in man.

Thus the Greeks enmeshed themselves in a basically false problematic. A chance-produced, finite mind must relate itself intelligently to chance-produced "things," things that change wholly into one another except for the fact they have no identity of their own, i.e., except as they turn into the opposites of themselves, by means of a changeless principle of unity which, as changeless, stands wholly over against the bottomless ocean of chance. Or, starting with the intellect of man as said to be "somehow" "remembering" in a way that no man can remember remembering, its derivation from an eternal principle of rationality, the mind seeks to return to its eternal home whence it has come, in order to be reabsorbed into it, leaving behind the "mud and hair and filth" of the world of space and time in which it was imprisoned.

This essentially Platonic version of the Greek form-matter scheme was modified, but not *basically* altered, by Aristotle. For Aristotle, as well as for Plato, knowledge is still of universals. He says that there cannot, strictly speaking, be any knowledge of the particulars of the world of space and time. If the particulars of the space-time world were represented by perpendicular lines unrelated to one another, then there can be no knowledge of them unless they be *wholly* horizontalized and as such made identical with the wholly horizontal line of logical relation. Goethe's winged dictum to the effect that if the individual is known it is, alas, no longer the individual that is known, would be applicable to Aristotle's notion of the relation of logic and fact.

It is the form-matter scheme of the relation of universals to particulars that comes to its fullest in Aristotle's philosophy.

The traditional form of Roman Catholic thinking builds the first story of its house by means of the form-matter scheme of Greek philosophy and then adds to this the second story by means of the creation-fall-redemption story of Christian teaching.

C. *Natural Theology-Analogy*

In its natural theology, traditional Romanist thought seeks to avoid univocism (i.e., Parmenidean identity philosophy), and equivocism (i.e., Heraclitean flux philosophy). The result is expressed in its notion of *analogy*. The entire false problematics of Greek philosophy may be expressed in this notion of analogy. Following

Aristotle, medieval scholasticism says that Being is analogical. There is in it the element of permanence that derives from Parmenides, and there is in it the element of chance that derives from Heraclitus. Plato had, Aristotle argues, a dualistic view of reality. There is the realm of flux, the realm of Heraclitus, the realm of which we can have no knowledge at all. This realm is *wholly* hidden to us. Then there is the realm of the changeless and eternal law. Here is absolute truth, absolute goodness, and absolute beauty. So far as man has, or rather is, intellect, man participates in this realm. Having fallen away from this realm by some demonic cause, man strives to return to it.

To overcome this dualism of Plato,[3] Aristotle softened the antithesis between the two realms. The dualism of Plato, he argued in effect, must be taken as operating within a monism that envelops it. Anticipating Hegel, Aristotle argued that finite, space-time facts had *some* reality, and of them there is *some* knowledge. The absolute claims of both Parmenides and Heraclitus must be sublated; the claims of both are valid only as correlative to one another. There is a dilemma here: man as an intellectual being knows everything about everything independently of having sense-experience of anything; but man as a volitional or affective being knows nothing of anything, even when he has had sense-experience of everything. The notion of analogy is introduced in an attempt to solve this dilemma. According to this notion of analogy, man is a border-line being. He has one foot in the realm of eternity and one foot in the realm of time.

As a member of the realm of Parmenides he swings the logician's postulate and demands that all reality, to be real, must be one eternal, changeless block of being. Then, as his individuality is being crushed by being *wholly* known, he remembers that he is under the law of Heraclitus as well as under the law of Parmenides. He turns his back on the realm of Parmenides toward the realm of Heraclitus. But as he rushes on into the realm of Heraclitus his individuality becomes water-logged and gradually sinks into oblivion.

His only hope, he thinks (if he can still think) would be to think of himself as being *wholly* revealed à la the demands of Parmenides, and *wholly* hidden à la the demands of Heraclitus. This, he thinks, will save him and science with him. It will make room for religion too. The realm of Parmenides will now be seen to have life and movement in it while the realm of Heraclitus will now be seen to have a measure of order in it. It is the Aristotelian notion of analogy that has saved us, on the one hand, from every form of determinism— or realism—and, on the other hand, from every form of pure indeterminism, or nominalism.

We return now to Kant. Kant found that neither Greek philosophy nor modern philosophy up to his time had really been able to save science and make room for religion. The Parmenidean-Spinozistic notion of absolute, exclusively analytic knowledge was never brought into real, harmonious interaction with the Heraclitian notion of exclusively synthetic knowledge. The question how synthetic-apriori judgments are possible had never been answered adequately. The scholastic notion of analogy had not managed to harmonize pure univocism and pure equivocism.

D. Kant's "Criticism"

Struggling with this situation, Kant's eyes were finally opened to the astounding insight that the reason for the failure of every dogmatic approach, whether rationalist or empiricist, lay in the fact that the empiricists were not empirical enough and the rationalists were not rationalist enough.

The empiricist's "stuff," or material of knowledge, had too much form in it. The "facts," even though still utterly unknown by the mind of man, were already structured to some extent. This already structured nature of facts acted like an immovable roadblock to the beginning, the progress, and the completion of man's knowledge of these facts. To know is to conceptualize. But the facts of empiricism were unconceptualizable. *To be conceptualizable the facts must be pliable, so pliable as to admit of complete formalization.*

In insisting on this point Kant merely expressed the demands of the Parmenidean position in relation to space-time factuality. How could the facts of the space-time world be *completely* conceptualized unless they had, previous to being known, no individual distinctiveness whatsoever?

Moreover, if the legitimate claim of the empiricist is to be met, then his "facts" must not only be without character before meeting the mind that knows them, but this mind itself must then not be thought of as passive. The only movement possible must spring from the subject of knowledge. The movement of things is movement of things because it is, first of all, a movement of mind.

The movement of cause and of purpose within and between things is what it is, because it is, first of all, a movement within the mind. If the empiricists wish to preserve and protect the objectivity of the knowledge of the acts of the space-time world in relation to one another, they had better give up looking for the holy grail of "facts in themselves" and find their objectivity within the organizing activity of the mind.

But while Kant, as it were, thus lectures the empiricists, he has also a criticism of the rationalists. The mind is inherently active. Would that the rationalists had understood this fact. Then they would have realized that objectivity of knowledge is inherently a matter of growth. If the rationalists wish to preserve and protect the objectivity of the knowledge of the facts of space and time in relation to one another, then they too must find this objectivity in the organizing activity of the mind. Only by looking for objectivity in the organizing activity of the mind, will they see that their notion of knowledge, as a universal changeless system, will forever stand dualistically over against a world of unrelated space-time factuality. They must think of their system as a growing and developing system.

II. *The Religion of Kant*

How then, finally, does Kant save science and make room for religion? How does Kant overcome the hopeless dilemma of pure univocism and pure equivocism involved in the scholastic notion of analogy?

If Kant were really the philosopher of Protestantism as he is often said to be, then he would have challenged the Greek-scholastic notion of analogy by means of the notion of analogy involved in Reformation thought.

Reformation thought is based on the scriptural doctrine that man is the image-bearer of God, that the world was created by God and is directed by God, that the evil in the world is the result of man's disobedience against the clear revelation of God within and about him, that Jesus Christ, the Son of God and Son of man, came to save men from the wrath of God resting upon them for this sin, and that the Holy Spirit gives the power to repent and believe to such as the Father through Christ would draw to himself.

If there is anything that is clear from the three Critiques of Kant, it is that his "system" of thought is diametrically opposed to this Reformation system. In his work on *Religion Within the Limits of Reason Alone*, Kant first demythologizes and then remythologizes this Reformation scheme of thinking. To this we shall return.

The basic defects of rationalism and empiricism, as Kant sees them, appear to him in magnified form in historic Protestantism. Traditional Protestantism has at the center of its thought the notion of the self-sufficient triune God of Scripture as the ultimate point of reference for all human predication. Nothing could be more diametrically opposed to the basic contention of all of Kant's thinking. According to Kant it is *man* as autonomous who, in effect, takes the place of the God of Luther and Calvin. As noted already, according to Kant all the ills of both rationalism and empiricism spring from the fact that they have not seen this point.

To save science and at the same time to make room for religion, we must clear out the last remnant of the idea that man is, as Scripture says, made in the image of God. In such a case man is not autonomous. We must also clear out the last remnant of the idea that it is *God's* ultimate, autonomous, organizing activity which, in the last analysis, makes the facts of the space-time world to be what they are. In such a case facts would not derive their character from *man's* ultimate organizing power. In such a case all space-time reality would not be rational for man. In such a case truth would be truth, right would be right, and beauty would be beauty because of the arbitrary assertions of God. In such a case man could not use the law of contradiction as a self-sufficient, if negative, test of truth. Socrates would be replaced by Calvin. Science would be destroyed instead of saved and religion would depend upon priestcraft.

A. *Kant "Saves" Science*

To save science and make room for religion means then that we must think of science as the field where our categories of thought create order in an utterly non-interpreted realm of pure contingency. Man's categorical thinking is absolutely legislative in the sense that it, and it alone, furnishes the forming element of experience.

Suppose you take the tray out of your refrigerator and fill it with water. Then you place a divider in the tray of water and return it to the refrigerator. When, after a while, you take the tray out of the refrigerator and the divider out of the tray, you have ice cubes. Are you surprised because all the ice cubes are of the same size? Not at all. Your divider has seen to that. *Similarly* in the world of science, the unbeliever will *always* see "raw stuff" ordered and arranged by himself by means of his logical activity. He will never find any providentially controlled facts such as the Reformers saw everywhere about them. He will never hear about such miracles as the virgin birth of Christ or his resurrection from the dead. There *could* be no such things as the regeneration of men's hearts by the recreating work of the Holy Spirit, or even providence.

This does not mean that you cannot be religious as well as scientific at the same time. On the contrary, science is saved by limiting it to the realm in which man's conceptual organizing activity rules, i.e., the realm of the *phenomenal*. But beyond the realm of the phenomenal is the realm of the *noumenal*. And, as before noted, in this realm of the noumenal man is negatively free from all conceptualizing control, and man is positively free to determine what is good and what is evil. In this realm of the noumenal man is free to determine the nature of the true, the good, and the beautiful in the way that Socrates insisted on doing it.

B. *Kant "Makes Room" for Religion*

Kant has undertaken to show us what kind of religion we, as rational men, can accept.[4] We may, argues Kant, continue to use such concepts as sin and grace, incarnation and atonement, but when we do so we must not attribute to them their traditional meanings.

The traditional meanings of these concepts were based upon a dogmatic rather than a critical view of the nature of reality, of knowledge, and of ethics. Accordingly, the traditional view failed to understand that man can have no knowledge, in the scientific sense of the term, of the realm of the noumenal. As a consequence, the traditional view fell into fanaticism and superstition with respect to its teaching of sin and salvation.

The traditional view fell into the notion that *some* men have *illumination* which others do not have. The traditional view fell into *thaumaturgy* when it dealt with the "means of grace." These points were "sheer aberrations of a reason going beyond its proper limits and that too for a purpose fancied to be moral (pleasing to God)."[5]

C. *Kant Demythologizes and Remythologizes Religion*

It is therefore of the first importance, argues Kant, that we have such a religion as is *moral*, i.e., in accord with the self-sufficient moral consciousness of man. We have made the great discovery that the self-consciousness of man, generically speaking, is sufficient to itself. Its freedom, or autonomy, cannot be affected by the laws of cause and effect that obtain in the phenomenal world. There can be no God who can have any effect on us *via* the relationships that obtain within the phenomenal world. We have saved science primarily by excluding the notion of the presence of such a god from the phenomenal world. We must not allow traditional religion to undo all that we, with great labor, have accomplished for the salvation of science. However unpopular our views may be with those who still cling to the traditional religion, we must insist that by our exclusion of fanaticism, superstition, thaumaturgy, and the like we are saving the only religion that any truly moral man should wish to have.

If we attend to the traits of the morally respectable religion as outlined by Kant, we are prepared to understand the nature of the religion of modern Protestantism, both in its liberal and in its neo-orthodox varieties.

1. *Works of Grace—Moral vs. Fanatic Religion*

Kant deals first with the indwelling "of the evil principle with the good" and particularly with "the radical evil in human nature."

There is in man, says Kant, in addition to a "Predisposition to animality" and a predisposition to humanity," also "a predisposition to *personality*." This predisposition to personality "is the capacity for respect for the moral law as *in itself a sufficient incentive of the will*."[6]

This disposition to *personality* "is rooted in reason which is practical of itself, that is, reason which dictates laws unconditionally."[7]

"All of these predispositions are not only *good* in negative fashion . . . ; they are also predispositions *toward good* (they enjoin the observance of the law). They are *original*, for they are bound up with the possibility of human nature."[8]

Considering this *original* good disposition in man, how did he become evil? To answer this question we must, says Kant, distinguish between an "*origin in reason*" and an "*origin in time.*" "In the former sense, regard is had only to the *existence* of the effect; in the latter, to its *occurrence*, and hence it is related as an event to its *first cause in time*."[9] Now it is all-important, if we are to have a moral view of religion that "Man *himself* must make or have made himself into whatever in a moral sense, whether good or evil, he is or is to become. Either condition must be an effect of his free choice; for otherwise he could not be held responsible for it and could therefore be *morally* neither good or evil."[10]

We must therefore demythologize both what Scripture says about man's being created good and what Scripture says about man's fall into evil. As to the former, the traditional view of man's *perfect* creation destroys his moral freedom. Man cannot be *created* good; he is not good unless by himself and by what is exclusively his own effort, he makes himself good."[11] We must, accordingly, not think of a temporal origin when we speak of human goodness.

The same holds true for the question of the origin of evil. If we are to have a *moral* view of evil, we must *not* think of it as having a temporal origin. Temporal origins take place in the realm of the phenomenal, and in that realm nothing in the way of *absolute* origins can take place. So far as man is a member of the realm of the phenomenal he is not free. He is free only as a member of the realm of the noumenal. As a member of the realm of the noumenal he originates both good and evil acts in an absolutely original fashion.

How this can be we do not know. We *know* only that which is phenomenal and therefore relative to ourselves. God cannot come into the realm of the phenomenal with absolute requirements. If he could and did, we could still not know that he was making such requirements. In any case, the very idea of God *commanding* man to do what is good and avoiding that which is evil is *immoral* in that *it attacks the autonomous freedom of man.*

We must therefore take the biblical narrative of the origin of man's evil as metaphorical. We cannot speak of absolute beginnings in the phenomenal other than by language taken from the world of the noumenal. We must realize that in all our assertions of the origin of good and evil in the realm of the phenomenal, we are merely pointing toward what takes place in the realm of the noumenal. If we take the narrative of the origin of evil as taking place in time, we, *ipso facto,* relativize what we say and defeat our purposes. Says Kant: "If an effect is referred to a cause to which it is bound under the laws of freedom, as is true in the case of moral evil, then the determination of the will to the production of this effect is conceived of as bound up in its determining ground not in time but merely in rational representation; such an effect cannot be derived from any *preceding* state whatsoever. Yet derivation of this sort is always necessary when an evil action, as an *event* in the world, is referred to its natural cause. To seek the temporal origin of free acts as such (as though they were operations of nature) is thus a contradiction. Hence it is also a contradiction to seek the temporal origin of man's moral character, so far as it is considered as contingent, since this character signifies the ground of the *exercise* of freedom; this ground (like the determining ground of the free will generally) must be sought in purely rational representations."[12]

Following out this line of reasoning, Kant speaks further of the origin of evil of individual men throughout the history of the human race. He says that "of all the explanations of the spread and propagation of this evil through all members and generations of our race, the most inept is that which describes it as descending to us as an *inheritance* from our first parents; . . ."[13] He adds: "In the search for the rational origin of evil actions, every such action must be regarded as though the individual had fallen into it directly from a state of innocence."[14]

To be responsible, man must be free. Even the disposition toward evil "must have been adopted by free choice, for otherwise it could not be imputed."[15] But there is no free choice found in the chain of causes that constitutes the realm of the phenomenal. Accordingly we must postulate freedom as that which constitutes man as a member of the noumenal realm.

Kant recognizes the fact that his view involves him in an idea of freedom that "surpasses our comprehension."[16] We cannot by our concepts grasp the notion of freedom either as the source of good or as the source of evil. How then are we to understand our "re-ascent from evil to good"? But, though we do not understand how it is possible, we must hold that it is. The "injunction that we *ought* to become better men" presupposes that "a seed of goodness still remains in its entire purity, incapable of being extirpated or corrupted. . . ."[17]

To have a moral view of our recovery from evil to good we must again replace temporal with rational relations. "The restoration of an original predisposition to good in us is therefore not the acquiring of a *lost* incentive for good, for the incentive which consists in respect for the moral law we have never been able to lose, and were such a thing possible, we could never get it again."[18] Having an evil disposition we must, as it were, put on a new man. Duty "bids us do this, and duty demands nothing of us which we cannot do."[19] Surely then "there is one thing in our soul which we cannot cease from regarding with the highest wonder, when we view it properly, and for which admiration is not only legitimate but even exalting, and that is the original moral disposition itself in us."[20]

In what we have heard Kant say about man's original goodness, about his disposition to evil and his restoration to the good, he has, in effect, already demythologized everything that the Reformation theologians said about the creation, the fall, and the redemption of man. Man is not created good in time, man does not fall in time, and man is not renewed in time. *But demythologizing involves remythologizing.* Kant speaks of his morally good man as "pleasing to God."[21] Kant uses the idea of the new birth as a *pointer* toward what takes place entirely and exclusively within the moral man.[22] He uses the idea of God for the ideal of the moral man who "penetrates to the intelligible ground of the heart. . . ."[23]

There are, says Kant, two kinds of religion: "those which are *endeavors to find favor* (mere worship), and *moral* religions, i.e., religions of *good life-conduct.* In the first, man flatters himself by believing either that God can make him eternally happy (through remission of his sins) without his having *to become a better man,* or else, if this seems to him impossible, that *God* can certainly *make him a better man* without his having to do anything more than to *ask* for it. Yet since, in the eyes of a Being who sees all, to ask is no more than to *wish,* this would really involve doing nothing at all; for were improvement to be achieved simply by a wish, every man would be good."[24]

Over against this type of religion which is an endeavor to win favor without deserving it, there is the moral type of religion. According to this moral type of religion, "it is a basic principle that each must do as much as lies in his power to become a better man, and that only when he has not buried his inborn talent (Luke XIX: 12-16) but has made use of his original predisposition to good in order to become a better man, can he hope that what is not within his power will be supplied through cooperation from above. Nor is it absolutely necessary for a man to know wherein this cooperation consists; indeed, it is perhaps inevitable that, were the way it occurs revealed at a given time, different people would at some other time form different conceptions of it, and that with entire sincerity. Even here the principle is valid: 'It is not essential, and hence not necessary, for every one to know what God does or has done for his salvation;' but it is essential to know *what man himself must do* in order to become worthy of this assistance."[25]

It is *this moral* kind of religion for which Kant claims to have made room.

Basic to this *moral* religion is, as noted, Kant's ethical dualism followed by his ethical phenomenalism. As a member of the noumenal realm, man is utterly free and therefore autonomous. He is negatively free from meeting the God of traditional Protestant Christianity. The *homo noumenon* is not the creature of God and is not subject to the law of God. God cannot visit him with punishment for breaking his law and cannot save him from the wrath to come by sending his Son into the world to bear the wrath of God in man's place.

In identifying what should be a transaction primarily with the moral consciousness of man seeking to do the good, with facts of the world of causal relations, men have, argues Kant, reduced the moral to mechanical relations. The result is *fanaticism*. As we must save science by thinking of its categories as having their source in self-sufficient man, so we must save religion by thinking of the transaction between sin and salvation as essentially within man's moral consciousness. We must insist that man cannot know anything about the God of such religions as historic Protestantism. That is, we must clear the ground for our moral religion by demythologizing fanaticism. After that, or even simultaneously with that, we must remythologize our whole approach to religion by insisting that *somehow*, in ways wholly unknown to us, the goodness of men will be rewarded by a god whom we postulate as almighty and all-gracious.

In this "moral" religion of Kant's we have the model for nineteenth and twentieth century Protestantism.

Before bringing out this fact directly a few more points must be added about Kant's religion. This is not strictly necessary; the essence of the matter is already before us. But it will corroborate what has been said about the nature of Kant's self-sufficient moral religion if we follow Kant's own exposition a bit further.

2. *Christ Demythologized and Remythologized*

It is of special interest to us to see what Kant says about Jesus Christ as the Son of God and Son of man.

Naturally Kant both demythologizes and remythologizes Christ. The Christ of *fanaticism* must be demythologized. Our *moral* religion demands that Christ cannot be identified directly in the space-time world. If he could, he would be *wholly* interwoven into the relativities of the world of ordinary history. He must as the Son of God be a member of the noumenal world. He must therefore be *wholly* beyond the interlacements of the phenomenal world. It is only after we have demythologized him till he is *wholly* beyond the space-time world, that it is safe to bring him back into this world. In fact then to bring him into this world is, in the nature of the case, to bring him *wholly* into it. As God, Jesus Christ is *wholly* beyond, as man he is *wholly* within. But since he is neither God nor man but is both God and man, i.e., as he is the God man, he must be both *wholly* revealed and *wholly* hidden to man in the world of space and time.

We must therefore demythologize the idea of Jesus Christ as with the Father and the Son having a decree according to which all things come to pass. We must turn this about. We must say that: "*Mankind* (rational earthly existence in general) *in its complete moral perfection* is that which alone can render a world the object of a divine decree and the end of creation. With such perfection as the prime condition, happiness is the direct consequence, according to the will of the Supreme Being. Man so conceived, alone pleasing to God, 'is in Him through eternity'; the idea of him proceeds from God's very being; hence he is no created thing but His only-begotten Son, 'the *Word* (the *Fiat!*) through which all other things are, and without which nothing is in existence that is made' (since for him, that is, for rational existence in the world, so far as he may be regarded in the light of his moral destiny, all things were made). 'He is the brightness of His glory.' 'In him God loved the world,' and only in him and through the adoption of his disposition can we hope 'to become the sons of God'; etc."[26]

According to Kant, then, Christ stands for the idea of mankind's moral perfection. As such he must be personified. Christ is "the personified idea of the Good Principle."[27] He is the "archetype of the moral disposition in all its purity."[28] It is "our common duty as men to *elevate* ourselves to this idea of moral perfection. . . ."[29]

We may say that "this archetype has *come down* to us from heaven and has assumed our humanity (for it is less possible to conceive how man, by nature *evil*, should of himself lay aside evil and *raise* himself to the ideal of holiness, than that the latter should *descend* to man and assume a *humanity* which is, in itself, not evil). Such union with us may therefore be regarded as a state of *humiliation* of the Son of God if we represent to ourselves this godly-minded person, regarded as our archetype, as assuming sorrows in fullest measure in order to further the world's good, though he himself is holy and therefore is bound to endure no sufferings whatsoever. Man, on the contrary, who is never free from guilt even though he has taken on the very same disposition, can regard as truly merited the sufferings that may overtake him, by whatever road they come; consequently he must consider himself unworthy of the union of his disposition with such an idea, even though this idea serves him as an archetype."[30]

We may, accordingly, "hope to become acceptable to God (and so be saved) through *a practical faith in this Son of God* (so far as He is represented as having taken upon Himself man's nature)."[31]

So conceived, the Son of God "is completely real in its own right, for it resides in our morally-legislative reason. We *ought* to conform to it; consequently we must be *able* to do so."[32]

Here, then, is the Christ that is constructed wholly in accord with the principles of the truly *moral* as opposed to the *fanatic* view of religion. It is through this Christ as a moral ideal that mankind is certain that it can and will eventually have the wholly holy life. "The law says: 'Be ye holy (in the conduct of your lives) even as your Father in Heaven is holy.' This is the ideal of the Son of God which is set up before us as our model."[33] And "man's moral constitution ought to accord with this holiness."[34] It follows that man can be holy, if not in degree then, at least, in principle. Christ as his projected ideal of perfection helps man on the way toward the ideal. With Socrates, Kant has seen the nature or essence of the holy regardless of what gods or men say about it. But the Son of God, standing for the ideal of perfect morality now *wholly* beyond man, also assures men of the fact that he is on the way toward that ideal because as his Archetype he is *wholly* within man.

Together with the demythologizing and remythologizing of Jesus Christ goes the demythologizing and remythologizing of *miracles*.

Together with *fanaticism* we must banish superstition. Says Kant: "If a moral religion (which must consist not in dogmas and rites but in the heart's disposition to fulfil all human duties as divine commands) is to be established, all *miracles* which history connects with its inauguration must themselves in the end render superfluous the belief in miracles in general; for it bespeaks a culpable degree of moral unbelief not to acknowledge as completely authoritative the commands of duty—commands primordially engraved upon the heart of man through reason—unless they are in addition accredited through miracles: 'except ye see signs and wonders, ye will not believe.' "[35]

Then when we have demythologized the miracles of a religion consisting merely in "dogmas and rites," we remythologize them so as to fit into our *moral* religion. Says Kant: "Yet, when a religion of mere rights and observances has run its course, and when one based on the spirit and the truth (on the moral disposition) is to be established in its stead, it is wholly conformable to man's ordinary ways of thought, though not strictly necessary, for the historical introduction of the latter to be accompanied and, as it were, adorned by miracles, in order to announce the termination of the earlier religion, which without miracles would never have had any authority. Indeed, in order to win over the adherents of the older religion to the new, the new order is interpreted as the fulfilment, at last, of what was only prefigured in the older religion and has all along been the design of Providence."[36]

Such remythologized miracles fit in perfectly with our scientific view of "the order of nature." Remythologized miracles give expression to our conviction that, somehow, our good will be rewarded in ways that we cannot now understand. The God and the Christ which Kant projects into the noumenal realm is, by definition, able to fulfill man's moral ideals. He is created for that purpose. Through him, man must accomplish victory over evil.

3. *The Church as Ethical Commonwealth*

Looking now briefly at Kant's ecclesiology, we see, as might be expected, that he demythologizes the traditional Protestant view of the church and then remythologizes it in accord with the principles of his *moral* religion.

The traditional view of the church depends upon the traditional view of the Christ as coming into the world to save his people from their sins through his life, his death, and his resurrection in Palestine almost 2,000 years ago.

This notion must again be demythologized and remythologized. To Kant a direct identification of Christ and of his work would mean that men must hear about this and believe in it or they are and will be lost. But a truly *moral* religion cannot be dependent upon any such eventuation in the world of temporal-spatial relativity. A truly *moral* religion is inherently universal. The idea of a moral religion involves the idea of *one* church. A moral religion allows for no sectarianism.[37] A true church, based upon a truly *moral* religion must be "purified of the stupidity of superstition and the madness of fanaticism."[38] *"Pure religious faith* alone can found a universal church; for only [such] rational faith can be believed in and shared by everyone, whereas an historical faith, grounded solely on facts, can extend its influence no further than tidings of it can reach, subject to circumstances of time and place and dependent upon the capacity [of men] to judge the credibility of such tidings."[39]

The organization of a church must therefore be subservient to the goal of establishing the one universal moral religion.[40]

A truly Protestant church is therefore one that protests against the claims of any organization that makes its profession of a revealed faith to be primary.[41] The Protestant principle of religion is that which we have spoken of as the moral religion. A truly Protestant church is, therefore, in the nature of the case, universal. A truly Protestant church is not interested in any doctrine except that they "conduce to the performance of all human duties as divine commands (that which constitutes the essence of all religion)."[42]

4. *The Moral View of Atonement and Election*

In this connection it interests us what Kant says about "the mystery of *atonement*" and "the mystery of *election*."[43]

The traditional doctrine of atonement is, for Kant, unacceptable:

"no one can, by virtue of the superabundance of his own good conduct and through his own merit, take another's place; or, if such vicarious atonement is accepted, we would have *to assume it* only from the moral point of view, since for ratiocination it is an unfathomable mystery."[44]

This rejection of vicarious atonement agrees with what Kant expressed earlier, when he said that if we are to have a moral religion, we must not think that God can make us better men without our having to do anything but ask him to do so.[45]

Then there is the "mystery of *election*." The traditional view of election is morally unacceptable. That salvation should come to man "not according to the merit of works but by an unconditioned *decree*; and that one portion of our race should be destined for salvation, the other for eternal reprobation—this again yields no concept of a divine justice but must be referred to a wisdom whose rule is for us an absolute mystery."[46]

Of such mysteries of atonement and election "God has revealed to us nothing and can reveal nothing since we would not *understand* it."[47]

Kant gives us an all-inclusive rule with respect to everything that presents itself in Scripture for man's acceptance. All that any Scripture of any religion teaches us must be interpreted "in a sense agreeing with the universal practical rules of a religion of pure reason."[48] The final purpose of reading the holy Scriptures "is to make men better." The "historical element" in these Scriptures "contributes nothing to this end." It "is something which is in itself quite indifferent, and we can do with it what we like."[49]

It is "the moral improvement of men" that "constitutes the real end of all religion of reason," and it will, therefore, "comprise the highest principle of all Scriptural exegesis." The moral improvement of man is the religion of "the Spirit of God, who guides us into all truth."[50]

Kant thinks of his moral religion as identical with Christianity. His moral religion is, he thinks, the true Christianity! It alone excludes *fanaticism, superstition,* and the *illumination* claimed by sectarians.

5. *The Moral View of the Means of Grace*

One more point must be added. It has to do with the "means of grace." Again, there is a right and a wrong way of thinking of what are called the means of grace. Thinking of them morally, as we should, we must realize that "*means* are all the intermediate causes, which man *has in his power*, whereby a certain purpose may be achieved."[51] Over against this morally acceptable use of the means of grace is that which springs from a "fetish-faith."[52] This "fetish-faith" fits in with the "fanaticism" which thinks that God will make us better men if only we ask him—we are not ourselves to do any thing.

True prayer, prayer "*in faith*," is such as fits in with religion as moral. Jesus taught us the true formula of prayer. "One finds in it nothing but the resolution to good-life conduct. . . ."[53] Only such a prayer can be sincere. Only such a prayer is certain to be heard, because only such a prayer accords with the truly moral view of religion.

D. *Kant vs. Historic Protestantism*

From the foregoing we note first that Kant has developed the principle of apostate thinking till it has attained a large measure of internal consistency. As noted before, Socrates expressed this principle well when he said he must know the nature of the holy regardless of what the gods say about it. Even so, when he sought to answer the scepticism of the Sophists, Socrates appealed to a self-existing realm of truth in which the knowing subject of man participated. Socrates did not yet dare to identify the knowing subject as *itself* the source, the goal, and the standard of knowledge. Nor did Descartes dare to go this far. He let the world of fact and the world of law stand dualistically over against the knowing subject. As for the rationalists and empiricists, though they, as followers of Descartes, were more subjective than the Greeks, yet they did not have the courage of their convictions. Their "science-ideal," as Dooyeweerd calls it, tended to swallow up the individual knowing subject. The activity, and with it the individuality, of the knowing subject was lost as soon as it was "successful" in reaching its object. It is not till the generating activity of the knowing self is thought of as the ultimate source of meaning that the spirit of apostasy reaches its climax.

All "objective" existence must be thought of as the projection of the self-sufficient self. Accordingly, even the "objective" existence of the self as phenomenal must be a projection of the noumenal self. All the "laws" of the space-time world, relating the "objects" of the space-time world to one another, must be projections of the noumenal self. As such these laws are *purely* formal. They are in consequence *purely* correlative to *purely* contingent stuff.

Only thus can Kant "save" science and make room for religion. As for Kant, both science and a truly moral religion would be destroyed if man had to think of a God such as historic Protestantism has. If the laws of science and of religion are to be valid for man, they must ultimately be projections of himself. The universals and the particulars of science cannot be thought of as properly related to one another unless they be thought of as deriving their differentiation from one another in the noumenal self. So too, the laws of God for morality and religion cannot be thought of as properly related to the particulars of man's space-time experience, unless they be thought of as deriving their differentiation from one another in the noumenal self. If science is to be taken for what it is, a growing system of knowledge, and if religion is to be moral, then they both must have their common source in the self-sufficient noumenal self. The noumenal self is the ultimate self-sufficient point of departure, the standard and the goal for anything that may or must be said by man about anything.

E. *Kant's Animosity to Christ*

It can be readily seen that Kant's chief target of opposition is the God and the Christ of Protestantism. If empiricism and rationalism are objectionable, then Protestantism, and particularly the historic Reformed faith, is much more so. Empiricism and rationalism can be cured. Historic Protestantism cannot be cured; it must be demolished.

Kant is so basically hostile to historic Protestantism that his description of it is, as seen earlier, largely a caricature. Nowhere does he present its teachings for what they claim to be. Its view of science and religion are portrayed as both contradictory and immoral.

But on what does Kant himself stand when he swings the logician's postulate and declares that historic Protestantism is contradictory? He stands on the noumenal self, and the noumenal self itself asserts that it stands on nothing.

Nothing less than this will do if Kant is to "save science and make room for religion." Kant needs the idea of pure contingency if he is to escape rationalism and empiricism and especially if he is to escape the everywhere-present claims of the God and the Christ of Christianity.

The idea of the noumenal self as the source of the idea of a genuine scientific development is admittedly utterly mysterious. This noumenal self, springing moment by moment from the womb of pure contingency, must therefore, on the one hand, know God, the world, and itself exhaustively, and, on the other hand, know nothing about God or the world or itself at all. All reality must be thought of as both wholly revealed and as wholly hidden to man.

Here we have the modern equivalent of the idea of Parmenides to the effect that *Being is One* and static. Here we have also the modern equivalent to the idea of Heraclitus that opposites turn into one another. Here, in short, the Greek notion finds its modern expression: All Being is One: change is ultimate, and therefore all things emanate from this One, and finally, all things that have emanated from the One return to the One.

Modern man, following Kant, now feels sure that the God and the Christ of the Reformers does not exist because he *cannot* exist. It is now *absolutely certain* that this God and this Christ *cannot* exist. All the assertions of Scripture to the effect that sinful man will come ino judgment for his rejection of God as his creator and of Christ his redeemer may now be safely set aside. We may now smile with condescension at the naïveté of early man who still fears a coming judgment in the way he fears spooks.

We now know that Santa Claus does not *really* exist; but at

Christmas season, we still think of him as we do of Christ, *as if* he were really able to save us from all things evil and bring us all things good. We may now write a Book of Confessions, in which the Westminster Standards are for the children and the *Confession of 1967* is for adults.

It is thus that apostate man has, in Butler's expression, curved himself inward upon himself by proclaiming himself that he knows all things, including the fact that he knows nothing.

NOTES

1. Richard Kroner, *Kant's Weltanschauung*, tr. John E. Smith (Chicago: 1956), p. 6.
2. Dooyeweerd brings out this fact clearly in his writings. He also points out the fact that there is an important difference between Greek thinking and the thinking of such pre-Kantian modern philosophers as Leibniz. We are not concerned to deny this. We simply emphasize the fact that all forms of apostate thinking have essentially the same structure and the same problematics.
3. Plato himself tried to overcome this dualism in his later dialogues.
4. Immanuel Kant, *Religion Within the Limits of Reason Alone*, tr. Theodore M. Greene and Hoyt. H. Hudson (Open Court Publishing Co., 1934).
5. *Ibid.*, p. 48.
6. *Ibid.*, pp. 22-23.
7. *Ibid.*, p. 23.
8. *Ibid.*
9. *Ibid.*, pp. 34-35.
10. *Ibid.*, p. 40.
11. *Ibid.*
12. *Ibid.*, p. 35.
13. *Ibid.*
14. *Ibid.*, p. 36.
15. *Ibid.*, p. 20.
16. *Ibid.*, p. 40.
17. *Ibid.*, pp. 40-41.
18. *Ibid.*, p. 42.
19. *Ibid.*, p. 43.
20. *Ibid.*, p. 44.
21. *Ibid.*, p. 42.
22. *Ibid.*, p. 43.
23. *Ibid.*
24. *Ibid.*, p. 47.
25. *Ibid.*
26. *Ibid.*, p. 54.
27. *Ibid.*
28. *Ibid.*
29. *Ibid.*
30. *Ibid.*, pp. 54-55.
31. *Ibid.*, p. 55.
32. *Ibid.*
33. *Ibid.*, p. 60.
34. *Ibid.*
35. *Ibid.*, p. 79.
36. *Ibid.*
37. *Ibid.*, p. 93.
38. *Ibid.*
39. *Ibid.*, p. 94.
40. *Ibid.*
41. *Ibid.*, p. 100.
42. *Ibid.*
43. *Ibid.*, p. 134.
44. *Ibid.*
45. *Ibid.*, p. 47.
46. *Ibid.*, p. 134
47. *Ibid.*
48. *Ibid.*, p. 100.
49. *Ibid.*, p. 102.
50. *Ibid.*, pp. 102-103.
51. *Ibid.*, p. 180.
52. *Ibid.*, p. 181.
53. *Ibid.*, p. 183.

Chapter IV

THE REFORMED PASTOR AND
MODERN PROTESTANTISM
(Twentieth Century Philosophy and Theology)

If the Reformed pastor has caught the significance of the Socratic-Kantian principle of inwardness, he is in a good position to understand the philosophy and theology of his own time. He will soon discover that the great variety of schools of philosophy and theology that confronts him need not lead to bewilderment.

The various great philosophers and theologians who seemingly stand in sharp opposition to one another are really like so many brothers of the same family. They all agree in building upon Kant's principle of inwardness. They vie with one another in their claims of being truer to this principle than Kant was himself. Kant, they contend, was not fully true to his own principle. He did not have the courage of his convictions. He was not prepared to say that there *could not possibly be* any fact or law or any combination of fact and law that was not wholly and exclusively an ideal projection into pure contingency of being. Kant claimed that his modern philosophical predecessors had not been thorough enough in excluding the presence of the activity of the Creator-Redeemer God of historic Protestantism from the world. So, in turn, Kant's followers charged him with lack of courage as he demythologized the realm of the metaphysical.

Kant was right in saying, in effect, that if God is to be known, he must be wholly known, and when wholly known, still be wholly unknown to man. But if this be true, then Kant's ethical dualism must be made more ethical and more dualistic than Kant made it, and Kant's ethical phenomenalism must be made both more ethical and more phenomenalistic than Kant made it. First, Kant's *Critique of Pure Reason* must teach us better than it taught Kant himself that

God can say absolutely nothing to man and that man can say absolutely nothing back to God. The relation of man to the beyond is *wholly* a matter of his own projection. The ideal of a scientific system must ever be and remain an ideal. That is the significance of the idea of pure contingency. Second, Kant's *Critique of Practical Reason*, his *Critique of Judgment*, and his *Religion Within the Limits of Reason Alone* must teach us better than they taught Kant himself that we may and should use such notions as God, creation, redemption, sin-salvation, and judgment as *limiting notions* which may help us to pursue the ideals of our moral religion. That is to say, we must make more use of the concept of the *productive imagination* than Kant himself did. We must lay greater stress on the "primacy of the practical reason" than Kant himself did.

We cannot give a survey here of the development of the post-Kantian idealism in such men as Fichte, Schelling, and Hegel.[1] One remark may be made in passing When Hegel says that the real is the rational and the rational is the real, he is not reverting to pre-Kantian rationalism. Hegel despises the *alte Metaphysik*. His is a post-Kantian "rationalism." It is a "rationalism" that has built the Kantian notion of contingency into its "system."

The very ideal of the *Concrete Universal* which constitutes the central notion of the idealism of such men as F. H. Bradley, Bernard Bosanquet, and Josiah Royce, presupposes that the irrational has been given its rightful place. Modern idealism, therefore, boasts of the fact that the individual and the universal, the temporal and the eternal are always present together in every experience of man. Space forbids an examination of the broad spectrum of modern Protestant thought. We will instead focus our attention on two influential and typical representatives of the twentieth century, post-Kantian thinking—Richard Kroner and Paul Tillich. The reader is referred to *Christianity and Barthianism*, and other publications by the present author, for treatment of other well-known modern theologians and philosophers.

I. *Richard Kroner: Philosopher-Theologian*

The works of Richard Kroner cover the entire field of philosophy

and theology from Kant to the present moment. A discussion of
Kroner's position gives us an admirable background for an understanding of current philosophy and religion.

First, argues Kroner, we must certainly build on Kant's ethical
dualism. What Kant called the phenomenal realm we now call the
"I-it" dimension. It is the realm of science and philosophy. Beyond
this I-it dimension is what Kant called the noumenal realm. We now
call it the "I-thou" dimension.

So far as knowledge goes, these two realms stand sharply over
against one another. But then we must also follow Kant and go
beyond Kant in his idea of ethical phenomenalism. The realm of
the I-thou dimension must be thought of as somehow being "above"
the realm of the realm of the I-it dimension.

Having said this, we have excluded all absolutism. No triune
self-subsistent God, such as the Reformers worshiped, can possibly
exist. No such God can possibly manifest himself in the world. There
can be no incarnation of the second person of this triune God in the
way the Council of Chalcedon spoke of him. When Jesus claimed
that he and the Father are one, he cannot have referred to such a
God. When on the cross he said, "It is finished," he cannot have
meant that he as God, in his assumed human nature, died vicariously
for those whom he came to save. There will not be because there
cannot be, any judgment coming, in which Jesus the Christ as judge,
will condemn those who have condemned him in the past. There
cannot be any meaning in "the past" that is not absorbed into the
present. It is the here and now, living, self-sufficient consciousness
of man, that draws all such concepts as God, creation, the fall, and
redemption out of itself. How could any of its own creations rule
over their creator?

The "absolutes" of our forefathers, we now see to be our own
projections, our own ideals by which we tried to encourage ourselves to be moral men. It is this that we have, in the first place,
learned from Kant.

Kant had, to be sure, already assigned a place to the productive
imagination, but he had done so only in the interest of connecting

the theoretical reason with sense-experience. But, says Kroner, the imagination also has a place in the realm of practical life: "Our inner life is determined by images produced by practical imagination."[2] "Practical imagination is the only means by which man can express his relation to reality thought of as a whole."[3] We cannot deal with the whole by means of the concepts of the theoretical reason. Not until concepts have turned to images does the real appear to the human mind. "It is the peculiar function and unique virtue of religious imagination to make *the real itself* enter the stage of our individual life, and address man."[4]

A. *Kroner on Christ*

The importance of this view of the imagination for the question of the relation of speculation and revelation is immediately apparent.

That the significance of the religious imagination is central for Kroner may be seen from his analysis of Jesus as the Christ. By our practical religious imagination, he says, we can understand how in Jesus both true individuality and true universality come to expression. "Jesus has discovered the individual and initiated a new era in history." At the same time, in him "God for the first time comes to true and full universality."[5] "Jesus *is* the Son of God because he *knows* himself to be so; being and knowledge are here inseparable, because both are imaginative. Knowledge is here not theoretical or objective, but *imaginative knowledge.* Imagination determines being and knowledge as well, because the whole existence of Jesus the Christ is formed and constituted by his *imagination*, and can therefore be understood and appreciated and 'assented' to only with the assistance of imagination. Being is here based on the mystical self-consciousness of Jesus because it is mystical itself. Therefore belief in the Sonship of Jesus must be based on mystical imagination also."[6]

It appears then that although Kroner seeks to go beyond Kant, and wants to stress the basic importance of religion as over against mere morality in human life, he goes beyond Kant in terms of the basic motif of Kant's primacy of the Practical Reason. Kroner follows Kant in holding that we must approach life as a whole in terms of the will, not as a metaphysical principle, but as an act which points toward a mystical type of being that can be spoken of only in terms of images.

Kroner speaks of this clearly Kantian method of making room for faith, as being identical in principle with the idea of historic Protestantism. True, Kroner does not fail to point out that there are deep differences between Luther and Kant. "Luther fought against human reason in general so far as it was not supported and inspired by the Word of God. Kant strove against the primacy of theoretical speculation in the whole fabric of human valuations, and propagated, instead, the primacy of practical or ethical reason. The interest of Luther was dictated by his belief in the activity of God alone; the interest of Kant by his critique of pure reason. An immense gap separates these two outlooks, the gap between two different ages."[7] Even so, according to Kroner, both Luther and Kant opposed the spirit of Greek philosophy with its love of speculation. In this, he says, they both expressed the true Christian spirit.[8] Kant was "the first to understand by purely philosophic means why Christian faith had been able to triumph over Greek philosophy, by showing the limit of pure reason in the realm of speculative theology."[9] Luther opposed scholasticism because it embodied the spirit of Greek philosophy, and "Kant finally gave philosophy a new foundation with faith as its basis."[10] The religious source of Kant's attitude is Protestantism. Luther's doctrine that faith, and faith alone, can constitute man's relationship to God has found an adequate philosophic ally and its expression in Kant's *Critique*."[11]

B. *Kroner on Greek Philosophy*

With this knowledge of Kroner's general post-Kantian position we turn to his analysis of Greek speculation. The final defect in this speculation, he says, as we even now surmise, is that it does not properly limit reason in order to make room for faith. This does not mean, of course, that Kroner evaluates Greek philosophy or speculation from the point of view of revelation in the historic Protestant sense of the term.

"Greek speculation is not only pre-Christian; it is outright un-

Christian. The very undertaking to discover the root of all things by means of human intuition and hypothesis is radically un-Biblical or even anti-Biblical."[12]

This statement would appear to be radical enough. But our eyes are opened at once to the platform from which this statement is made when we continue to read, "It is hardly necessary today to emphasize this fact. Indeed, Kierkegaard has made it so compellingly evident that one has to be blind or deaf not to recognize it."[13] But Kierkegaard is himself Kantian in his approach to the idea of speculation.[14] In contradistinction from what, as we noted earlier, Calvin holds, Kierkegaard does not find any direct revelation of God in nature or in history. He has, in effect, with Kant, excluded the possibility of such a revelation. From the point of view of Calvin, Kierkegaard's own position would be speculative. The roots of Kant's thinking are found in the soil of human autonomy. We are, therefore, not surprised to hear Kroner say that Kant "saw more clearly than any other thinker before him that the limitation of reason for the sake of faith was the primary and central task of European Philosophy."[15] But to say this is to drive out demons by means of Beelzebub. How can modern speculation drive out ancient speculation? To be sure, Kant makes room for faith, but he is careful to make room for only such a faith as drives out the Christian faith. The Christian faith is based upon the idea that the answer of God in Christ to the problems of human life have been within the reach of man's apprehension from the beginning. When Kroner says that man is not accidentally but essentially religious, he did not have this true Protestant view in mind. If he had had this true Protestant view in mind, he should have said that any form of speculation since the fall was, in its deepest root, a Satanic attempt to suppress man's proper acknowledgement of God.

The story of the fall, says Kroner, reveals the fact that man is forbidden to know the truth as God knows it.[16] However, Kroner interprets this story in Kantian terms. He says that it signifies the idea that man must not attempt to know "as much as God knows." But this analysis of the fall is itself of a speculative nature. It does not appreciate the deeply ethical implication of the fall. When we speak of the *ethical* implication of the fall, we mean the direct opposite of what Kroner means by the same term. Kroner, following Kant, uses the term *ethical* to mean that man's intellectual or conceptual manipulation is, in the nature of the case, unable to cover the whole of reality, and that man must therefore, on the basis of his moral consciousness, simply postulate the existence of a God who will bring to realization the ideals of man. The Reformers, however, understood the fall of man to indicate his hostility to God as Creator. Because of this hostility, man is unwilling to submit himself in covenant obedience to his Creator. According to this view, the whole history of Greek and of modern speculation manifests, for all its "honest" endeavors to find the truth, a rationalization of man's efforts to *cover up* the truth. In paradise man walked and talked with God. God revealed his will to man by direct communication. Man was to subdue the earth. He was to be a prophet, priest, and king under God, his Creator. The revelation of God within him and about him was, from the beginning, supplemented by the revelation of direct communication of thought by God to man. Supernatural and natural revelation together constituted what Polman calls *foundational* revelation.

It was in this atmosphere of revelation that man from the beginning lived and moved and had his being. It was not only that man had some *intimation* within himself of the origin of his being; he *was told* immediately of his goal as well as of his origin. The goal was not set before him in detail, however; he was to find his way toward it by means of constant reference to the continued revelation of God. His "speculation" was always to be subject to word revelation. His hypotheses concerning the relation of any one fact of the universe to any other fact were always to be made within the limits of the presupposition that God rules and directs all things and that all things will serve the final purposes of God as revealed in Scripture. Thus, speculation, i.e., intellectual articulation, was consciously subject to the sovereign directing activity of God.

Satan suggested to man that he think of God as a fellow-speculator with himself. Man should think of God's command as though it were based merely on a hypothesis that God entertained as to which way *reality* would go. No one had as yet experimented with the eating of the fruit of the tree that God forbade to man. Why should not Satan's theory with respect to the effect of such eating be placed on a par with that of God? It was up to man to assert his freedom from authority, to begin asking questions, and to find answers for himself. Man must set aside a god who pretended that he already had the answer to any question the creature could ask.

The result of this rebellion from divine authority was that man had to ask his questions in the void. And yet he could not ask them in the void. *Every question that he asked, therefore, implied the denial of its proper answer.* Futility and frustration was the only possible result. The history of philosophy is itself the evidence of this fact. With great aplomb, apostate man asks himself *whether* there is a God. But by thus asking whether God exists he has assumed the possibility of the non-existence of God. If he should then conclude that God does exist, it would be a god who might as well not exist. Such a God is of no possible use to man. He has no answers to man's questions. He is made in the image of man. Even when man asserts the impossibility of the non-existence of God by means of the onto-logical proof, as variously formulated, he is still, in effect, asserting the non-existence of the God of the Bible. Of course, the followers of Kant would also say this, and thus they too seem to oppose every form of speculation, yet they do so on a purely speculative founda-tion. They do so merely on the ground that reality is ultimately irrational. When Kroner, with Kant, says that God is incompre-hensible, he does so because, with Kant, he believes that man cannot by conceptualization penetrate the whole of reality. He does not, with the Reformers, hold to the incomprehensibility of God because God is absolutely self-contained, and has clearly revealed himself as such through Christ in Scripture. In other words, the very term *incomprehensibility* means one thing for the Reformers, but it means quite another for the Kantians. The Kantians assume that man as autonomous can properly interpret the realm of phenomena inde-pendently of God. The Reformers hold that man must confess his sin of assumed autonomy to his Redeemer, and then interpret all things, the phenomenal as well as the noumenal, in terms of this Creator-Redeemer.

C. *Kroner Opposes Reformation Philosophy*

We are now in a position to understand why Kroner's seemingly very sharp rejection of Greek speculation does not rest on the basis of the Reformation idea of revelation. It rests rather on the basis of modern speculation. The Greek philosopher assumed that it would be possible for man actually to penetrate the whole of reality, God as well as man, by means of his intellect. He wanted to do this in order to keep the voice of God his Creator from sounding in his ears. Apostate man's whole cultural effort, whatever else it is, whatever good has come out of it, is still basically an effort to suppress the revelation of God within and about him. His philosophizing springs from an evil conscience. *Deep down in his heart every man, since he is made in the image of God, knows that he is a creature of God and that he should worship his Creator and bountiful Benefactor.* God has given man rain and sunshine and fruitful seasons. He has given him the good things of the earth freely to enjoy. But man wants them wholly for himself. He wants to disown God, even the God of love. He does this out of hatred, hatred Satanically inspired. It is this *ethical* suppression of the situation as it really is, that underlies Greek speculation. Kroner has no eye for this. Whatever weakness he finds in Greek thought, he sees no sin in this basic suppression of the truth. In consequence, when he speaks of Christianity in relation to Greek speculation, the former is in the last analysis merely supplementary to the latter. Kroner has not really transcended the Roman Catholic view at all.

When, therefore, Kroner says that "biblical religion is more averse to speculation and metaphysics than any other religion," he says this from the point of view of a Christianity that has itself been Kantianized.

Kroner's own position is still speculative. The starting-point of his approach is still the starting-point of human autonomy. He, as well as the Greek philosophers, works on the assumption that man did not from the beginning of history stand in covenant relation to God. Kroner, following Kant, starts man off in a bottomless ocean of irrationalism. At the same time, also with Kant, he virtually ascribes to man the power of putting order into the irrational by means of man's logical activity. It is this irrationalist-rationalist starting-point that controls Kroner's thought. Over against this, the Greek position may be called rationalistic irrationalism. *All apostate thought exhibits a combination of rationalism and irrationalism.* With the Greek philosophers it was rationalism that prevailed over irrationalism. In modern times it is irrationalism that prevails over rationalism. Nevertheless the one always involves the other. The difference between the modern and the ancient approach is merely one of emphasis.

The rationalist-irrationalist approach works on the assumption that the distinction between the Creator and the creature is not basic. If this distinction is introduced at all, it is introduced *after* the attempt is first made to predicate about *being in general* by means of laws of logic in general. We may call this the *monistic assumption* of apostate thought.

It has been well said that for Greek philosophy all is at bottom one; all comes out of the one, and all returns to the one. But this is as true of modern philosophy as it is of Greek philosophy. Even the ethical dualism of Kant has back of it this monistic assumption. Kroner speaks of Christianity as being incompatible with the speculative nature of Greek philosophy. Says Kroner: "The living God of the Bible deters all conceptual knowledge, and yet in some way he stands for the ultimate truth which speculation tries to grasp in its own right. In spite of the diversity separating their form and content, speculation and revelation meet. The religious and the speculative Ultimate are in the final analysis the same Absolute."[17]

In this brief quotation the whole of Kroner's view of the relation of Greek speculation to Christianity is expressed. Regarded from the historic Protestant point of view its basic weaknesses are as follows:

(1) Kroner says that the God of the Bible deters all conceptual knowledge. If this were true, then this God would not be man's Creator and Redeemer. The God of the Bible has made man in his image; man must therefore use *all* his gifts, including his power of conceptualization, to the praise of his Creator and Redeemer. This means that man's conceptual activity must be employed only upon the

presupposition of the primacy of man's Creator-Redeemer. If man subjects his whole being, including his intellect, to his Creator-Redeemer, then he knows this God and knows all things in the light of his knowledge of God. There is then a concrete and living inter-action between man's knowledge of the world, of himself, and of his God. His body of knowledge then has internal coherence.

(2) Involved in Kroner's idea that the God of the Bible deters conceptual knowledge, is the idea that conceptual knowledge func-tions properly in the created universe without any reference to the God of the Bible. This functioning is spoken of as speculation, and is said to function *in its own right*. Yet how can conceptual operation on the part of man be said to be functioning in its own right? The conceptual functioning of a creature made in the image of God presupposes the religious recognition of Jesus Christ as his Re-deemer and Lord. Strictly speaking, no conceptual operation of man can exist except in religious ethical subordination to, or else in religious ethical rebellion against, the Redeemer-Creator. Is not man, as Kroner himself said, *essentially religious?* The speculation of the Greeks was therefore the false conceptualization of covenant-breakers.

(3) Such being the case, it is quite impossible that the god of this speculation should be the same as the God of Christianity. Kroner says that the religious and the speculative ultimates are the same. We should, rather, say that there are two religious ultimates opposing one another. There is the ultimate of Christianity, the triune God and Redeemer of Scripture. Any man who knows this ultimate, that is, who knows "it" existentially, knows not an *it* but knows *Him*. He then knows this ultimate as the one who has raised him from death to life so that in all his activity he has come alive, whereas he was formerly spiritually dead. In his spiritual deadness he had made himself the goal of all his efforts. His conceptual activity, too, was employed for the purpose of maintaining the respectability of the monistic assumption on which he was working. But now he has come alive through the death and resurrection of Jesus Christ, his substitute, and through the regenerating power of the Holy Spirit, who takes the things of Christ and gives them unto us. Now he submits himself, and therefore his powers of conceptualization, too,

captive to the obedience of Christ. Speculation is therefore the activity of spiritually dead men, men religiously hostile to their Creator and Redeemer. These men create gods in their own image. And, if they speak of a god as *ultimate*, this ultimate is an *it* and not *He*. This ultimate is without power or love. This ultimate is the projection and hypostatization of man's love of himself apart from God. Even when apostate man speaks of this God as having or being love, this love is love of the sinner for himself and therefore implies hatred of the God and the Christ of the Bible. The ultimate of Greek and of modern post-Kantian speculation and the Ultimate of Christianity cannot possibly be the same.

(4) It must be noted finally, that, according to Kroner, these two ultimates of religion and speculation are *somehow* the same. Somehow the world of speculation and the world of faith *must* be brought together. That is the demand of Kant's *Critique of Practical Reason*. Yet the two worlds stand over against one another in absolute opposition; or, in other words, no intelligible meaning can be placed in the idea of their conjunction. Consequently, no reason can be given why the world of the spirit should be placed above the world of the mechanical. It is simply blind faith when men assert that *somehow* the world has purpose and victory over its evil when they first assume that the world works independently of God. This implies, therefore, that the whole of human predication falls to the ground unless one presupposes the God and the Christ of the Reformers. This also implies that the world of speculation cannot in any intelligible way be said to be the same as the world of revelation. In the former, the world of science is first abstracted from God by man and then returned to God by man. In the world of revelation, everything is always related to God and seen to be intelligible only because of this relation.

We must therefore hold that Kroner's own position is that of speculation. And it is no marvel that he rejects the idea of Dooyeweerd when the latter asserts that Greek speculation has a religious root, namely, that of apostasy from God. Says Kroner: "In our time the thesis has been defended that a religious 'ground motive' was always operative within metaphysical systems and that the history of philosophy can be best understood and interpreted when we reflect upon this motive and make it overt. Only then can the ground motive of a Christian philosophy be rightly appreciated. After such reflection full justice can be done to a Christian philosophy in its struggle with other philosophical systems and schools. The representative of this thesis, Herman Dooyeweerd, asserts that all Greek speculation was based upon the contrast of matter and form, a contrast that has a religious origin and significance."[18] Over against this view of Dooyeweerd's, Kroner maintains that that Greek attitude toward the world and life in which Greek philosophy had its roots was "not religious but artistic."[19] "Hence within Greek civilization philosophy could desert religion with greater facility than is possible in the Christian Era."[20] "And even if the contrast of matter and form ever had a religious connotation, it was not expressed philosophically or expounded philosophically; such connotation had been lost entirely in the scheme of Aristotle. As far as I can see, there is no religious ground motive within Aristotle's system. I shall show that Aristotle's emphasis upon form is not religious but aesthetic in origin. Even though the Greeks originated the idea of autonomous *theoria,* they did not formulate the ideal of autonomy because their religion was not dogmatic; it did not censor their thought."[21]

It is obvious that Kroner does not appreciate Dooyeweerd's basic approach. When Dooyeweerd speaks of a religious motive as lying back of all speculation, he is not thinking of some self-conscious view developed by philosophers. Rather, he is thinking of *that which controls their motivation,* even in their philosophical speculation, as the children of Adam, as covenant-breakers. If not *self*-consciously, then *sub*-consciously the Greek philosophers worked on the monistic assumption spoken of earlier. They assumed that at bottom all being, both divine being and human being together, is one. They assumed that it was possible to say something intelligible about *being in general* without distinguishing between the Creator's being and the creature's being. They assumed that the plurality of the created world and all the evil that is in it, is somehow an outflow of the being of God. They assumed that *somehow* man, together with the whole temporal process, participates in the very life and being of God.

Kroner's approach acknowledges none of this. He even asserts that Dooyeweerd "does not reflect upon the difference between a religious motive, deliberately assumed and ostentatiously proclaimed by a philosopher, and historical conditions more or less unconsciously influencing individual thought or communal thinking."[22] In reality Dooyeweerd presupposes a religious motive that lies deepr in human nature than all self-consciously adopted positions and all historical conditions that have influenced philosophers "more or less unconsciously." It is the attitude of apostasy which controls the "natural man." It is this that constitutes the driving force of his self-conscious conceptualization. It is his evil heart that controls his intellect, his imagination, and his every other gift.

Accordingly, the Greeks were not "free" in the sense in which Kroner thinks they were. On the contrary, they were slaves of sin. And this kept them from giving any consideration to the idea of God as Creator-Redeemer. They could not tolerate such a notion even as an hypothesis. All their thinking took place within the restrictive limits of their monistic assumption.

On the other hand, the Christian church did not restrict freedom of thought by introducing the notion of heresy, as Kroner claims. True, the church has much abused the idea of heresy; but when the church *restricted true* freedom of thought by means of heresy trials, it was then no longer the true church. The idea of heresy, properly conceived, presupposes both the fact of God's revelation to man in Christ, and his charge to the church to proclaim the truth. Therefore only those who believe the Christ as the one through whom the world is created and directed, and who has saved them from their sin, can, properly, be members of the church. Satan tries desperately to stifle the witness of the church to Christ. He therefore seeks to confuse the issue between belief and unbelief. His most plausible argument is that no absolute truth can be found in history and that, therefore, no group of human beings should claim to possess it. Is it not the acme of pride, he insinuates, to hold that one group of people should exclude others from their fellowship when such men as Kant have shown the subjective foundation of all "truth"?

In all thought opposed to the idea that the truth of Christ is present in history, and that his church has the responsibility of maintaining an unsullied testimony to the fact and substance of that truth, men still speak as slaves to the monistic assumption. They assume that all "being" is one and that, in consequence, "god" is himself immersed both in evil and in change. They assume that God *cannot* exist free in himself and freely in control of the world of history. They assume that Jesus Christ cannot have been the Son of God and Son of man who died to set his people free from sin. They assume that the Holy Spirit *cannot* exist and cannot cause the spiritually blind to see.

All this is purely formal and *a priori* reasoning, reasoning that, in effect, does what Parmenides did when he said that the reach of consistent logical human thought can control what can and cannot be. *True freedom of thought is found only among those who proclaim Christ in their thought.*

One more point must be made in this connection. Kroner says, in criticism of Dooyeweerd, that "though the Greeks originated the idea of autonomous *theoria*, they did not formulate the ideal of autonomy because their religion was not dogmatic; it did not censor their thought."[23]

Yet what Dooyeweerd means by autonomy, as we have already noted, is the sinful unwillingness of apostate man to submit all thought to the obedience of God in Christ. This came into the world at the beginning of history. In consequence *all* men, the Greeks as well as Kant and his followers, are controlled by the principle of apostasy unless they are redeemed by Christ.

D. *Kroner: Exponent of New Protestantism*

In what way then could Kroner view Greek philosophy as a preparation for the coming of the gospel of salvation through Jesus Christ? Kroner himself says that "a seemingly impossible chasm exists between the Greek spirit of contemplation and the Biblical spirit of action and active faith." In spite of this, however, he says that the Greeks themselves "have built a connecting link" between Greek popular religion and Christianity.[24] It was the historic mission of Greek speculation "to bring about the destruction of the popular religion, thereby paving the way for the recognition of the Lord of the Bible."[25] "The whole system of ancient culture had to give way to the new spirit and the new truth of revelation."[26]

Is the preparatory significance of Greek philosophy for the coming of the gospel then primarily a negative one? It would seem on the surface that this is at least the point that Kroner is most concerned to stress. He would seem to be taking a position quite different from that of Romanism. "If the term 'theism' means the doctrine implied in Biblical faith and revelation, philosophy can never be theistic for it can never come into contact with the living God but can only conceive of the idea of a divine being."[27] "Greek speculation never went beyond the idea of a world-mind."[28]

But if this be true, how then, we may ask, can Kroner say that "speculation dislodged the polytheistic gods and approached Biblical monotheism . . ."?[29] Kroner speaks of Greek speculation with the idea of God as the world-mind of pantheism.[30] Then he thinks of this pantheism as the instrument by which polytheism "was transformed into monotheism."[31] Greek philosophy, he says, overcame polytheism not only by means of criticism but also "by a constructive theological doctrine."[32] "The Hellenic Logos was thus eventually transformed into the Christian Logos."[33] "The power of revelation was present from the very beginning, when speculation set out to gain knowledge of the divine, although this power was not yet known as that of revelation. There was within speculation a kind of substitute for revelation, namely, intuition as contrasted with analysis."[34] By logical analysis the Greeks could reach nothing higher than the duality of form and matter as this attains its climax in the philosophy of Aristotle. Nevertheless this was unsatisfactory even from the point of view of analysis itself, since logical thought must always seek for a unity back of every duality. Still, this idea of logical unity at once leads back to that of logical duality. Thus no concept of an original unity can be gained except one that stands in correlation with an equally original plurality. "All these grave and central questions brought about the final ruin of speculation and coerced the mind to accept another source of truth."[35] For Kroner, intuition lies as a connecting link between speculation and this other source of truth, namely, revelation.

May we not ask Kroner how this can be, since speculation and revelation are, on his view, mutually exclusive totalitarian views? Kroner himself speaks of Greek speculation as pantheism. Speculation, he says, "implies an impersonal comprehension or vision and an understanding by critical analysis. It leads, therefore, to an abstract relation between the thinking mind and the Absolute, as its object."[36] "The avenue of human thought docs not lead to an encounter with the living God."[37] "And yet history proves that human wisdom is an avenue toward revealed wisdom."[38] Speculation had "to be frustrated in the end."[39] "And religion based on speculation or consonant with it is impersonal and pantheistic."[40] Yet, "The philosophers moved toward the Biblical primacy of the ethical in its contest with the aesthetic. They moved in the direction of a more rigorous separation of 'flesh' and spirit, of man and God, of the temporal and the eternal, a separation achieved by means of logical distinction, but also making for the truth of revelation. Speculation thus 'prepared' for the gospel. It pointed to the transcendence of the Highest without fully arriving at the Biblical starting point. The employment of logic simultaneously enhanced the ethical standards of religion and applied the latter to the representation of the divine. This trend culminated in Plato. It set in with Xenophanes and Heraclitus. Xenophanes did not yet announce the God of Genesis, but he had an intuition of the oneness and spirituality of the Biblical Creator. 'There is one god, the greatest amongst gods and men, not resembling the mortals in figure or in thinking. . . . He sets in motion the All without any toil, by the power of his mind alone. What a sublime image! While preserving a Homeric trait, it reminds one of the psalms. It represents a striking synthesis of Greek and Biblical insight, before Biblical insight was brought to the Greeks. . . .' "[41]

We recall at this point that for Kroner, Kant's concept of the "primacy of the ethical" is virtually identified with the main contention of the Protestant Reformation. He sees in the philosophy of Plato, as over against that of Aristotle, a tendency toward the primacy of the ethical such as is held by Kant. It is on this basis that Kroner can think of Greek speculation as being a preparation for the gospel.

This preparation for the gospel, Kroner argues, finds its most striking expression in the Platonic notion of intuition. "Speculation and revelation were related to each other, even though revelation played only a negative role in this development. The power of revelation was present from the very beginning when speculation set out to gain knowledge of the divine, although this power was not yet known as that of revelation. There was within speculation a kind of substitute for revelation, namely intuition as contrasted with analysis."[42] Yet it is not only in the Platonic idea of intuition but also in speculation itself that Kroner finds a tendency toward the truth of revelation. "There is a kind of affinity between logical clarity and moral purity, between speculative profundity and spiritual sublimity, between the truth attainable by thought and the truth revealed by God. And to the extent of this affinity, the Greek thinkers did attain knowledge of the divine being. To that degree Plato advanced in the direction of revelation. The more consistently speculation proceeded, the more logical its arguments, the more did philosophical concepts approximate to the incomprehensible. There is an inner coincidence between the truth of one realm and that of another. What is true in thought cannot be false in faith. And, therefore, Greek thought went as far as thought could go in the right direction of the true faith. It failed only when it transgressed its limits."[43]

If now we analyze the various elements in Kroner's position, there appears to be a basic ambiguity. Speculation is said to lead to pantheism. Surely, then, the more consistent speculation is, the more consistently pantheistic will be its result. Then, also, the more obvious will be the fact that the god of speculation and the God of Christianity are utterly opposed to one another. Rather, if there is to be any mention of speculation as preparatory to the coming of the gospel, this should be considered purely negative because the Christianity for which speculation would actually prepare would be one of pure irrationalism.

When Kroner speaks in this connection of speculation as failing only when it transgresses its limits, he is again speaking from the

Kantian point of view. He thinks that more than Aristotle Plato to some extent (though not as fully as Kant), recognizes the proper limits of speculation. But who is finally to set the limits to speculation? Speculation itself will not. Its inherent nature, according to Kroner himself, is to give a totalitarian interpretation of reality. The proper limits of human thought cannot be ascertained unless one first takes one's stand upon the position of revelation. Only then is it possible to think of human thought as that of the creature who is made in the image of God. The speculative method of Plato's thinking is just as definitely exclusive of the biblical view of creation and redemption as is the philosophy of Aristotle.

The basic difficulty in Kroner's view springs from the fact that he thinks the Kantian idea of the primacy of the ethical to be consonant with, or even constitutive of, the Christian position. But Kant does not limit speculation properly. He does not base "speculation" on revelation. He merely marks the inability of speculation to cover the whole of reality. He assumes that that aspect of reality which human speculation cannot control is unknowable to God as well as to man. In other words, his method still implies the ability of human speculation to determine negatively, if not positively, what can or cannot exist. *The idea of creation and redemption in the Christian sense of the term is as impossible with the Kantian view as it is with the Aristotelian.*

In particular, it should be observed that the Kantian notion of the primacy of the ethical, and the Platonic notion of intuition, are still controlled by the principle of speculation. In both cases it is speculation that determines what can or what cannot be intuited. In both cases it is a foregone conclusion that what is intuited is not the Creator-Redeemer God of Christianity.

It appears then that Kroner's "Protestant" evaluation of Greek speculation is not radically different from that of Romanism. As Romanism builds positively upon the form-matter scheme of Aristotle's philosophy, Kroner seeks to build positively upon the philosophy of Kant, and between these there is only a gradational difference. The modern Protestant view as represented by Kroner is faced with the same impasse that faces Romanism. Both accept the principle of speculation as based on the idea of human autonomy. Both think this principle needs supplementation by revelation. Both fail to see that the principle of speculation is inherently totalitarian and therefore does not allow for supplementation. Consequently, in both cases the Christianity that is added to speculation is an emasculated Christianity. It is a Christianity without the basic framework of creation, the fall, and redemption through Christ in history. In both cases it is only after the speculative principle has exhausted itself that Christianity is assigned its place. Its place is then only in the area of the purely irrational. Only such a Christ as cannot in any intelligible sense be said to challenge man's whole being, his thought as well as his action, can be allowed to speak. When he speaks, he speaks in a vacuum, and then man need not pay any attention to him.

The historic Protestant view of Greek speculation is therefore quite the opposite both of the Romanist view and of the modern Protestant view. The historic Protestant view starts frankly from the point of view of totalitarian revelation. Starting thus, we have at once a positive view of the relation of God to the world as a whole and to man. Starting from the God and the Self-attesting Christ of Scripture as the one who posits himself, we have the basic unity in terms of which all that takes place in history is given its opportunity of making a positive contribution to the kingdom of God. All men know God. The Greeks knew God too. Every man in the world knows, deep down in his heart, that he is a creature of God and a sinner before him. Man's thinking takes place, as a matter of fact, within the atmosphere of revelation. His own consciousness is revelational of God. His self-awareness presupposes his awareness of his relation to God, his Creator. Paul speaks of man as thus "knowing God" in Romans 1:21.

It is in terms of this original positive relation of every man to God that the Greeks, as well as all other men, could and did make (even though indirectly) their positive contribution to the development of the kingdom of God and of his Christ. How is this possible?

Did we not see that when carried out consistently, apostate thinking leads to idols instead of to the living God? This is true. But even the wrath of man must praise God. When Joseph revealed himself to his brothers at Pharaoh's court, he told them that what they intended for evil, God, the Redeemer, overruled for good (Gen. 50:20; cf. Gen. 45:4ff.). So it is also with the spirit of speculation. All speculation seeks is to suppress the truth that speaks to all men everywhere and all the time. The systems of thought as elaborated by speculation are marvelously beautiful idols which men worship as substitutes for the true God. Kroner is quite right when he says that these systems end up with a god who is nothing but an abstract principle. If the sinner could satisfy himself that the only God that exists is such a principle, he would not need to repent of his sin. Paul the apostle confronts these systems when he cries out that they have been made foolishness with God. They have themselves demonstrated the fact that speculation, as inspired with sinful man's desire to suppress the truth, has shown itself to be folly. Sin-inspired as it is, speculation cannot solve a single problem. It can only create artificial questions, and, of course, cannot solve these. It sets out boldly on its way to bury the idea of revelation by means of the vague notion of *thought-in-general*. It sets out boldly on its way to bury the idea of God's authority by means of *behaviour-in-general*. By virtue of its uncritical monistic assumption, it takes for granted that human being, human knowledge, and human action are not what Christianity says they are, namely, as confronted always and everywhere with God the Creator-Redeemer.

The complete rejection of the principle of speculation presupposes that even this rejected speculation itself cannot help but make a positive contribution to the development of the kingdom of God. Suppose that I have poor taste in arranging the furniture of my home. Suppose further that during my vacation an intruder came into my home and rearranged my furniture. When I return, I may be greatly surprised at the improvement made in my house. The intruder, though he was in my house illegally, was nevertheless a man of good taste; and, even if this intruder hated me with an incurable hatred, he could still, in virtue of his being an artist, arrange the furniture of my house in such a way as to make me approve of what he had done, in spite of his hatred for me. Even so, the natural man, hating God and out to repress every trace of the presence of God, may yet arrange the things of the Creator-Redeemer's universe, which has been defaced by sin, in such a way as to further the progress of the cultural mandate given to man at the beginning of history.

We must go one step further. The natural man hates God. When he speaks of the primacy of the ethical, he does this only in the interest of making his own moral consciousness the ultimate source of right and wrong. Even by means of this primacy of the ethical, the natural man is still engaged in his speculative enterprise, the enterprise of repressing the truth. But though this be so, the very frustration to which all his speculation leads him is an indirect contribution toward the progress of the gospel. The captain of a ship may have planned to murder all its passengers on a lonely island in the Pacific Ocean. His crew may be in agreement with him. But just as he is about to turn the course of the ship away from its proper destination and toward this island, the owner of the ship, aware of the evil intentions of the skipper all the while, has him locked in the hold of the ship and replaced by one who guides it to the desired haven. In the same way even the hostile efforts of Satan and all his hosts must finally serve the Christ and his coming kingdom. All this is true simply because in the first place, the relation of God, the Creator-Redeemer, to man has been positive. From the time the first man, Adam, came to be aware of himself, God was speaking directly to him as well as being presented to him in the facts of the universe and of his mind. God revealed his task to him. Adam lived on God's estate. Every tree and shrub, every fact in it, was marked with the sign that it belonged to God and was to be used freely by man but used only in recognition of God as his Lord.

For this original positive relation of God to man, Kroner has no eye. And because he has no eye for this, he regards the Platonic and the Kantian systems as being consonant with, or at least directly preparatory to, the Christian outlook.

Kroner has not indicated the dilemma that faces both Romanism and modern Protestantism. Whether we say that the existence of God can or cannot be proved by means of speculation based on the idea of human autonomy makes no basic difference. So long as we do not say that the very possibility of proof and the very possibility of intelligible human predication presupposes the historic Protestant framework of thought, we are faced with the necessity of making abstract unity correlative to abstract particularity, and abstract particularity correlative to abstract unity. But a God or a Christ who is the correlative of man is of no help to man in his distress.

II. *Paul Tillich: Theologian-Philosopher*

We now take Paul Tillich as a second representative of what is often called the "Principle of the Reformation."[44] There are several other outstanding thinkers of the recent past and of the present from whose writings we might learn about the nature of this principle. But a rapid survey of a number of them would not help us as much as a more penetrating analysis of one or two of them. We choose Tillich because he, perhaps more thoroughly than any other besides Kroner, has attempted to relate theology, philosophy, and science into one systematic whole. Moreover, a discussion of Tillich may properly be taken as a supplement to a discussion of Kroner. Kroner shows us what kind of theology is consonant with modern philosophy and science. Tillich shows us what kind of philosophy and science is consonant with modern theology. Both are digging the same tunnel under the same river. Perhaps we shall find that each is *wholly unaware and wholly aware* of what the other is doing.

We have spoken of Kroner's three-volume work on *Revelation and Speculation* as the chief source of our information about Kroner's views of the relation between theology on the one hand and philosophy and science on the other. We shall now think of Tillich's three-volume work on *Systematic Theology* as the chief, but not exclusive, source of our information.

A. *Tillich on The Protestant Era*

In chapter XIII of his work on *The Protestant Era* Tillich discusses "The Protestant Message and the Man of Today."

"Protestantism," says Tillich, "is understood as a special historical embodiment of a universally significant principle."[45] Therefore, it may also be said that "Protestantism as a principle is eternal and a permanent criterion of everything temporal. Protestantism as the characteristic of a historical period is temporal and subjected to the eternal Protestant principle."[46]

We may therefore expect ever-new interpretations of the historic Protestant notion of justification by faith. Tillich himself early discovered that "the principle of justification through faith refers not only to the religious-ethical but also to the religious-intellectual life. Not only he who is in sin but also he who is in doubt is justified through faith. The situation of doubt, even of doubt about God, need not separate us from God. There is faith in every serious doubt, namely, the faith in the truth as such, even if the only truth we can express is our lack of truth. But if this is experienced in its depth and as an ultimate concern, the divine is present; and he who doubts in such an attitude is 'justified' in his thinking."[47]

Here we have what Tillich himself calls a "radical and universal interpretation of the idea of justification through faith. . . ."[48] "It was natural that on the basis of these presuppositions the history of religion and of Christianity required a new interpretation."[49] Tillich was especially concerned to apply the idea of his Protestant principle to the interpretation of history.[50] No genuinely Protestant interpretation of history was available to him.[51]

Tillich speaks of the ideas of *theonomy, kairos,* and the *demonic* as basic to his view of history.[52]

In these ideas, "the Gestalt of grace, and the latent church—the Protestant principle appears in its revealing and critical power."[53] For in them we have expressed the idea of Jesus Christ as the *New Being.*[54] "Here the Protestant principle comes to an end. Here is the bedrock on which it stands and which is not subjected to its criticism."[55]

Tillich says that his position thus characterized attempts to overcome the conflict between the Neo-Orthodox and the Liberal approaches to theology.[56] The "Protestant principle itself prohibits old and new orthodoxy, old and new liberalism."[57]

In view of these remarks of Tillich's, it is easy to see why the Protestant message to modern man "cannot be a direct proclamation of religious truths as they are given in the Bible and in tradition, for the situation of the modern man of today is precisely one of doubt about all this and about the Protestant church itself."[58] "The message of the Protestant church must take a threefold form. First, it must insist upon the radical experience of the boundary-situation; it must destroy the secret reservations harbored by the modern man which prevent him from accepting resolutely the limits of his human existence."[59] Second, the Protestant church must pronounce the 'Yes' that comes to man in the boundary-situation when he takes it upon himself in its ultimate seriousness. Protestantism must proclaim the judgment that brings assurance by depriving us of all security; the judgment that declares us whole in the disintegration and cleavage of soul and community; the judgment that affirms our having truth in the very absence of truth (even of religious truth); the judgment that reveals the meaning of our life in the situation in which all the meaning of life has disappeared."[60] "Third, Protestantism must witness to the 'New Being' through which alone it is able to say its word in power, and it must do this without making this witness again the basis of a wrong security."[61]

Here we already have the gist of what Tillich thinks the principle of a true Protestantism to be. It implies the rejection of the idea of a directly ascertainable presence of God in history, such as was entertained by the Reformers. It requires the idea of God as both *wholly* hidden and *wholly* revealed to man in Jesus Christ.

We now turn to Tillich's most comprehensive statement of the Protestant principle as expressed in his *Systematic Theology*. In his introduction Tillich again speaks of the *message* and the *situation*. "The 'situation' theology must consider is the creative interpretation of existence, an interpretation which is carried on in every period of history under all kinds of psychological and sociological conditions."[62] Again, "The 'situation' to which theology must respond is the totality of man's creative self-interpretation in a special period. Fundamentalism and orthodoxy reject this task, and, in doing so, they miss the meaning of theology."[63]

We soon discover what Tillich means by the "creative self-interpretation" of our period. It is the self-sufficient reflective mind of modern post-Kantian thought that analyzes its own resources and its own needs. It is this mind that is assumed to be able to interpret itself and the world and then to call upon God afterwards. It is this mind that is assumed to be able to ask proper questions about itself and the world, requiring merely that the answers to these questions be given by God. But God, as he speaks in Christ, will give no answers unless he is permitted to inspire in men the proper questions; and further, even improper questions, such as are asked by the would-be autonomous man, can be asked only because God has, in Christ, given negative answers to them.

Tillich is a profound philosopher as well as a profound theologian. It is his aim to give a totality picture of the human situation. He does not seek for such a picture by means of a pre-Kantian rationalist method. He assumes that Kant was right in holding that there is an ultimate mystery surrounding man. His totality picture is therefore similar to that of the *ethical* idealism of such men as Fichte and Hegel. His "system" differs from that of such men in that, together with Kierkegaard and other existentialists, he stresses more than they did the depth of the mystery or contingency surrounding man.

B. *Tillich Opposes Reformation Theology*

Tillich therefore shares the bitter hostility of modern existentialism against every form of orthodox thought. For him the idea of Jesus Christ as being directly identifiable with the man who walked in Galilee, or the idea of Scripture as the direct and final revelation of God in Christ, is intolerable. How could the depth of the mystery of being be exhaustively set forth in a form of words that finite man has produced and can understand? How could a revelation, pretending to be final and comprehensive, do anything but injustice to the freedom of man which is the very nature of his being? In other words, Tillich has two reasons, or rather a twofold reason, for regarding the idea of a final or direct revelation of God to man as impossible. This twofold reason springs from the assumption that he has in common with post-Kantian man, namely, that reality is at the same time infinitely contingent and that yet it is somehow possible for man to say that it cannot be of a certain nature. In other words, Tillich, together with modern man in general, holds that the God and the Christ of the Scriptures, and therefore of the Reformation, *cannot* exist.

It is clearly impossible to deal with the position of Tillich adequately unless one sets over against it the bold challenge of the God of the Scriptures, the one who claims that without him no intelligible questions can be asked any more than answers can be given in any field of human endeavor. In Tillich's "system" a mighty effort is made to present an all-inclusive system in terms of a principle that confessedly presupposes man himself as able to ask the right questions about himself and his fate. It is to be expected that he will therefore reinterpret Christianity and with it the Reformation, in terms of his self-sufficient method. Tillich is quite right when he asserts that a method is an expression of the system it produces.[64] His own method, not taken from the "system" of biblical thought, produces a system which swallows up biblical thought.

The traditional method of apologetics based on the *Summae* of Aquinas and on the *Analogy* of Butler is futile in dealing with Tillich. This traditional method would have to agree with Tillich that the natural man can analyze his own situation adequately by himself, and that all he needs is for Christ to give him the answers to his questions. On the basis of the Aquinas-Butler type of apologetics the patient diagnoses his own case and prescribes to the doctor the kind of medicine he needs. The method that is needed for a conversation with Tillich is that by which Christ is shown to be the great Physician who alone can diagnose the nature of man's disease in terms of the healing *he* has prescribed.

Tillich's system, as set forth in his *Systematic Theology*, comprises five parts: *Being and God, Existence and Christ, Life and the Spirit, Reason and Revelation,* and *History and the Kingdom of God*.[65]

C.   *Tillich's Method of Correlation*

If the message of Christianity is to be brought to the modern situation, it is important, Tillich argues, that we use the proper method in the construction of our system. "The following system is an attempt to use the 'method of correlation' as a way of uniting message and situation. It tries to correlate the questions implied in the situation with the answers implied in the message. It does not derive the answers from the questions as a self-defining apologetic theology does. Nor does it elaborate answers without relating them to the questions as a self-defining kerygmatic theology does. It correlates questions and answers, situation and message, human existence and divine manifestation . . . ," and since "system and method belong to each other,"[66] the system produced by the method of correlation could be discovered by no other method than that of correlation.

In speaking of Tillich's method of correlation, Walter Leibrecht asserts its aim to be a "synthesis, in which the split between Greek wisdom and Christian faith is overcome."[67] Speaking of Tillich himself, Leibrecht adds, "He is one of the few great men in our age who have the courage to venture beyond prophetic criticism and existential analysis and to forge a new synthesis and therewith provide a new possibility for creative action. With a singleness of mind perhaps unique among the true thinkers of our time Tillich devotes his work not only to the pondering but also to the answering of man's ultimate questions."[68]

We agree with Leibrecht's estimate both with respect to Tillich's great powers of thought and with respect to his "system" as being a great synthesis, but we cannot agree with Tillich when he says that "in the initial sentences of his theological system Calvin expresses the essence of the method of correlation."[69] It is not out of accord with Tillich's own method of correlation to make such a claim, for he need not agree with any of Calvin's teachings with respect to God, to man, to sin, and to salvation through Christ to say this. In fact, Tillich agrees with none of Calvin's teachings on these points, although for all that, he says that Calvin already employed the method of correlation. Calvin, according to Tillich, does not wish to speak of God *as such* and of man *as such.*[70] Calvin sought to think of God and man as together from the outset. "Man as existing, representing existence generally and asking the question implied in his existence, is one side of the cognitive correlation to which Calvin points, the other side being the divine majesty."[71]

However, even in these very words it is apparent that Tillich is attributing to Calvin the modern, post-Kantian view of man, and that it is for this reason that he can speak of Calvin as using the method of correlation. On Tillich's own view it is man who by his creative self-interpretation can properly fathom his own situation and ask the questions that need to be asked about it. Since he thinks Calvin holds a similar view of man, he also thinks of him as using the method of correlation. Notwithstanding, it was this point precisely that the first paragraph of Calvin's *Institutes* set out to deny. Not for a moment does Calvin assume that man can intelligently "represent existence generally." Calvin had been confronted by this sort of notion in the scholastic point of view and he was out to destroy it. For Calvin, God is the Creator-being and man is the creature-being. Moreover, God the Creator spoke to man the creature in paradise and told him of the goal of his being. This goal was not his absorption into a unity of being with God, but the realization of his potentiality as a creature on the created level of existence and all to the praise of God. Taking his "system" from the Scripture Calvin knew that God intended from the beginning that mankind should reach this goal through Christ, the God-man, as man's redeemer from sin. Calvin knew that no sinner will accept salvation through Christ but by the regenerating power of the Holy Spirit.

Thus it appears that what Calvin says on revelation and reason (i.e., on method), on God, on Christ, and on the Holy Spirit is diametrically opposed to what Tillich has so far said on those same subjects.

In Calvin's "system" the triune God, as sufficient in himself and as revealed by Christ, is primary. In Tillich's system it is man, man as "free" from God, who is primary. To be sure, this free man himself asserts his need of "god." But then the "god" of which Tillich's "free" man asserts his need is like a genie that is supposed to make the world over magically according to the free man's wish.

The method of correlation, then, produces, and is produced by, the ideal of making a synthesis between the biblical and the modern idealist views of life. It is essential to note this point if we would understand what Tillich means by the message of Protestantism to the modern situation.

When Tillich explicitly discusses the method of correlation he again mentions the fact that "method and system determine each other."[72] "In using the method of correlation, systematic theology proceeds in the following way: it makes an analysis of the human situation out of which the existential questions arise, and it demonstrates that the symbols used in the Christian message are the answers to these questions. The analysis of the human situation is done in terms which today are called 'existential.' "[73]

Thus Tillich begins with a philosophical analysis of the human situation. After this is completed he relates the "Christian Symbols" to this analysis. The analysis of the human situation, even if from the beginning it is carried on by those who already know the meaning of the Christian symbols, is none the less a wholly independent enterprise. If we think of a man who is both a theologian and a philosopher and ask how such a man relates his philosophical analysis to his theological answers, Tillich replies: "As a theologian he does not tell himself what is philosophically true. As a philosopher he does not tell himself what is theologically true. But he cannot help seeing human existence and existence generally in such a way that the Christian symbols appear meaningful and understandable to him. His eyes are partially focused by his ultimate concern, which is true of every philosopher. Nevertheless, his act of seeing is autonomous, for it is determined only by the object as it is given in his experience. If he sees something he did not expect to see in the light of his theological answer, he holds fast to what he has seen and reformulates the theological answer. He is certain that nothing he sees can change the substance of his answer because this substance is the logos of being, manifest in Jesus as the Christ. If this were not his presuppositon, he would have to sacrifice either his philosophical honesty or his theological concern."[74]

Tillich is here struggling to hold, on the one hand, to the idea that there is "a mutual dependence between question and answer," and, on the other hand, to safeguard the autonomy of philosophical analysis of the human situation.

To the first consideration, Tillich says that "God is the answer to the question implied in human finitude," and, he adds, "This answer cannot be derived from the analysis of existence."[75]

When Tillich makes such statements as these then we might perhaps think that he is proceeding according to the method of Calvin. But then we would also expect him to say that even philosophical analysis of man's existence must be undertaken in the light of God in Christ as the answer. Yet we hear nothing of the sort from Tillich. In fact, we hear the reverse. We hear him define the very nature of God in terms of a philosophical analysis of being made quite independently of God's answer in Christ. "God must be called the infinite power of being which resists the threat of non-being."[76] Here the God of Luther and of Calvin is reduced in one stroke to the god of Kant. And the god of Kant is also the god of Plato and Aristotle. There is in Scripture no such thing as a threat of non-being. There is death, but death is the wages of sin. Together with Greek and modern philosophical thought, Tillich virtually identifies sin with finitude, and involved in this virtual reduction of the ethical to the metaphysical is the idea that salvation is absorption into Christ, the manifestation of the New Being. "If anxiety is defined as the awareness of being finite, God must be called the infinite ground of courage. In classical theology this is universal providence."[77] We would rather say that in classical theology such identification of the idea of providence with a mystical ideal of absorption into the being of God, as Tillich offers, would be called a monistic heresy!

Meanwhile we have had the opportunity to observe how impossible it is for Tillich to speak of his method of correlation without showing that it produces a "system" which is, in all basic respects, the opposite of the theology of the Reformation.

D. *Tillich's Theological System*

"The structure of the theological system follows from the method of correlation."[78] The system is derived from the "structure of existence in correlation with the structure of the Christian message."[79]

It is not our purpose to follow the details of Tillich's argument. We seek merely to illustrate how he produces his system by means of his method of correlation in order to find, as he thinks, the Christian message for the situation today. We merely note how he does this when he deals with reason and revelation.

Tillich speaks of subjective and objective reason. "Subjective reason is the rational structure of the mind, while objective reason is the rational structure of reality which the mind can grasp and according to which it can shape reality. Reason in the philosopher grasps the reason in nature."[80] Neither subjective nor objective reason is static. Tillich is not a pre-Kantian rationalist. He wants to do justice to the dynamics of reason both as subjective and as objective. "Reality itself creates structural possibilities within itself. Life, as well as mind, is creative. Only those things can live which embody a rational structure. Living beings are successful attempts of nature to actualize itself in accordance with the demands of objective reason. If nature does not follow these demands, its products are unsuccessful trials. The same is true of legal forms and social relations. New products of the historical process are attempts which can succeed only if they follow the demands of objective reason. Neither nature nor history can create anything that contradicts reason. The new and the old in history and nature are bound together in an overwhelming rational unity which is static and dynamic at the same time."[81]

Believing in the *dynamic character* of both objective and subjective reason, Tillich also speaks of the "depth of reason." "The depth of reason is the expression of something that is not reason but which precedes reason and is manifest through it."[82] This "depth of reason" could "be called the 'substance' which appears in the rational structure, or 'being-itself' which appears in the rational structure, or 'being-itself' which is manifest in the logos of being, or the 'ground' which is creative in every rational creation, or the 'abyss' which cannot be exhausted by any creation or by any totality of them, or the 'infinite potentiality of being and meaning' which pours into the rational structures of mind and reality, actualising and transforming them."[83] "The depth of reason is essentially manifest in reason. But it is hidden in reason under the conditions of existence."[84] Finally we must speak of "actual reason." "Reason as the structure of mind and reality is actual in the processes of being, existence, and life. Being is finite, existence is self-contradictory, and life is ambiguous. Actual reason participates in these characteristics of reality. Actual reason moves through finite categories, through self-destructive conflicts, through ambiguities, and through the quest for what is unambiguous, beyond conflict, and beyond bondage to the categories. The nature of finite reason is described in classical form by Nicolaus Cusanus and Immanuel Kant."[85]

Tillich needs these distinctions between subjective reason, objective reason, the depth of reason, and actual reason in order to make his independent existential or philosophical analysis of the "situation," and in order then to relate reason as a whole to revelation.

If his total view of reason is to stand in intelligent relation to revelation, we must not have the orthodox view of revelation.[86] Revelation deals with mystery. "The genuine mystery appears when reason is driven beyond itself to its 'ground and abyss,' to that which 'precedes' reason, to the fact that 'being is and non-being is not' (Parmenides), to the original fact (Ur-Tatsache) that there is *something* and not *nothing*. We call this the 'negative side' of the mystery."[87] "The positive side of the mystery—which includes the negative side— becomes manifest in actual revelation. Here the mystery appears as ground and not only as abyss. It appears as the power of being, conquering non-being."[88]

Here then we can relate reason to revelation. "The threat of non-being, grasping the mind, produces the 'ontological shock' in which the negative side of the mystery of being—its abysmal element—is experienced. 'Shock' points to a state of mind in which the mind is thrown out of its normal balance, shaken in its structure. Reason reaches its boundary line, is thrown back upon itself, and then is driven again to its extreme situation. This experience of ontological shock is expressed in the cognitive function by the basic philosophical question, the question of being and non-being."[89] "In revelation and in the ecstatic experience in which it is received, the ontological shock is preserved and overcome at the same time. It is preserved in the annihilating power of the divine presence (*mysterium tremendum*) and is overcome in the elevating power of the divine presence (*mysterium fascinosum*). Ecstasy unites the experience of the abyss to which reason in all its functions is driven with the experience of the ground in which reason is grasped by the mystery of its own depth and of the depth of being generally."[90]

It appears, then, that we have in Tillich's position the post-Kantian view of reason and the post-Kantian view of revelation. Together with all post-Kantian idealism Tillich seeks for a principle of identity which, both in subjective and in objective reason, is both static and dynamic. However much Tillich stresses the dynamic or irrational side of being, his system is not radically different from that of Hegel's idea of the self-realization of the Absolute Spirit. With Hegel, Tillich puts movement into logic in order to have it keep pace with reality, which is dynamic. But he has to do this, as even Hegel did, by postulating an Absolute Individual as a limiting concept. As for subjective reason, the cognitive function of finite man, it is meaningless unless it be viewed as ideally unified with absolute or objective reason.

On this view of the relation of reason to revelation it is quite natural that Tillich should scout the idea of the "Word of God" as containing "information about otherwise hidden truth."[91] The idea of revelation as information "would lack all the characteristics of revelation. It would not have the power of grasping, shaking, and transforming the power which is attributed to the 'Word of God.' "[92] The sound of ultimacy would be lacking. Revelation as information would offer no intimation of a "new reality."[93] So also "there are no revealed doctrines, but there are revelatory events and situations which can be described in doctrinal terms. . . ." "The 'Word of God' contains neither revealed commandments nor revealed doctrines; it accompanies and interprets revelatory situations."[94] "Knowledge of revelation does not increase our knowledge about the structures of nature, history, and man. Whenever a claim to knowledge is made on this level, it must be subjected to the experimental tests through which truth is established. If such a claim is made in the name of revelation or of any other authority, it must be disregarded and the ordinary methods of research and verification must be applied."[95] "If revealed knowledge did interfere with ordinary knowledge, it would destroy scientific honesty and methodological humility. It would exhibit demonic possession, not divine revelation. Knowledge of revelation is knowledge about the revelation of the mystery of being to us, not information about the nature of beings and their relation to one another. Therefore, the knowledge of revelation can be received only in the situation of revelation, and it can be communicated—in contrast to ordinary knowledge—only to those who participate in this situation."[96] "Revealed truth lies in a dimension where it can neither be confirmed nor negated by historiography. Therefore, theologians should not prefer some results of historical research to others on theological grounds, and they should not resist results which finally have to be accepted if scientific honesty is not to be destroyed, even if they seem to undermine the knowledge of revelation. Historical investigations should neither comfort nor worry theologians. Knowledge of revelation, although it is mediated primarily through historical events, does not imply factual assertions, and it is therefore not exposed to critical analysis by historical research. Its truth is to be judged by criteria which lie within the dimension of revelatory knowledge."[97]

Tillich does not deny the idea of final revelation but reinterprets its meaning. "The first and basic answer theology must give to the question of the finality of the revelation in Jesus as the Christ is the following: a revelation is final if it has the power of negating itself without losing itself. This paradox is based on the fact that every revelation is conditioned by the medium in and through which it appears. The question of the final revelation is the question of a medium of revelation which overcomes its own finite conditions by sacrificing them, and itself with them. He who is the bearer of the final revelation must surrender his finitude—not only his life but also his finite power and knowledge and perfection. In doing so, he affirms that he is the bearer of final revelation (the 'Son of God' in classical terms). He becomes completely transparent to the mystery he reveals. But, in order to be able to surrender himself completely, he must possess himself completely. And only he can possess—and therefore surrender—himself completely who is united with the ground of his being and meaning without separation and disruption. In the picture of Jesus as the Christ we have the picture of a man who possesses these qualities, a man who, therefore, can be called the medium of final revelation."[98]

Jesus therefore is the Christ insofar as he "sacrifices what is merely 'Jesus' in him."[99] "The revelatory event is Jesus as the Christ. He is the miracle of the final revelation, and his reception is the ecstasy of the final revelation. His appearance is the decisive constellation of historical (and by participation, natural) forces. It is the ecstatic moment of human history and, therefore, its centre, giving meaning to all possible and actual history."[100] And "the history of revelation is history interpreted in the light of the final revelation."[101]

It is thus that "revelation is the answer to the questions implied in the existential conflicts of reason."[102] "The church as the community of the New Being is the place where the new theonomy is actual. But from there it pours into the whole of man's cultural life and gives a Spiritual centre to man's spiritual life."[103]

This may suffice to indicate how in Tillich's thought the method of correlation produces a post-Kantian type of ethical idealism. All the main elements of Kant's three *Critiques* are found in it. There is first what Kroner calls the ethical dualism. The ethical autonomy of man is set dualistically over against the inevitable fate of the world of nature. Then, to overcome this dualism, the idea that God in Christ redeems all the world and all men from all ill is introduced as a limiting concept. It is thus that the primacy of the personality ideal as Dooyeweerd speaks of it and the primacy of the practical reason as Kroner speaks of it are boldly asserted. It is thus that what Bavinck calls the ethical concept of the relation between God and man is even more thoroughly reduced to a self-constructed system of metaphysics that was done in Roman Catholicism. And this is done in the name of a truly *ethical* idea of God and his relation to man. The modern post-Kantian view of ethics seeks thus to destroy the historic Protestant biblical view of ethics and theology. At the same time this New Protestantism reveals itself to be more closely related to Roman Catholicism than it is to the theology of Luther and Calvin. In both Romanism and New Protestantism it is the idea of *being as such* and *reason as such* that makes the analysis of the situation and therefore determines the nature of revelation and the answers to be given by it.

E. *Tillich on "Being and God"*

That the method of correlation produces the sort of ethical idealism so prevalent in post-Kantian thought, is still more clearly manifest in the second section or part of Tillich's work than it is in the first. We need only to devote brief space to it now. In this section Tillich speaks of the ontological polarities of individualism and participation, dynamics and form, and freedom and destiny. In discussing these the idea of ethical dualism, as with Kant, is his starting point. "Man's vitality lives in contrast with its intentionality and is conditioned by it."[104] "Freedom in polarity with destiny is the structural element which makes existence possible because it transcends the essential necessity of being without destroying it."[105] "The methodological perversion of much ontological inquiry is more obvious in the doctrine of freedom than at any other point."[106] It is only by the method of correlation that we can see the true relation between freedom and fate. "Freedom is experienced as deliberation, decision, and responsibility."[107] "In the light of this analysis of freedom the meaning of destiny becomes understandable."[108] "Destiny is not a strange power which determines what shall happen to me. It is myself as given, formed by nature, history, and myself. My destiny is the basis of my freedom; my freedom participates in shaping my destiny."[109]

Here we have typical post-Kantian ethical dualism. But, going beyond Kant, Tillich at once weaves the notion of ethical phenomenalism into that of ethical dualism. The decision of man is from the outset made to participate in the decision of God.

It is thus that by conjoining the primacy of man with the primacy of God over nature and destiny that Tillich is able, as he thinks, to discover what man is and ought to be.[110] "Being precedes non-being in ontological validity, as the word 'non-being' itself indicates."[111] But we can say this only because we hold that "infinity is a directing concept, not a constituting concept. It directs the mind to experience its own unlimited potentialities, but it does not establish the existence of an infinite being."[112] It is by thus making infinity a limiting rather than a constitutive concept that Tillich can retain his notion of God as the abyss and as the ground of being. It is thus also that he can postulate the idea of God in Christ as the New Being which overcomes the threat of non-being. "The potential presence of the infinite (as unlimited self-transcendence) is the negation of the negative element in finitude. It is the negation of non-being."[113] "Infinity is a demand, not a thing. This is the stringency of Kant's solution of the antinomies between the finite and the infinite character of time and space."[114] It is thus that man's destiny can be transformed from that of impersonal fate to the full self-realization of man. "Destiny is not a meaningless fate. It is necessity united with meaning."[115] Finitude thus becomes merely the possibility of "losing one's ontological structure."[116]

Tillich may be said, in effect, to be teaching here what Karl Barth speaks of as the ontological impossibility of sin. Both Barth and Tillich reduce the Reformation teaching with respect to the wrath of God upon sinners to the abstract, ethically harmless notion of the threat of non-being. Nevertheless, according to Scripture there are those who because of their failure to repent would gladly fall into non-being; to them non-being is in the last analysis not a threat but their only hope of escape from the wrath of God's Christ. But there is no possible escape for sinners into that mythical realm. They must face the judgment seat of God. They will enter into eternal punishment for their sins. It is true that Barth and Tillich do say that there is no real possibility of falling into non-being. But their explanation for this fact is that every man must, because of his essential nature, enter into participation with divine being. The "fall" of man does not, for either Barth or Tillich, mean that man can be permanently separated from God.

If this position of universal absorption of man's being into the *New Being* is to be maintained, then the idea of God as *existing* must be rejected. "It is as atheistic to affirm the existence of God as it is to deny it. God is being-itself, not *a* being. On this basis a first step can be taken toward the solution of the problem which usually is discussed as the immanence and the transcendence of God. As the power of being, God transcends every being and also the totality of being—the world. Being-itself is beyond finitude and infinity; otherwise it would be conditioned by something other than itself, and the

real power of being would lie beyond both it and that which conditioned it."[117] The idea that God exists must be rejected for the same
reason that the idea of revelation as information must be rejected.
In the latter case we should not have *the sound of ultimacy* and in
the former case we should not have the *presence of ultimacy*; and
these two are at bottom one.

Combining then the idea of revelation discussed in the first section
and the idea of God as the abyss and as the ground of being discussed in the second section of Tillich's *Systematic Theology* we
realize that "any concrete assertion about God must be symbolic, for
a concrete assertion is one which uses a segment of finite experience
in order to say something about him. It transcends the content of
this segment, although it also includes it. The segment of finite
reality which becomes the vehicle of a concrete assertion about God
is affirmed and negated at the same time. It becomes a symbol, for
a symbolic expression is one whose proper meaning is negated by
that to which it points."[118] Here, says Tillich, "the crucial question
must now be faced. Can a segment of finite reality become the basis
for an assertion about that which is infinite? The answer is that it
can, because that which is infinite is being-itself and because everything participates in being-itself. The *analogia entis* is not the property
of a questionable natural theology which attempts to gain knowledge
of God by drawing conclusions about the infinite from the finite. The
analogia entis gives us our only justification of speaking at all about
God. It is based on the fact that God must be understood as
being-itself."[119]

It is thus that while Barth denies the idea of *analogy of being* Tillich affirms it. But Barth's denial and Tillich's affirmation are alike
made in the interest of setting what they call the truly Protestant
notion of the relation of God to man over against the *analogia entis*
idea of Romanism. But, as it turns out, Barth's denial and Tillich's
affirmation of the idea of analogy of being are both made in the interest
of the idea that man's essential nature is that of participation in the
being of deity. On this point they are both in basic agreement with
Roman Catholicism, and by that token are both out of agreement
with historic Protestantism. Any form of correlation in which man

is made primary, as is the case with Romanism, with Barth, and with Tillich, is bound to be out of accord with Luther and with Calvin. The ultimate concern of the Reformers was to bring the fullness of grace in its purity to men. They therefore sought to set it free from the encrustations of Greek metaphysics which are the metaphysics of fallen man. Tillich, Barth, Kroner, and many others have enmeshed Christianity even more deeply in apostate philosophy than Romanism has done.

F. Tillich on "Existence and Christ"

We turn now to the third section of Tillich's system, namely, that of the Existence of Christ. In this section the method of correlation is still employed and its destructive significance is brought out, if possible, still more clearly than in the first two sections. For in this section the formal similarity between the historic Christian or Protestant position and that of Tillich is even more striking than it was in the former sections.

The second part of Tillich's system must, says Tillich, "give an analysis of man's existential self-estrangement (in unity with the self-destructive aspects of existence generally) and the question implied in this situation; and it must give the answer which is the Christ. This part, therefore, is called 'Existence and Christ.' "[120] But of course this analysis must be made in conjunction with the "analysis of man's essential nature (in unity with the essential nature of everything that has being), and of the question implied in man's finitude and finitude generally; . . ."[121]

The Idea of Existence deals first with man's estrangement from his essence. Christianity expresses this idea of estrangement by its symbol of "the fall."[122] "Although usually associated with the biblical story of the 'Fall of Adam,' its meaning transcends the myth of Adam's Fall and has universal anthropological significance."[123] Of course, when Scripture speaks of the fall it does not pretend to give us historic information.[124] We have already seen that the idea of historic information and revelation exclude one another. The story of the fall is *revelation*, not historical information. "Theology must clearly and unambiguously represent 'the Fall' as a symbol for the human situation universally, not as the story of an event that happened 'once upon a time.' "[125]

Of course we cannot remove the temporal element from human speech altogether. Even when we speak of the fall as a "transition from essence to existence" we have still not escaped time entirely. "Complete demythologization is not possible when speaking about the divine."[126] Even Plato knew "that existence is not a matter of essential necessity but that it is a fact and that therefore the 'Fall of the soul' is a story to be told in mythical symbols. If he had understood existence to be a logical implication of essence, existence itself would have appeared as essential."[127]

Of course, the possibility of the fall is to be found in human freedom.[128] "Man's freedom is finite freedom. All the potentialities which constitute his freedom are limited by the opposite pole, his destiny."[129]

Unfortunately, traditional theology did not realize that the "freedom of turning away from God is a quality of the structure of freedom as such."[130]

We enquire next into the motives of the fall. Why should there be any transition from essence to existence at all? "In order to answer this, we must have an image of the state of essential being in which the motifs are working. The difficulty is that the state of essential being is not an actual stage of human development which can be known directly or indirectly. The essential nature of man is present in all stages of his development, although in existential distortion."[131]

Tillich speaks of the essence of man as being that of "dreaming innocence." "Dreaming is a state of mind which is real and non-real at the same time—just as is potentiality. Dreaming anticipates the actual, just as everything actual is somehow present in the potential. . . . For these reasons the metaphor 'dreaming' is adequate in describing the state of essential being. The word 'innocence' also points to non-actualized potentiality."[132]

Now "dreaming innocence drives beyond itself."[133] This is to be explained by the fact of man's freedom. This freedom is in the nature of the case "finite freedom." And man's awareness of his "finite freedom" spells anxiety. Through Søren Kierkegaard the word *Angst* has become a central concept of existentialism. It expresses the awareness of being finite, of being a mixture of being and non-being, or of being threatened by non-being. All creatures are driven by anxiety; for finitude and anxiety are the same.[134] "In man freedom is united with anxiety. One could call man's freedom 'freedom in anxiety' or 'anxious freedom' (in German, *sich ängstigende Freiheit*). This anxiety is one of the driving forces toward the transition from essence to existence. Kierkegaard particularly has used the concept of anxiety to describe (not to explain) the transition from essence to existence."[135]

Combining now "the structure of finite freedom," with the idea of finitude as anxiety, "one may show in two interrelated ways the motifs of the transition from essence to existence."[136]

(1) "In the state of dreaming innocence, freedom and destiny are in harmony, but neither of them is actualized."[137] But tension between them develops when "finite freedom becomes conscious of itself and tends to become actual. This is what could be called the moment of aroused freedom."[138] But at the same time a reaction takes place. "Dreaming innocence wants to preserve itself. This reaction is symbolized in the biblical story as the divine prohibition against actualizing one's potential freedom and against acquiring knowledge and power. Man is caught between the desire to actualize his freedom and the demand to preserve his dreaming innocence. In the power of his finite freedom, he decides for actualization."[139]

(2) "The same analysis can be made, so to speak, from the inside, namely from man's anxious awareness of his finite freedom. At the moment when man becomes conscious of his freedom, the awareness of his dangerous situation gets hold of him. He experiences a double threat, which is rooted in his finite freedom and expressed in anxiety. Man experiences the anxiety of losing himself by not actualizing himself and his potentialities and the anxiety of losing himself by actualizing himself and his potentialities."[140]

It is obvious to Tillich that traditional theology had no appreciation for this explanation of the fall of man, just as it was unable to explain its possibility. "In myth and dogma man's essential nature has been projected into the past as a history before history, symbolized as a golden age or paradise."[141] Thus traditional theology precluded itself from ever understanding the true structure of finite freedom and its concomitant, anxiety, and therewith also precluded itself from understanding the motivation of the fall.

But with this background of understanding both the structure of finite freedom and the motif of the fall we also understand the *fact* of the fall. "The transition from essence to existence is the original fact. It is not the first fact in a temporal sense or a fact beside or before others, but it is that which gives validity to every fact. It is the actual in every fact. We do exist and our world with us. This is the original fact. It means that the transition from essence to existence is a universal quality of finite being. It is not an event of the past; for it ontologically precedes everything that happens in time and space. It sets the conditions of spatial and temporal existence. It is manifest in every individual person in the transition from dreaming innocence to actualization and guilt."[142]

We understand then that a "cosmic myth" is hidden behind the Genesis story.[143] "But the most consistent emphasis on the cosmic character of the Fall is given in the myth of the transcendent Fall of the souls. While it probably has Orphic roots, it is first told by Plato when he contests essence and existence. It received a Christian form by Origen, a humanistic one by Kant, and is present in many other philosophies and theologies of the Christian Era. All have recognized that existence cannot be derived from within existence, that it cannot be derived from an individual event in time and space. They have recognized that existence has a universal dimension."[144] "The motif of the myth of the transcendent Fall is the tragic-universal character of existence. The meaning of the myth is that the very constitution of existence implies the transition from essence to existence. The individual act of existential estrangement is not the isolated act of an isolated individual; it is an act of freedom which is imbedded, nevertheless, in the universal destiny of existence."[145]

It is thus that Tillich's method of correlation synthesizes Greek and biblical motifs in his discussion of the fall of man.

In line with what he has said about the possibility, the motif, and the fact of the fall, Tillich finally explains its consequences. "Biblical literalism would answer that the Fall of man changed the structures of nature. The divine curse upon Adam and Eve involves a change of nature in and around man. If such literalism is rejected as absurd, then what does the term 'fallen world' mean? If the structures of nature were always what they are now, can one speak of the participation of nature, including man's natural basis, in his existential estrangement? Has nature been corrupted by man? Does this combination of words have any meaning at all?"[146]

If we are to have an answer to the question pertaining to the consequence of man's "first" sin, then we must, he argues, again insist that there was no such thing as a fall in the temporal sense of the term. "The first answer to these questions is that the transition from essence to existence is not an event in time and space but the transhistorical quality of all events in time and space. This is equally true of man and of nature. 'Adam before the Fall' and 'nature before the curse' are states of potentiality. They are not actual states. The actual state is that existence in which man finds himself along with the whole universe, and there is no time in which this was otherwise. The notion of a moment *in* time in which man and nature were changed from good to evil is absurd, and it has no foundation in experience or revelation."[147]

We need not follow the further details of what Tillich himself calls his reinterpretation of the idea of the fall.[148] Our reinterpretation, says Tillich, must sometimes go so far as to reject even the terms used by traditional theology. Such is the case when the words "original" and "hereditary" are employed in relation to sin. Both of these words "are so much burdened with literalistic absurdities that it is practically impossible to use them any longer."[149]

It would seem, however, that it makes very little difference whether or not Tillich rejects the words of traditional theory. At every point he sets his view *over against* that of what he speaks as the traditional point of view. The one great mistake of the traditional view is its literalism. Because of its literalism the traditional view has no eye for the fact that what is told in the form of ordinary history must be demythologized or de-temporalized and that on the basis of experience and revelation. The traditional literalist and therefore

historicist view of the fall is out of accord with the proper view of
revelation no less than it is out of accord with experience. "The notion
of a moment *in* time in which man and nature were changed from
good to evil is absurd, and it has no foundation in experience or
revelation."[150]

Would it not then be better, asks Tillich, to drop the concept of a
"fallen world" altogether? Tillich's answer is decidedly in the negative. Complete demythologization would lead right back into pure
essentialism. Sin must not become a "rational necessity." We need
the idea of "the leap from essence to existence"[151] as an original fact.
And the idea of a leap (freedom) is the opposite of "structural
necessity."[152] On the one hand the idea of "leap" must not destroy
the idea of structure and, on the other hand, the idea of structure
must not destroy the idea of the leap. The leap presupposes the
structure. "Therefore, even destruction has structures."[153] "There
are always structures of destruction in history, but they are possible
only because there are structures of finitude which can be transformed
into structures of estrangement."[154] These "structures of destruction"
are suprapersonal and therefore demonic.

In accordance with the idea of sin as the transition from essence to
existence we must now look at the question of salvation. We are
already prepared by such a view of sin to realize that to speak of
"eternal condemnation . . . is a theologically untenable combination of
words."[155] We should "eliminate the term 'eternal condemnation'
from the theological vocabulary. Instead, one should speak of condemnation as removal from the eternal. This seems to be implied
in the term 'eternal death,' which certainly cannot mean everlasting
death, since death has no duration. The experience of separation
from one's eternity is the state of despair."[156] "The negative can be
experienced and spoken of only in union with the positive. Both for
time and for eternity, one must say that even the state of separation
God is creatively working in us—even if his creativity takes the way
of destruction. Man is never cut off from the ground of being, not
even in the state of condemnation."[157]

We must, to be sure, go out in quest of the "New Being," but as we
search for it we must not forget that the "quest for the New Being

presupposes the presence of the New Being, as the search for truth presupposes the presence of truth."[158] Therefore Christ represents "to those who live under the conditions of existence what man essentially is and therefore ought to be under these conditions."[159] And, since this is true we must also revise the traditional view of the incarnation.[160] "The Christian assertion that the New Being has appeared in Jesus as the Christ is paradoxical. It constitutes the only all-embracing paradox of Christianity."[161] Traditional theology did not realize this fact. It said that God has become man. But this is non-sensical, not paradoxical.[162] God cannot become man. "The word 'God' points to ultimate reality, and even the most consistent Scotists had to admit that the only thing God cannot do is to cease to be God."[163] On the other hand, in the incarnation God need not become finite. "God is infinite, in so far as he is the creative ground of the finite and eternally produces the finite potentialities in himself. The finite does not limit him but belongs to the eternal process of his life."[164] If we use the word "incarnation" at all it should mean that "God is manifest in a personal life-process as a saving participant in the human predicament."[165] The basic concept that controls us as we speak of the incarnation is that of "essential man appearing in a personal life under conditions of existential estrangement. This restricts the expectation of the Christ to historical mankind. The man in whom essential man has appeared in existence represents human history; more precisely, as its central event, he creates the meaning of human history. It is the eternal relation of God to man which is manifest in the Christ. At the same time, our basic answer leaves the universe open for possible divine manifestations in other areas or periods of being."[166]

It is this, argues Tillich, that is demanded by our method of correlation.[167]

Using this method for the interpretation of the incarnation we have been enabled to understand what the Christ *must* be. We now ask about the reality of this Christ. "If there were no personal life in which existential estrangement had been overcome, the New Being would have remained a quest and an expectation and would not be a reality in time and space. Only if the existence is conquered in *one* point—a personal life, representing existence as a whole—is it conquered in principle, which means 'in beginning and in power.' "[168] Of course the question of the "manifestation of the New Being in time and space" is a difficult one.[169] But here as well as everywhere we must reject "supernaturalistic literalism."[170] "Jesus as the Christ is related to that historical development of which he is the center, determining its beginning and its end."[171] Such a beginning and such an end cannot be directly identified with anything in ordinary history.[172] "Theology has learned to distinguish between the empirically historical, the legendary, and the mythological elements in the biblical stories of both Testaments."[173] In consequence systematic theology now has "a tool for dealing with the christological symbols of the Bible. Systematic theology cannot escape this task, since it is through these symbols that theology from the very beginning has tried to give the 'logos' of the Christian message in order to show its rationality."[174] Systematic theology is now in a position to show the "rationality" of the Christian message.[175] When theology now deals with "christological symbols" such as the *Son of man* it avoids literalism which imagines "a transcendent being who, once upon a time, was sent down from his heavenly place and transmuted into a man."[176] The title *Son of man* actually points to an "original unity between God and man."[177]

Thus, when theology deals with the title *Son of God*, it realizes that this too presupposes that in his essential nature, in his dreaming innocence, man is related to God as a son is to his father.[178] Of course this relation has been lost by the fall.[179] "Sonship to God has ceased to be a universal fact."[180] And therein lies the necessity of the Christ as the one in whom "the essential unity of God and man has appeared under the conditions of existence."[181] In him the "essentially universal becomes existentially unique." At the same time "this uniqueness is not exclusive." "The son re-establishes the child character of every man in relation to God, a character which is essentially human."[182]

It is thus that "historical criticism is largely responsible for our understanding of the development of christological symbols. They can be used again by theology, for they are liberated from literalistic connotations which made them useless for theology and an unnecessary stumbling block for those who wanted to understand the meaning of the Christian symbols."[183]

Of course, though we thus throw out the "literalistic distortion of the messianic paradox"[184] we should realize that it is only faith that can guarantee the truth about Christ as the New Being.[185] Faith guarantees the foundation on which it stands. This is possible because its own existence is identical with the presence of the New Being. Faith itself is the immediate (not mediated by conclusions) evidence of the New Being within and under the conditions of existence. Precisely that is guaranteed by the very nature of the Christian faith. No historical criticism can question the immediate awareness of those who find themselves transformed into the state of faith."[186] It is "participation, not historical argument," which "guarantees the reality of the event upon which Christianity is based."[187]

Faith even "guarantees a personal life in which the New Being has conquered the old being. But it does not guarantee his name to be Jesus of Nazareth. . . . (This is an historically absurd, but logically necessary consequence of the historical method.) Whatever his name, the New Being was and is actual in this man."[188]

"The concrete biblical material is not guaranteed by faith in respect to empirical factuality; but it is guaranteed as an adequate expression of the transforming power of the New Being in Jesus as the Christ. Only in this sense does faith guarantee the biblical picture of Jesus. And it can be shown that, in all periods of the history of the church, it was this picture which created both the church and the Christian, and not a hypothetical description of what may lie behind the biblical picture. But the picture has this creative power, because the power of the New Being is expressed in and through it."[189]

Of course the "New Testament witness is unanimous in its witness to Jesus as the Christ. This witness is the foundation of the Christian church."[190] Even so "the risk of faith is existential; it concerns the totality of our being, while the risk of historical judgments is theoretical and open to permanent scientific correction."[191]

We may therefore speak of Jesus as the Christ, in whom the New

Being has "eternal significance also for those who caused his death, including Judas."[192]

By this analysis of the Christological symbols Tillich has tried, he says, to perform the task of Protestantism in our day. He has sought for new forms "in which the christological substance of the past can be expressed."[193] In the three sections of his system discussed Tillich has constantly set "the structure of existence in correlation with the structure of the Christian message."[194] His message as a whole is that "there are supra-individual structures of goodness and supra-individual structures of evil. Angels and demons are mythological names for constructive and destructive powers of being, which are ambiguously interwoven and which fight with each other in the same person, in the same social group, and in the same historical situation. They are not beings but powers of being dependent on the whole structure of existence and involved in the ambiguous life. Man is responsible for the transition from essence to existence because he has finite freedom and because all dimensions of reality are united in him."[195] We must, on the one hand, take seriously "the participation in the ambiguities of life, on the part of him who is the bearer of the New Being."[196] We must also, on the other hand, speak of the "conquest of existential estrangement in the New Being, which is the being of the Christ," and which takes away "the negativities of existence into unbroken unity with God."[197]

G. Tillich on the "Spiritual Presence"

In what has preceded, Tillich dealt with God the Father and God the Son, and with their work of creation and redemption. His *system* requires that he now, toward its conclusion, write on God the Holy Spirit. As there has been a transition from essence to existence, so there must be a transition from existence to the New Being. Of course, the New Being has been present even in the transition from essence to existence. How else could man have any consciousness of the New Being? The historic trinitarian doctrine failed to see this fact. It spoke of God as a being and of the three persons as three beings within this one being. Failing to see that God is the ground of all beings and the depth of being, it failed to have unity within its trinity and therefore also failed to relate its trinity intelligently to the consciousness of man.

If we are to strive with intelligence for the unambiguous life we must subject Protestant theology to a "positive revision of its whole tradition."[198] We must remove without residue the inveterate habit of traditional Protestantism of identifying the absolute with individual entities.

In particular we must cast out the traditional view of Scripture. Traditional Protestant theology objectifies all its individual doctrines about God and man because it objectifies its view of Scripture. We must get away from "the false elevation of human words to the dignity of the Word of God."[199]

If we are to have an intelligible grasp of "the answer revelation gives to the quest for unambiguous life"[200] then we must catch the significance of what the Protestant Principle really is. "Unambiguous life can be described as life under the Spiritual Presence, or as life in the Kingdom of God, or as Eternal Life."[201]

As in the case of the historic notion of Scripture, so also with the historic notions of justification and regeneration; we must restate them in accord with the true nature of the Protestant Principle.

The "central doctrine of the Reformation, the article by which Protestantism stands or falls" is "the principle of justification by grace through faith." Says Tillich: "I call it not only a doctrine and an article among others but also a principle, because it is the first and basic expression of the Protestant principle itself."[202] It should "be regarded as the principle which permeates every single assertion of the theological system."[203]

Naturally it is at this central point of the application of the work of Christ to the hearts of men that Tillich again sets his Protestant principle squarely over against the teachings of historic Protestantism. The whole house of historic Protestantism must be demolished if we are to make significant progress on the way toward the unambiguous life.

In opposition to Romanism the Reformers insisted on the doctrine of " 'justification by faith'—and not by 'works.' " Did they by doing this express what is really the Protestant principle? Not at all. Their teaching "led to a devastating confusion." The catholic teaching was soon "replaced by the intellectual work of accepting a doctrine."[204] "It should be a serious concern in the teaching and preaching of every minister that this profound distortion of the 'good news' of the Christian message be remedied."[205] The true nature of the Protestant principle has now come into view. "It should be regarded as the Protestant principle that, in relation to God, God alone can act and that no human claim (especially no religious claim), no intellectual or moral or devotional 'work,' can reunite us with him."[206] Again: "The courage to surrender one's own goodness to God is the central element in the courage of faith. In it the paradox of the New Being is experienced, the ambiguity of good and evil is conquered, unambiguous life has taken hold of man through the impact of the Spiritual Presence."[207] It was the Spiritual Presence in Jesus of Nazareth that drove "his individual spirit."[208] "The faith of the Christ is the state of being grasped unambiguously by the Spiritual Presence."[209] Thus we see that the Lord is the Spirit, and we see how we are in that Spirit.

H. Tillich on "History and the Kingdom of God"

We proceed now to the fifth and last part or section of Tillich's *Systematic Theology*. We have seen how God as the depth, the ground and the power of Being, is present in all things. As we deal with the question of our relation to this depth of Being, we must think of essence as falling into existence and of the New Being as restoring man back into essence, and leading him beyond essence and existence into the true unambiguous life. It remains only to indicate more definitely than has so far been done that the process of the fall and redemption envelops the whole course of history.

The Protestant principle is, says Tillich, inherently cosmical in nature. It enables us to see "that Jesus, the Christ, is the keystone in the arch of Spiritual manifestations in history."[210] "Spirit-Christology acknowledges that the divine Spirit which made Jesus into the Christ is creatively present in the whole history of revelation and salvation before and after his appearance." Thus "the Spiritual Presence in history is essentially the same as the Spiritual Presence in Jesus as the Christ. God in his self-manifestation, wherever this occurs, is the same God who is decisively and ultimately manifest in the Christ. Therefore, his manifestations anywhere before or after Christ must be consonant with the encounter with the center of history."[211]

It is thus, argues Tillich, that the Protestant principle, in using the symbols of the Spiritual Presence, the Kingdom of God and eternal life gives expression both to the true idea of faith and of hope. By means of the Protestant principle we know, i.e., know absolutely, that the New Being has, from "the beginning" been present in all of history. Thus the Protestant principle enables us to see that the church of Christ "is not a religious community but the anticipatory representation of a new reality, the New Being as community." The Protestant principle releases us from the idea that faith means adherence to a set of beliefs. Faith is "the state of being grasped by that which concerns us ultimately. . . ."[212] It is by seeing this vision that the profanization and demonization of Christianity are conquered.

"Our problem is the interpretation of history," says Tillich, "in the sense of the question: What is the significance of history for the meaning of existence in general?"[213] There is no answer to this question except in terms of the Protestant principle. First in terms of the Protestant principle do we see that God as the ground and power or depth of being and of history is always wholly hidden to man. Accordingly, the revelation of God in Jesus Christ to man is never unambiguously present to him. Man can never identify anything absolute in history. Orthodox Protestantism failed to see this point. Secondly, in terms of the Protestant principle, we see that while wholly hidden, God is the ground, the power, and the depth of being; yet he is also wholly revealed to man. Accordingly, the revelation of God in Jesus Christ to man is surely present to all men everywhere. Orthodox Protestantism did not see this point.

It is therefore of basic importance for us to reject the orthodox Protestant view. On its view we cannot have the sovereign, universal grace of God to man in Jesus Christ. On the orthodox view God is not free to give himself freely and unconditionally to man. On the orthodox view God cannot give his grace to man unless there be a directly identifiable transition from wrath to grace in history in the death and resurrection of Christ. This is a profane and demonic notion. It acts like a dam holding back the grace of God as it seeks to flow down freely to men.

Secondly, orthodox Protestantism demands that to be saved a man must hear about, and believe in, what happened in Palestine when Jesus was crucified and rose from the dead. The orthodox view makes man's ultimate concern pertain to something that is, in the nature of the case, relative and ambiguous. Only if reality is not what orthodox Protestantism holds it to be can man's religion be a genuine, authentic, and ultimate concern about the unconditional or sovereign, universal grace of God in Christ.

Keeping this basic contrast between the Protestant principle and the beliefs of historic Protestantism in mind it is easy to understand why the final subject of discussion in Tillich's *Systematic Theology*, namely the subject of the "end of history," should again lead him to set the Protestant principle over against the historic belief of Protestants. Says Tillich: "The theological problem of eschatology is not constituted by the many things which will happen but by the one 'thing' which is not a thing but which is the symbolic expression of the relation of the temporal to the eternal. More specifically, it symbolizes the 'transition' from the temporal to the eternal, and this is a metaphor similar to that of the transition from the eternal to the temporal in the doctrine of creation, from essence to existence in the doctrine of the fall, and from existence to essence in the doctrine of salvation."[214]

It is thus that Tillich's *Systematic Theology* is consistent in rejecting historic Protestantism "in toto" in the name of his Protestant principle.

Tillich's Protestant principle is patterned after what Kroner calls the primacy of the practical reason in Kant's philosophy and religion. Tillich and Kroner have built the same tunnel both wholly aware and wholly unaware of the basic significance of their own efforts. Both know with *absolute* certainty that nothing absolute can be identified in history. That is, they both *know* that *nobody* knows anything about anything. By this token historic Protestantism is certainly both contradictory and demonic. God and Christ and Scripture, the death and resurrection, justification, regeneration, faith and hope, the regeneration of all things cannot be what the Reformers thought they were. Then, though *nobody* knows anything because the depth of being is *wholly* mysterious, man knows by "faith," as a leap backwards into this depth of being, that there will be progress toward the ideals which moral man sets before himself. It is thus that the Protestant principle, remade after the pattern of Kant's philosophy, has, as it thinks, completely destroyed the claims of God the creator and Christ the redeemer of man.

As the Reformed pastor watches the construction of the Protestant principle by such men as Kroner and Tillich, he notes how self-deception could scarcely go further. Kroner and Tillich, together with many other modern Protestant thinkers, seek with great earnestness and with deep concern for the truth about man and his environment. They do not sense the fact that in it all they are concealing the truth in unrighteousness. Even when they are driven to the position where, on their view, man as a product of pure contingency must by his chance-produced powers of logic make universal negative assertions about all future possibility (thus virtually claiming both omniscience and utter ignorance), they continue to maintain that such is the only tenable position to hold.

Looking anew at this depth of self-deception as found in the works of modern Protestant philosophers and theologians such as Richard Kroner and Paul Tillich, the Reformed pastor realizes anew that the efforts of Mr. Grey,[215] the Arminian, are futile as he seeks to win modern men to the gospel. Modern Protestantism has given up the entire content of the gospel in order to bring it to man. Only a fully Reformed, and therefore biblical, method of apologetics can effectively challenge the natural man. Arminian Protestantism assumes that it has an area of common interpretation with modern Protestantism. The result is that Arminian Protestantism has no power to resist the argument of modern Protestantism as it leads ever-onward toward the acceptance of the so-called Protestant principle in place of the faith of the Reformers. Relinquishing its own strength, Arminian Protestantism can no longer challenge the natural man to forsake his faith in his own autonomy.

NOTES

1. Cf. the writer's *Christianity and Idealism* (Philadelphia: Presbyterian and Reformed Publishing Co., 1958).
2. R. Kroner, *The Religious Function of Imagination* (New Haven, 1941), p. 8.
3. *Ibid.*, p. 11.
4. *Ibid.*, p. 29.
5. *Ibid.*, p. 61.
6. *Ibid.*
7. R. Kroner, *The Primacy of Faith* (New York, 1943), p. 24.
8. *Ibid.*, p. 27.
9. *Ibid.*
10. *Ibid.*
11. *Ibid.*, p. 31.
12. R. Kroner, *Speculation in Pre-Christian Philosophy*, p. 11.
13. *Ibid.*
14. See the writer's *The New Modernism*, 1937, out of print.
15. *Ibid.*, p. 12.
16. *Ibid.*, p. 19.
17. *Ibid.*, pp. 21-22.
18. *Ibid.*, p. 24.
19. *Ibid.*, p. 25.
20. *Ibid.*
21. *Ibid.*, p. 26.
22. *Ibid.*
23. *Ibid.*
24. *Ibid.*, p. 60.
25. *Ibid.*
26. *Ibid.*, p. 61.
27. *Ibid.*, pp. 61-62.
28. *Ibid.*, p. 62.
29. *Ibid.*
30. *Ibid.*
31. *Ibid.*
32. *Ibid.*
33. *Ibid.*, p. 63.
34. *Ibid.*
35. *Ibid.*
36. *Ibid.*, p. 65.
37. *Ibid.*
38. *Ibid*
39. *Ibid.*
40. *Ibid.*, p. 66.
41. *Ibid.*, p. 67.
42. *Ibid.*, p. 63.
43. *Ibid.*, p. 64.
44. Paul Tillich, *The Protestant Era*, tr. James L. Adams (Chicago, 1948).
45. *Ibid.*, p. xi.
46. *Ibid.*, p. xii.
47. *Ibid.*, p. xiv.
48. *Ibid.*, p. xv.
49. *Ibid.*, p. xvi.
50. *Ibid.*, p. xvii.
51. *Ibid.*, p. xix.
52. *Ibid.*
53. *Ibid.*, pp. xxi-xxii.
54. *Ibid.*, p. xxiii.
55. *Ibid.*, pp. xxii-xxiii.
56. *Ibid.*, pp. xxvi-xxvii.
57. *Ibid.*, p. xxvii.
58. *Ibid.*, p. 202.
59. *Ibid.*, p. 203.
60. *Ibid.*, p. 204.
61. *Ibid.*
62. Paul Tillich, *Systematic Theology* (London: Nesbet & Co., Ltd., 1955), Vol. I, p. 4.
63. *Ibid.*
64. *Ibid.*, p. 8.
65. *Ibid.*, pp. 74-75.
66. *Ibid.*, p. 8.
67. *Religion and Culture*, Essays in honor of Paul Tillich, ed. W. Leibrecht (New York, 1959), p. 27.

68. *Ibid.*
69. *Systematic Theology*, Vol. I, etc., p. 71.
70. *Ibid.*, p. 70.

71. *Ibid.*, pp. 70-71.
72. *Ibid.*, p. 67.
73. *Ibid.*, p. 70.
74. *Ibid.*, p. 71.
75. *Ibid.*, p. 72.
76. *Ibid.*
77. *Ibid.*
78. *Ibid.*, p. 74.
79. *Ibid.*
80. *Ibid.*, p. 86.
81. *Ibid.*, p. 87.
82. *Ibid.*, p. 88.
83. *Ibid.*
84. *Ibid.*, p. 89.
85. *Ibid.*, p. 90.
86. *Ibid.*, p. 97.
87. *Ibid.*, p. 122.

88. *Ibid.*
89. *Ibid.*, p. 126.
90. *Ibid.*
91. *Ibid.*, p. 138.
92. *Ibid.*
93. *Ibid.*, p. 139.
94. *Ibid.*
95. *Ibid.*, p. 143.
96. *Ibid.*
97. *Ibid.*, p. 144.
98. *Ibid.*, p. 148.
99. *Ibid.*, p. 150.
100. *Ibid.*, p. 152.
101. *Ibid.*, p. 153.
102. *Ibid.*, p. 163.
103. *Ibid.*, p. 164.
104. *Ibid.*, p. 200.

105. *Ibid.*, p. 201.
106. *Ibid.*, p. 202.
107. *Ibid.*, p. 203.
108. *Ibid.*, p. 204.
109. *Ibid.*
110. *Ibid.*, p. 75.
111. *Ibid.*, pp. 210, 211.
112. *Ibid.*, p. 211.
113. *Ibid.*, p. 212.
114. *Ibid.*
115. *Ibid.*, p. 223.
116. *Ibid.*
117. *Ibid.*, p. 263.
118. *Ibid.*, p. 265.
119. *Ibid.*, p. 266.
120. *Ibid.*, p. 74.
121. *Ibid.*

122. Paul Tillich, *Systematic Theology* (Chicago: The University of Chicago Press, 1957), Vol. II, p. 29.

123. *Ibid.*
124. *Ibid.*
125. *Ibid.*
126. *Ibid.*
127. *Ibid.*
128. *Ibid.*, p. 31.
129. *Ibid.*, p. 32.
130. *Ibid.*
131. *Ibid.*, p. 33.
132. *Ibid.*
133. *Ibid.*, p. 34.
134. *Ibid.*
135. *Ibid.*, pp. 34, 35.
136. *Ibid.*, p. 35.
137. *Ibid.*
138. *Ibid.*
139. *Ibid.*
140. *Ibid.*, pp. 35, 36.
141. *Ibid.*, p. 33.
142. *Ibid.*, p. 36.
143. *Ibid.*, p. 37.

144. *Ibid.*
145. *Ibid.*, p. 38.
146. *Ibid.*, p. 40.
147. *Ibid.*, pp. 40, 41.
148. *Ibid.*, p. 46.
149. *Ibid.*
150. *Ibid.*, p. 41.
151. *Ibid.*, p. 44.
152. *Ibid.*
153. *Ibid.*, p. 60.
154. *Ibid.*, p. 74.
155. *Ibid.*, p. 78.
156. *Ibid.*
157. *Ibid.*
158. *Ibid.*, p. 80.
150. *Ibid.*, p. 93.
160. *Ibid.*, p. 94.
161. *Ibid.*, p. 90.
162. *Ibid.*, p. 94.
163. *Ibid.*
164. *Ibid.*, p. 91.

165. *Ibid.*, p. 95.
166. *Ibid.*, pp. 95, 96.
167. *Ibid.*, p. 93.
168. *Ibid.*, p. 98.
169. *Ibid.*
170. *Ibid.*, p. 100.
171. *Ibid.*
172. *Ibid.*
173. *Ibid.*, p. 108.
174. *Ibid.*
175. *Ibid.*
176. *Ibid.*, p. 109.
177. *Ibid.*
178. *Ibid.*
179. *Ibid.*, p. 110.
180. *Ibid.*
181. *Ibid.*
182. *Ibid.*
183. *Ibid.*, p. 112.
184. *Ibid.*, p. 111.
185. *Ibid.*, p. 114.

186. *Ibid.*
187. *Ibid.*
188. *Ibid.*
189. *Ibid.*, p. 115.
190. *Ibid.*, p. 118.
191. *Ibid.*, p. 117.
192. *Ibid.*, p. 134.
193. *Ibid.*, p. 145.
194. P. Tillich, *Systematic Theology*, Vol. I, p. 74.
195. *Ibid.*, Vol. II, p. 40.
196. *Ibid.*, p. 133.
197. *Ibid.*, p. 134.
198. *Ibid.*, Vol. III, p. 7.
199. *Ibid.*, p. 125.
200. *Ibid.*, p. 108.
201. *Ibid.*
202. *Ibid.*, p. 223.
203. *Ibid.*, p. 224.
204. *Ibid.*
205. *Ibid.*
206. *Ibid.*
207. *Ibid.*, p. 226.
208. *Ibid.*, p. 146.
209. *Ibid.*
210. *Ibid.*, p. 147.
211. *Ibid.*
212. *Ibid.*, p. 243.
213. *Ibid.*, p. 349.
214. *Ibid.*, p. 395.
215. Cf. Chapter I.

Chapter V

THE REFORMED PASTOR AND
MODERN ROMAN CATHOLICISM*

I. *Introduction*

In presenting the Conservative or Orthodox Protestant point of view of Christianity, we should note something of the difference that exists between what is called "Modern Protestantism" and what is called "Traditional Protestantism." Dr. J. Gresham Machen, the founder of Westminster Theological Seminary, wrote a book entitled *Christianity and Liberalism*, in which he made plain the difference between these two approaches. The Liberalism or Modernism of which Dr. Machen spoke in his book is the theology of Friedrich Schleiermacher, Albrecht Ritschl, and their theological descendants. At the turn of the century such men as Adolph von Harnack and Wilhelm Herrmann were among the leaders of this modern theology.

Dr. Machen's contention was that this modern Protestantism is not to be identified with historic Protestantism at all. Liberalism, Machen argued, is not the Protestantism of Martin Luther and of John Calvin. True Protestantism, Machen contended, believes that Jesus Christ the Son of God and the Son of man effected a change from wrath to grace through his death and resurrection in history. On the contrary, modern Protestant theology follows modern philosophy in holding that there need not and cannot be such a completed work of redemption in history. True Protestantism, Machen observed, believes that Christ himself, by his Spirit and through his servants the prophets and apostles, has given us in Scripture both a historical record and a final interpretation of his work in history. Modern Protestantism holds that no such record and final interpreta-

---

* The content of this chapter was given as an address before a Roman Catholic audience under the auspices of LaSalle College, Philadelphia, on January 5, 1966.

tion of the person and work of Christ need or can come directly into history from a God who transcends history.

It is of particular importance to observe that in saying these things about Christ and his speech to man in Scripture, Machen, rightly or wrongly, was dealing with *ultimate issues*. Nothing less than a complete philosophy of history is involved in the great debate between modern and historic Protestantism.

Modern Protestantism has reinterpreted the triune God's work of redemption in history in terms of a modern epistemology, a modern ontology, and a modern ethic. Consequently, those who adhere to historic Protestantism do so in the interest of preserving for themselves, for the church of Christ, and for the world, the memory and present power of the Christ who alone saved men from sin and by his Spirit saves them now.

Orthodox Christians today preach and teach the Christ of the Scriptures as the Savior of the *whole* man with his *entire* culture. In doing this they desire to follow the example of St. Peter as he confessed the name of Christ fearlessly before the Sanhedrin. Peter had seen how the Jewish council, while claiming to speak for Moses and the prophets, had condemned Jesus. The Pharisees viewed their own ethical consciousness as the ultimate standard of right and wrong. The council condemned Peter as it had condemned his Lord, again setting the human subject above the Word of Christ.

Orthodox Christians seek also to follow the example of the Apostle Paul as he wrote to the Greeks at Corinth: "Where is the wise? Where is the scribe? Where is the disputer of this world? Hath not God made foolish the wisdom of this world? For after that in the wisdom of God the world by wisdom knew not God, it pleased God by the foolishness of preaching to save them that believe" (I Cor. 1:20, 21).

Conscious of the wiles of Satan, orthodox Christians pray, above all else, both for something of the true humility of their Redeemer as they view the great "mystery of godliness" and for something of the compassion which their Savior manifested when he shed his blood for them. As they argue among themselves, they do so in the interest of stirring up their faith in their common Lord and in the interest of presenting him more faithfully to a world that is "without hope and without God." As they stir up one another for the purpose of reaching a consistent and faithful presentation of that only name which is given under heaven whereby men must be saved, they look everywhere within the professing church of Christ for help, fellowship, and consolation. Confessing their own frequent failures in presenting the Christ of the Scriptures properly, they hope and pray that the "mother" church may, with them, go forth to Mexico, to South America, to Africa, and to Asia and tell these peoples that there is now no condemnation for those who believe and trust in him who, knowing no sin, was made sin for men that they might be made the righteousness of God in him.

II. *Vatican II*

It is in this spirit that those of us who cling to the Christ of the Scriptures in distinction from modern Protestantism have watched the proceedings of the Second Vatican Council and now will watch what its effects will be. The chief question for us is: What will Vatican II indicate as to the theological trend in the "mother" church? "Among the *periti*" present at the council, *Life* (Dec. 17, 1965) tells us, "were some leaders of the recent revolution in Catholic theology that prepared the way for this council." *Life* mentions the names of Karl Rahner, Bernard Häring, Yves Congar, Henri de Lubac, Hans Küng, Edward Schillebeeckx, and John Courtney Murray.

Not being adequately informed with respect to the theology of all these theologians, I single out the name of Hans Küng. It is well known to all that Hans Küng, following the example of Hans Urs von Balthasar, has concerned himself with Karl Barth, perhaps the most influential neo-orthodox "Protestant theologian" of our day. Küng knows, of course, that Karl Barth's theology must not be identified with that of Schleiermacher and Ritschl. Karl Barth speaks of Schleiermacher and his followers as "consciousness theologians." These consciousness theologians start, says Barth, with the human consciousness as essentially sufficient unto itself. They start from beneath (*von unten*), and from within. Barth, however, would start with God who, in Christ, tells us who man is and what he needs. Barth would start from above (*von oben*). Barth wants to be *Christological* through and through. Aiming to be *wholly* Christological, Barth constructs what he calls a "Theology of the Word." He holds to the *primacy of Christ speaking through his Word*.

Hans Küng knows further that for many years Barth has been critical of the theology of the "mother" church. Rightly or wrongly, Barth has seen in the *analogia entis* idea both the source and the expression of a synthesis-theology which compromises the Christ of the Word. A true Christian theology, Barth has argued, requires us to substitute the idea of the *analogia fidei* for the idea of *analogia entis*. Without the substitution of the *analogia fidei* for the *analogia entis* we cannot have, says Barth, a true concept of justification by faith. Here, Barth maintains, is the heart of Protestantism. Here, he says, is he talking of the theology of Luther and Calvin. Here is the theology officially condemned by the Council of Trent. How then can there be *aggiornamento*? It would seem to be pretty near impossible!

Nothing daunted, Küng has Barth write the introduction to his book on justification. In this introduction Barth comments that Küng has presented his views fairly and that if Küng's views on justification are truly those of his church, then his (Barth's) own views are also in basic agreement with those of the church.

The prospects at this point are exhilarating. For many years Barth has seen in the Roman Catholic theology a threat to the biblical idea of the sovereign grace of God toward man and to the true nature of man's faith as his response to this sovereign grace. Is it not man himself who, in the Roman Catholic view, really justifies himself inasmuch as he cooperates with justification?[2]

But Küng has apparently satisfied Barth on these basic points. Küng has shown him, and shown him from the history of the doctrine, that Roman Catholic theology too interprets the God-man relation in terms of Christ's act of redemption. Roman Catholicism, says Küng, is not a closed but an open system. Dogmatic truths do indeed set forth the truth infallibly, but they never express truth exhaustively. The church, therefore, seeks constantly to set forth the truth in ever-more inclusive perspectives. It is thus that the embodiment of the truth as the outworking of the incarnation (*Auswirkung der*

Menschwerdung) is accomplished in the church through the working of the Holy Spirit.[3] Apply this now, says Küng, to the Council of Trent and its rejection of the theology of the Reformation. When the church formulated its own view of justification over against that of the Reformers it did, indeed, employ a certain anthropomorphism. But this was not done in the interest of the primacy of man. On the contrary, it was done in the interest of truly saving the primacy of God's grace in Christ to man. For how can the primacy of Christ in saving man be maintained if there is no real man to be saved?[4] Does not Barth himself, in order to save the primacy of the faith, reject the deterministic idea of the *Alleinwirksamkeit Gottes*, of the Reformers in relation to man?

Throughout its history, then, the church has held to the primacy of Christ.[5] Barth is right in saying that our justification must be brought into relationship with our election in Christ from all eternity.[6] From all eternity God has in his Son thought of the salvation of all men.[7] From the beginning, the whole of world history is determined by God's plan of salvation. Through God's grace world-history becomes the history of salvation (*Heilsgeschichte*) and of the church.[8] All temporal eventuation happens in fulfillment of the eternal plan of salvation for men in Jesus Christ.[9] The whole of creation bears the form of Christ (*Christusformig*) and as such, has a hidden trinitarian structure.[10] Of course, creation has its own existence, but its ground of being is factually in Jesus Christ.[11] To say that the ground of all creation is in Jesus Christ is not to deny the fact of gradation. Material creation is not conscious of existing in Christ. The sinner who rebels in Christ exists in Christ in a different manner than the righteous man. The damned are in Christ in a different manner than the blessed. But though the idea of gradation must be maintained, this must never reduce the fact that all things are in Christ.[12]

Look at the ecumenical possibilities that are latent in this approach of Küng to Barth. The United Presbyterian Church in the United States of America has adopted a new Confession. It is called *The Confession of 1967*. This *Confession of 1967* is new *negatively* in that it rejects what it considers to be the determinism of the old

Westminster Confession. The *Confession of 1967* is new *positively* in that it has largely incorporated the theological principles of Karl Barth.

Dr. George Hendry of Princeton Theological Seminary makes the contrast between the theology of the old and the theology of the new confession very clear. Hendry says that with its determinism and particularism, the old confession is not truly Christological and biblical. In consequence, it has no eye for the sovereign, universal grace of God to all men in Christ. This appears especially, he says, in what the old confession teaches concerning justification. Calvin spoke of Christ as fully discharging the debt that man owes to God and as making "a proper, real, and full satisfaction to his Father's justice."[13] The Westminster Divines adopted this idea. But, says Hendry, "if God's grace is contingent on 'a proper, real, and full satisfaction' of his justice, grace is not sovereign, and justification cannot be said to be 'only of free grace.' "[14]

But this is not all. Correlative to the idea of genuinely *sovereign* grace, argues Hendry, is that of *universal* grace. With its particularism, the old confession reduces "the freedom of grace to sheer caprice."[15] "The salvation provided in the covenant of grace is in God's eternal purpose intended for all men."[16] Therefore "the absence of a Christian profession" should not be held against those who have not heard the gospel. To "assert that 'good pagans' " cannot "be saved surely overlooks Romans 2."[17]

III. *Confessing Christ*

It will not seem strange that we orthodox Protestants cannot express our faith in terms of *The Confession of 1967.* It will be clear that the theology underlying this Confession is as much a consciousness-theology as that of Schleiermacher ever was. The theology of Barth, no less than the theology of Schleiermacher, presupposes the autonomy or self-sufficiency of the growing ethical consciousness of man. The God of Barth's theology, like the God of Schleiermacher's theology, is a projection of the supposedly free moral consciousness as this is taken from Immanuel Kant's *Critique of Practical Reason.* The idea of sovereign universal grace as Hendry, following Barth, sets it before us, is the religious expression of a critical philosophy in which the idea of pure contingency and abstract determinism interpenetrate one another. In terms of this theology no transition from wrath to grace *in history* is thinkable.

How could we fulfill our task of proclaiming the name of Jesus Christ in the framework of such a philosophy? To be known, the Christ of this theology must be exhaustively known and can be exhaustively known only as absolutely hidden. How can such a Christ have any meaning for men?

On the basis of Kant's philosophy, man must, to be free, project himself into the realm of the noumenal. But as such he cannot know himself at all. When, in order to know himself, Kant thinks of his free man as manifesting himself in the realm of the phenomenal, man loses his freedom. Moreover, what holds for man in general holds also for God. To be God to man, he must first be wholly free, i.e., unknown and unknowable to man. On the other hand, he must be wholly determined and therefore wholly known if he manifests himself to man at all. The Son of God of whom Kant speaks is not the Christ of the Scriptures. Yet, amazing as it may seem, recent dialectical theologians, led by Barth, have sought to press the biblical teachings of creation, of sin, and of redemption into the phenomenal-noumenal distinctions of Kant's essentially non-historical thought.

It is true that some recent philosophers, for example, Robert Collingwood, make the assertion that it is precisely Kant's philosophy which, for the first time, shows us how history can and does have genuine meaning. But they who assert this can only do what Collingwood actually does, namely, absorb the whole of history as past into the present. This does away, once and for all, with the idea that Jesus Christ, the Son of God and the Son of man, died and rose again from the dead in a past which is truly historical (and not merely our present encounter with, and self-imposed structure upon, records which have come down to us). Naturally, Collingwood's position, at the same time, does away both with the authority of the Christ and his word in Scripture, and with the authority of the church as speaking officially in the name of Christ.

Modern thinkers now follow the example of the Jewish Sanhedrin in their antagonism to the Christ of the Scriptures. Together with the Sanhedrin, modern Protestant thinking simply assumes that it is the self-sufficient, ever-advancing, ethical consciousness of man which must sit in judgment upon the Christ and his claim to be the Son of God come in the flesh. Together with the Pharisees, the modern Protestant philosopher and theologian, disclaiming all knowledge of ultimate reality, makes, in effect, a universal negative statement about it. Assuming first that *nobody knows* what God is he then adds, in effect, that God *cannot* be anything like what the historical Christian creeds have said that he is and that he must be identical with the process of advancing human ideals. He assumes that Christianity must be interpreted in terms of a schematism of categories which *any* man, whatever his metaphysical presuppositions, *must* accept to be rational.

As orthodox Protestants we would therefore, first of all, repent for our sin if we have allowed ourselves to be carried away with this Kantian schematism of thought, a schematism that stands foursquare against Scripture. Then we would plead with our fellow Protestants to forsake this scheme. We would plead with our fellow Protestants to repent *with us* and bow before the Christ of the Scriptures before he returns in judgment and we plead for mercy in vain.

Then, insofar as we must follow the injunction of the Apostle to contend for the faith once for all delivered to the saints, we shall seek to convince our fellow Protestants that to be truly Protestant they must be truly Christian, and that to be truly Christian they must see all things in the light of the revelation given us by God through Christ in Scripture. How else, we shall ask them, can you find unity in human experience? We must really do what Karl Barth has insisted that we must do but has not done, namely, start our interpretation of the whole of life *von oben*. We must begin our meditation upon any fact in the world in the light of the Son of God, the light which is as the light of the sun, the source of all other light.

How could we know anything legitimately about the facts of the world unless we see that through the Son the facts were made? How shall we sinful men, "dead by reason of your offenses and sins" (Eph. 2:1-3, *Confraternity Version*), be able to see the teleology that pervades the world unless our Savior's words be true that to him all power is given in heaven and on earth? How shall we, as "blinded by the God of this world" (II Cor. 4:3-5, C.V.) see anything aright unless we see it through the Holy Spirit who takes the things of Christ and gives them to us, unless "God who commanded the light to shine out of darkness has shown in our hearts, to give enlightenment concerning the knowledge of the glory of God, shining on the face of Christ Jesus" (II Cor. 4:6, C.V.). Have you forgotten, we say to our neo-Protestant friends, the words of the Apostle when he says that the "sensual man does not perceive the things that are of the Spirit of God, for it is foolishness to him and he cannot understand, because it is examined spiritually" (I Cor. 2:14, C.V.)? And then, placing ourselves for the sake of the argument upon the position of those who reject the idea that God has in Christ redeemed men in history, we shall ask them to show us how, on their assumption of human autonomy, they can expect to find any meaning in human experience. "Here you start," we say to them in all kindness but with a persistence that springs from our contract of submission to Christ, "with man as though he were intelligible to himself in terms of himself and in terms of an environment which is not directed by the redemptive providence of God directly active in history. Here you place man in an environment of *ultimate* contingency, or chance. You want no part of the idea that human experience must be interpreted from the very start from above. But then, having said this, you turn about and make what amounts to a universal negative judgment about all past, present, and future possibility. You claim that you are nothing but a whitecap on a wave of the bottomless and shoreless ocean of chance and then you presume to say that there *cannot be any evidence* of the existence of God anywhere in all the world. Such an internally contradictory and meaningless position is, I believe, my friends, the only alternative to starting frankly with the authoritative word of Christ in the Scriptures."

We know, of course, what our neo-Protestant friends will tell us as we contend that we must presuppose the idea of the Scriptures as being the clear and final words of Christ with respect to the creation, the fall, and the redemption of man through Christ himself.

To speak of the *necessity* of such a revelation of God through Christ in history, they have said repeatedly, is to speak of what is impossible. *Absolutes cannot appear in history.* History is the realm of the relative. All interpretation by man is relative to man the interpreter. It is well, they say, to use the idea of the necessity of an absolute revelation in history as a *limiting concept.* In fact, we do need the principle of absolute rationality of all being as an *ideal.* But then we *also* need, as correlative to this ideal of absolute rationality, the principle of *pure* contingency. Science and philosophy alike need both of these ideals: comprehensive, rationally inter-related knowledge, and absolute contingency.

The Greeks did not have a vision of the relativity of all knowledge to the mind of man. Accordingly they did not have the idea of the *correlativity* of pure rationality and pure irrationality. Hence, they either followed the example of Parmenides, denying all change, or of Heraclitus, claiming that there is nothing but change. Or if, with Aristotle, they seemed to begin to see something of the need of combining pure change with pure rationality and therefore spoke of being as of *analogical* and of human knowledge as *analogical*, they still continued to look for a reality and a rationality that is prior to and independent of the organizing acts of the human mind. It is Kant who, in principle at least, has liberated us from the idea of the thing in itself. It is Kant who, in principle at least, has saved us from what Hegel called the "*alte Metaphysik.*" We have now learned in science, in philosophy, and in theology to seek for *objectivity*, not by reaching for the moon, but by the ever-deepening penetration of a reality which always beckons us on as an ideal. Kant has shown us true objectivity in science and has given us a place for a religion consonant with free human personality.

I am not hiding the fact that Protestantism is indeed divided within itself. In fact, I am pointing out that the rift within Protestantism is much deeper than you perhaps have realized. We are speaking of the many ecclesiastical divisions found in Protestantism. We are ashamed of them. But let that pass for the moment, as I call to attention the deep perpendicular theological rift that cuts all the horizontal lines of demarcation which figure so largely in our surface ecclesiastical debates. There are those who follow Descartes and more particularly Kant, and there are those who continue to follow the Reformers. The issue between them is all-inclusive. The gulf between them cannot be crossed. There is not a fact in the field of science, or of philosophy, or of theology that is not in dispute between them. The followers of Kant have done precisely what the Pharisees did in Jesus' day, i.e., reject the Christ of God as speaking in the Scripture. They have made a Christ who speaks through the *Critique of Pure Reason.* By their own confession, the followers of Kant assert that they can say nothing about God and then also assert that they know that God *cannot* be what historic Christianity says that he is. Having adopted a totality view of being on *purely non-rational grounds*, they then use the *law of contradiction* as a tool with which to *prove* that the totality view of Christianty *cannot* be what it claims to be.

Seeing this, those of us who continue to believe in historic Christianity do not then claim that we by some self-existent abstract principle of logic as such can prove the truth of what the Bible teaches. We have frankly taken our totality view from the revelation of God through Scripture. We start *von oben.* We start with the absolute authority of Christ speaking in Scripture. And we have done this not, in the first place, because we claim to be wiser than other men. We have been saved by grace. By the regenerating power of the Spirit we have been enabled to see that the foolishness of God is wiser than men. But having been saved by grace we now also see that there is no place for the fruitful exercise of the human intellect except within the totality view granted us in Scripture. There is no logic or reality, neither is there any relation between the two which we as creatures may consistently hold to, unless both logic and reality have their very being in the Creator-Redeemer God of the Scriptures. If men do not accept this totality view by faith in the absolute authority of Christ, then there is nothing left to them but the fearful looking forward toward the crucifixion of the intellect by which they are seeking to defend themselves against the approaching judgment of the self-attesting Christ, who shall judge all men by the words which he has spoken (cf. John 13:44-50, C.V.).

IV. *Dialogue*

I might well stop at this point. I have tried to give you a survey of what traditional Protestants believe. I have taken some pains to point out that those who hold this view do so in self-conscious relation to neo-Protestantism. We hold to our position, first, because it is revealed to us by the self-attesting Christ of Scripture; and, secondly, because we think that the only alternative to it is solipsism or pure subjectivism. The only alternate to our position, we are bound to think, is a man-centered interpretation of life. And we think that the man who stands at the center of neo-Protestantism can in no wise identify himself, let alone say anything intelligible about the world, God, or Christ. If the modern Protestant thinker first rejects and then refuses to return to the traditional Protestant view of things, it is not that he has found any facts to disprove this position or any logical reasons for saying that it is out of accord with the laws of human thought. Neither is it because he has found facts or logical reasons that even point to the intelligibility of his own position. If a man swims in the ocean next to an iceberg and wants to move it, he may push against it with all his might but, even if he does not notice it, it is he, not the iceberg, that is moving. This illustration is still too weak to indicate the real state of affairs with respect to new Protestant thought. The man of new Protestantism is himself made of water, or rather, he is not *made* of water because he *is* water, water concentrated as a whitecap on a wave of a bottomless and shoreless ocean. Come out of chance, he disappears in his environment of the endless blue.

But let us now go beyond this point, for I may perhaps assume that in a certain sense, at least, you agree with my analysis of modern Protestantism. If I read a book like that of Dr. Michael Mahoney on *Cartesianism* then I am established in this opinion. All modern philosophical subjectivism, argues Mahoney, is but a development of the Cartesian starting-point. This starting-point is basically mistaken because it assumes that man can find objectivity within himself. Once more, if I read a book like *Present Day Thinkers and the New Scholasticism* edited by John S. Zybura, I am again confirmed in this view.

Summing up what many of the contributors to this volume say, Dr. Zybura himself asserts that the modern approach to philosophy is centered in man as over against scholasticism, which is centered in God.[18] Once more, in his popular work, *The Faith of Millions*, Father John O'Brien says the "Principle of the supremacy of private judgment in the interpretation of Scripture" has led to the extremes of modern subjectivism.[19]

Thus we seem, at first blush, to agree on the sad state of modern Protestant theology and of modern post-Cartesian philosophy in general.

We now come to the most important question as to what we think the answer is to this modern subjectivism. Here, on the surface at least, we might still seem to be in agreement. We must believe, says Father O'Brien, in the "mystery of the Blessed Trinity." We believe in this mystery, he adds, "because it has been divinely revealed to us in the Holy Scriptures. God the Father is the Creator of the world, Jesus Christ is the Redeemer of mankind, and the Holy Ghost is the Sanctifier."[20] Then more specifically with respect to Christ, Father O'Brien adds:

> Our Christian faith teaches that Jesus Christ is divine in his personality and possesses two distinct natures, human and divine. "He is God of the substance of the Father, begotten before time," says the Athanasian creed formulated in the fourth century, "and He is man of the substance of His mother, born in time." In order to redeem us from our sins, the Son of God became incarnate, being conceived by the power of the Holy Ghost in the womb of the virgin Mary, and was born in a stable at Bethlehem on Christmas day over nineteen hundred years ago.[21]

This in itself is encouraging enough. Surely this is essentially the official position of the Church as expressed, for instance, by the Council of Trent, is it not? Did not Vatican II encourage the study of Scripture anew in the interest of the ecumenical ideal?

We must, however, have the total picture before us. It is all-important to ask what reasons we give for rejecting the subjective position of modern Protestantism. Modern Protestantism also claims to believe in the "mystery of the trinity." Modern Protestantism also claims to believe in the incarnation. Modern Protestantism too claims to get its teachings on the trinity and the incarnation from the Bible as the Word of God. For all that, it remains true that modern Protestantism starts from man instead of from God. Modern Protestantism has reduced the objective facts of Christianity to projections of the human mind. It has done this because it is wedded to a philosophy which is man-centered. Modern Protestantism is wedded to a philosophy that cannot account for the meaning of history at all. It rejects the idea that there is any objective meaning in history. Modern philosophy cannot allow for the biblical idea of creation, the fall, the incarnation, the resurrection, and the return of Christ on the clouds of heaven. So far as modern Protestantism has accepted these biblical teachings it has virtually *allegorized* them. It speaks of them as *myths* or *symbols* or, with Barth, as *Saga*, i.e., non-temporal events. So far as the facts of the Bible are said to be temporal, they are said to be merely *Hinweise*, pointers, to the realm of *Geschichte*, the non-temporal sphere equivalent to Kant's noumenal realm.

But now the critical question in our dialogue is this: What do *you* and what do *we* mean when we speak of "objective truth" in terms of which we wish to escape from modern subjectivism? If we are to ask men to truly repent and turn to Christ, then we must be able to tell them who Christ is and where he may be found. We must present Christ as the one who has first identified himself in terms of himself and then identifies man and gives man freedom through his redeeming work.

It is obvious that some of your own modern thinkers, as well as some of the past, do not think that we, orthodox Protestants, have the wherewithal to challenge modern subjectivism. So for instance, Father O'Brien thinks Luther was more individualistic than was Descartes. Father O'Brien quotes Luther as saying "whoever teaches otherwise than I teach, condemns God, and must remain a child of hell." As for Calvin, he "claimed infallible authority, regarding himself as the mouthpiece of God, in saying: 'God has conferred upon me the authority to declare what is good and what is bad.' In consonance with this premise, he demanded death by fire or sword for all who differed with him." Such intolerance, says Father O'Brien, "was implicit in the system."

V. *Jacques Maritain*

As for the nature of that system, Dr. Jacques Maritain tells us more particularly what it is. It is, says he, a system of anthropocentric humanism. This anthropocentric humanism merits the name of "inhuman humanism."[22] This modern inhuman humanism is, says Maritain, derived in part from the Renaissance. It "severs itself more and more from the incarnation."[23] According to this humanism of the Reformers, man is "taken to be essentially corrupt." Yet somehow this corrupt nature is said, by this humanism, to cry out to God. Man is walking corruption; but this irremediably corrupt nature cries out to God, and the initiative, do what one will, is thus man's by that cry.[24]

Thus there is, says Maritain, inherent in the system of Protestantism a basic antinomy. Man is "bound down, annihilated under a despotic decree" and yet this same man is sure of his salvation. Barth's error, says Maritain, "is that of Luther and of Calvin: it is to think that grace does not vivify."[25] In the various schools of Protestantism we have a "theology of grace without freedom."

Where then are we to look for true objectivity? Where obtain true freedom, true freedom in terms of the primacy of the incarnation of Christ? The answer Maritain gives is that "the theology of St. Thomas will govern" the age of the new humanism that is truly Christian and truly sets man free.[26] Speaking in a similar vein, the writers of the volume on New Scholasticism insist that the *Philosophia Perennis* is bound to be the philosophy of the future. To win men away from their fatal subjectivism toward the idea of analogy as formulated by "the prince of Scholastic thinkers" we must, with him, go back to the best of Greek philosophy. According to Maritain, says Dr. Martin Grabmann, "Aristotle has laid the foundation of true philosophy for all time."[27] We may therefore, he says, speak of the "Christian Aristotelianism of Albert the Great and particularly of St. Thomas Aquinas."[28]

It is, accordingly, by the combination of a true philosophy and a true theology, as found especially in St. Thomas, that we must meet modern subjectivism. When we discover a true philosophy then we discover also that such a true philosophy naturally looks upwards to its supplementation by revelation. In this, says Etienne Gilson, there "lies the whole secret of Thomism, in this immense effort of intellectual honesty to reconstruct philosophy on a plan which exhibits the *de facto* accord with theology as the necessary consequence of the demands of reason itself, and not as the accidental result of a mere wish for conciliation."[29]

There are, therefore, two points at which such writers of your church as I have quoted would disagree with what I have said or assumed. In the first place, they would disagree with my contention that modern subjectivism in theology and philosophy began with Descartes and Kant but not with the Reformers. Your writers contend that individualism and solipsism of modern post-Kantian thought is but the logical outworking of the principle of private judgment introduced by the Reformers.

It follows, secondly, the above writers contend, that the theology and philosophy of the Reformation cannot serve the servant of Christ as a means by which to bring modern man back to God. On the contrary, those who follow *historic* Protestantism, no less than those who follow *modern* Protestantism, must, we are told, themselves be called to repentance from their rejection of God's revelation to man through Christ. How can they who themselves have no objective criterion of truth call others to an acknowledgement of their need of God as revealed in Christ? In speaking of the Reformation point of view, Father O'Brien says that "there is left no rational means by which error can be demonstrated or the vagaries of a capricious nature, effectively checked."[30] The individual's own subjective reaction, he adds, "has become supreme and infallible."[31] "It is this principle which the prolific mother of modern religious indifferentism, in which vague half-truths and obvious contradiction dressed up in pleasant sentimental garb are eagerly pressed to the bosom without so much as being questioned for their credentials."[32] "According to this generally Protestant view, argues Father O'Brien, each of the hundreds of millions of readers of the Bible becomes a Pope, while the only one who is not a Pope is the Pope himself."[33] Or, "if you don't claim to be infallibly certain that your interpretation of the whole Bible is correct, then of what value is it to have an infallible Bible without an infallible interpreter?"[34]

Is it any wonder then, asks Father O'Brien, that in recent times many "intellectuals turn to Rome"? Take the case of Arnold Lunn. He was seeking for truth "with his intellect and not with his feelings." In this he followed the example of St. Thomas. Doing this he soon learned that the Catholic Church alone retains the medieval heritage appealing to reason instead of to both emotion and alleged intuition to establish the validity of her belief. She battles single-handedly a vast array of heresies which agree only that they must flee from reason and seek refuge in the dark cave of subjectivism in which they find security, because no one can discover either where or what they are.[35] Let the separated brethren then say with Lunn that "the Catholic Church alone has remained true to the mind of Christ" or with Chesterton that there are ten thousand reasons for entering the Church, "all amounting to one reason: that Catholicism is true."[36]

Are you waiting now for me to come forth with a vigorous emotional and negative response to what I have just quoted from Father O'Brien? I trust you are not. If there is to be any fruitful dialogue between us, then we must do exactly what Father O'Brien and others have done, namely, start from the conviction that we have, in what we believe, the answer to modern skepticism and solipsism. We must hold that in our totality view we have discovered for ourselves, after the most careful and basic intellectual examination, the proper place for reason, the proper place for authority, and the proper concept of the relation between the two. Only then can our dialogue be truly existential. I shall respect you most if you call me to repentance for the part I have taken in furthering modern subjectivism with all its evil consequences for the individual and for society, for the present life and for the next. I want to take no comfort for the moment in the fact that, in your kindness, you are including me in the *soul* of the church though I am not a member of her *body*. For whatever else may be the case, it is certainly true that I claim to be a member of the body of Christ. I claim to make Christ primary in my life and thought. I too claim to be a minister of the gospel of Christ. I too claim to have the remedy for subjectivism and the medicine that alone can heal the diseases of men's lives. Has Satan then so enveloped me and drugged my spiritual perception that I am really *his* servant while I think of myself as the servant of Christ? Am I so self-deceived that I do not know myself for what I am at all? Have I set myself above Christ and his church as having in myself the standard of absolute truth of right and wrong?

In any case, in the call to repentance that comes from the mother church to me through its official documents and through its theological spokesmen today and in particular through the Pope, I must, first of all, hear the voice of Christ, the head of the church, calling me to renewed repentance and faith. This means that I must, whatever else I must do, first ask myself with deep searching of heart whether in all my orthodoxy, in all my negative attitude to the neo-Protestant, and in all my criticism of the theology of St. Thomas, I have been unaware of a large measure of speculation in my own thinking that has its source not in Christ but in Satan. Have I perhaps sought to indicate contradiction in positions that are not my own in the interest of showing that I or my fellow orthodox Christians have infallible solutions for all problems? Do I, in myself, claim to have penetrated the "mystery of the trinity" and the "mystery of the incarnation" or any other mystery?

VI.   *Following Jacques Maritain*

Let me now with patience listen to the spokesmen for mother church as they seek to show me how to attain true objectivity in Christ. To lead modern subjectivism toward an acceptance of the truth as it is in Christ, Maritain leads us on gently by way of a true philosophy. A truly objective philosophy, a philosophy that really satisfies the demands of reason, will, says Maritain, naturally point toward the need of faith in Christ.

Maritain seeks to show that Thomistic thinking alone adequately meets the needs of the modern situation. There is nothing wrong in starting with the human subject, says Maritain, so long as you show that in its first breath this subject is directed toward the objective world that envelops it.

Maritain would replace the *cogito* of Descartes by the phrase *aliquid est* as indicating the "first movement of the mind" and therefore as the "starting point of all philosophy."[37] Then when I pay particular attention to my own awareness of something as existing, I may say *cognosco aliquid esse.*[38]

By this approach Maritain has already, he thinks, placed us on solid ground. The *cogito* is now no longer the primary but rather the secondary movement of the mind. We are now operating *within,* not over against, objective being. "Being" is the first and simplest of all notions. Reason feels satisfied now, for "being" as the first and simplest notion, is also the first in logical order. In the logical order, everything depends upon the principle of identity, and given with the notion of being is that of identity.[39]

Of course, when we assert this, says Maritain, we are speaking of adults. A child first meets being as "embodied in the sensible quiddity, being 'clothed' in the diverse natures apprehended by the senses, *ens concretum quidditati sensibili.*[40] But when, as adults, we see that the object of metaphysics is "being as such, *ens in quantam ens,* being not clothed or embodied in the sensible quiddity, the the essence or nature of sensible things, but on the contrary abstractum, being disengaged and isolated, at least so far as being can be taken in abstraction from more particularized objects. It is being disengaged and isolated from the sensible quiddity, being viewed as such and set apart in its pure intelligible values."[41]

Thus by means of intellectual abstraction the intellect draws forth being from the things of sense. Yet in our conceptual abstraction from sense reality, we do not, as Plato did, deal *merely* with abstractions. The profound philosophy of St. Thomas "leads the intellect and therefore philosophy and metaphysics, not only to essences but to existence itself, the perfect and perfecting goal, the ultimate fulfilment of being."[42] In short, the being that impresses itself upon us as we become intellectually aware of ourselves is *analogical.*

As *analogical,* being has within it both the element of necessity and of contingency. As such it is both luminous and mysterious. Being is not exclusively luminous. If it were, it could be caught exhaustively by our concepts. But being appears in all its riches and fecundity as overflowing all our conceptual ability to grasp it. It is not enough to say "being." "We must have the intuition, the intellectual perception of the inexhaustible and incomprehensible reality thus manifested as the object of this perception. It is this intuition that makes the metaphysician."[43]

The general notion of being as analogical implies a definite *method* of approach to God. This method, the method of St. Thomas, may also, argues Maritain, be called a new method. This method of approach to God is based upon "the intuition of the basic intelligible reality of being, as analogically permeating everything knowable; and especially the intuition of existence as the act of every act and the perfection of every perfection."[44]

Thus, instead of setting itself over against being, the self, from the outset of its self-awareness, is taken hold of by the intuition of being as analogical. Note how, according to Maritain, this intuition of being, as objective and as satisfying reason at the same time, gives man the true vision of his relation to God. Says Maritain:

> So the prime intuition of Being is the intuition of the solidity and inexorability of existence; and secondly, of the death and nothingness to which my existence is liable. And thirdly, in the same flash of intuition, which is but my becoming aware of the intelligible value of Being, I realize that the solid and inexorable existence perceived in anything whatsoever implies—I don't know yet in what way, perhaps in things themselves, perhaps separately from them—some absolute irrefragable existence, completely free from nothingness and death. These three intellective leaps—to actual existence as asserting itself independently from me; from this sheer objective existence to my own threatened existence; and from my existence spoiled with nothingness to absolute existence—are achieved within that same and unique intuition, which philosophers would explain as the intuitive perception of the essentiallly analogical content of the first concept, the concept of Being.[45]

This approach to God is new but yet not new. "This is no new approach," says Maritain. "It is the eternal approach of man's reason to God. What is new is the manner in which the modern mind has become aware of the simplicity and liberating power, the natural and somehow intuitive characteristics of this eternal approach."[46]

With deep conviction, Maritain presents this "eternal approach of man's reason to God" as the answer to all forms of subjectivism.

> The cogitatum of the first cogito is not cogitaum, but ens. One does not eat the eaten, one eats bread. To separate the objects from the thing, the objective logos from the metalogical being, is to violate the nature of the intellect, at once rejecting the primary evidence of direct intuition and mutilating reflective intuition (that same reflective intuition on which everything is made to depend) in the first of its immediate presentations. Idealism sets an original sin against the light in the very heart of its whole philosophical construction.[47]

Maritain would replace a modern anthropocentric humanism with an integral God-centered humanism as the fruit of a true, a rational, method of approach to God. Modern subjective or idealist thought has sought in vain to escape the first and natural judgment by which we know that if we "accord to a point of moss, to the smallest ant, the value of their ontological reality, . . . we cannot escape any longer from the terrifying hands which made us all."[48]

Herewith we have reached "the very mystery of knowledge."

> The Thomists, following Aristotle, recognize the intellect as having in it an active light, which disengages the intelligibility that is enclosed in sense impression. And as active light drawing intelligible species from sense impression the intellect becomes, intentionally the object. Through its activity the intellect brings the object to its sovereign decree of actuality and intelligible formation "and thus becomes itself in ultimate act this object."[49]

Thus Maritain leads reason on beyond itself to the adoration of that which is wholly beyond itself. "The process by which reason demonstrates that God is puts the reason itself in an attitude of natural adoration and intellectual admiration."[50] The whole tradition of wisdom, Maritain contends, repeats incessantly "that apophatic theology, which knows God by the mode of negation and ignorance, knows him better than *cataphatic* theology, which proceeds by that that of affirmation and science. Nevertheless this implies an essential condition, that this apophatic or negative theology should not be that of a pure and simple ignorance, but of an ignorance which knows, in which lies its mystery."[51]

Herewith we have reached "theological faith, the root of all life."[52] This faith must itself "first advance cataphatically, making known the mysteries of the Godhead to us in communicable enunciations in order then to lead us on to mystical contemplation."[53]

If this be theism, Christianity is immediately involved in it. By grace the soul is "made infinite" when the intellect becomes one in intention with its object. The Apostle Peter tells us that through grace we participate in the divine nature (II Pet. 1:4).

> How can we thus being made gods by participation, receive the communication of what belongs to God alone? How can a finite subject participate *formally* in the nature of the Infinite?

> The Thomists answer: it is by right of *relation to the object* that the soul is so made infinite. A formal participation in the divine which would be impossible if it meant to have the deity as our essence (that what is not divine should have the divine for its essence is a rank absurdity), is possible in that it means to have the divine for object: that what is not God should be raised in the depths of its nature and in the energies which precede its operations, so that it has God as the object of its intelligence and its love, God as he is in himself, is impossible by the force of nature alone, but not an absolute impossibility. Grace supernaturally confers on us the intrinsic power of laying hold of the Pure Act as our object; a new root of spiritual action which gives us as our specific and proper object the divine essence in itself.

> In the intuitive vision of the divine essence the beautified creature will receive—and with no shadow of pantheism— infinitely more than the most audacious pantheism has ever dreamed: the infinite and transcendent God himself, not that miserable totem-god tangled in matter and dragging himself forth by our efforts imagined by pantheism and the philosophies of becoming, but the true God, eternally self-sufficient, infinitely blessed in the Trinity of the Three persons—in this vision the creature becomes the very God himself, not in the order of substance, but in that of that immaterial union which fashions the intellectual act.[54]

By this modernization of the Thomistic approach to philosophy, natural theology, and grace, Maritain has not only answered current idealistic subjectivism but also, he thinks, the pessimistic inhuman humanism of the Reformers. The Reformers were determinists *pur sang.* Their God controls whatsoever comes to pass by an absolute, irresistible, and arbitrary decree. Their man is a helpless victim of sin as constitutionally one with his very being. Yet, in spite of this absolute determinism, this man can claim the mercy of God and be sure of his salvation. Thus pure determinism and pure indeterminism together formed for the Reformers a meaningless dialectic. The issue was decided on the side of the former against the latter. So, they thought, the Scriptures teach.

But now, with our metaphysical intuition of being, argues Maritain, both God and man are genuinely free. We now have a scale of being. In his book on *St. Thomas and the Problem of Evil*, he develops this idea further. According to St. Thomas, says Maritain, the idea of perfection in the universe requires that there be in it all degrees of being and goodness.[55] This idea of the necessity of the existence of every type of being provides us, Maritain contends, with a principle of continuity which replaces the Reformation principle of determinism. For this principle of continuity does not suppress but rather assumes both the freedom of God and the freedom of man. We can now see that if there is to be genuine nihilation, it has to be effected by man, who, while participating in being, is yet effected by non-being. An act of man is evil in that it is "wounded or corroded by nothingness." This happens when the will withdraws in some measure from being. This free withdrawal from being is not itself evil, but is the precondition of evil.[56]

But the victory over evil and sin is sure. Though sinners, men are still persons. As persons, they want to be free without sinning.[57] In the state of nature this aspiration would remain forever unsatisfied. But grace enables man to reach up toward a final realization of man through participation in deity.[58] Thus we see a true, *integral humanism* in which man is what he becomes by becoming united with God. God attains his purposes of grace for man. He alone knows

all that which is causable or caused by Him, that of which he is absolutely not the cause like the evil of the free act and like the free nihilating which is its precondition, these God does not know in the divine essence considered alone but in the divine essence in as much as created existence are seen therein, and in as much as in *them* is seen that nihilating and privation of which their freedom is the first cause.

How then does the will of God stand related to this free nihilating act of man? Does not God attain to his purposes of grace for man? "I answer that He knows in Himself alone all that which is causable or caused by Him, though it be only by accident (like the evil of nature). But what is not causable nor caused by Him, that of which He is absolutely not the cause, like the evil of the free act and like the free nihilating which is its precondition, these God does not know in the divine essence in as much as in *them* is seen that nihilating and privation of which their freedom is the first cause. In other terms, He knows that nihilating and that priva- tion *in* the created existents whom He knows *in* His essence. It is in this sense that I said that the 'non-consideration of the rule' which precedes the evil option (that nihilating whose importance is crucial for the present discussion because it is a pure non-being due solely to the freedom of the existent) is known to God in the actually deficient or nihilating will."

Thus the eternal plan of God is realized and the free will of man is fully maintained. "Thus we can conceive, by the aid of the moments of reason which our human mode of conceiving is forced to distinguish in the divine will, that the variegated drama of his- tory and humanity, with its infinite interweavings, is immutably fixed from all eternity by the perfectly and infinitely simple domi- nating act of divine knowledge and free will, account being taken of all free existents and of all the free nihilations of which these existents have or have not the initiative, throughout the whole succession of time whose every moment is present in eternity. Let no one say that man alters the eternal plan! That would be an absurdity. Man does not alter it. He enters into its very compo- sition and its eternal fixity by his power of saying, No!"[59]

VII.   *Etienne Gilson*

We turn now briefly to the interpretation Etienne Gilson gives of "the spirit of medieval philosophy," which is, he says, "the only Christian philosophy."[60] Before St. Thomas, says Gilson, medieval thought was in danger of falling into idealism. Matthew of Aquasparta argued that "the essence of things are not bound up with any existing thing." They "take no account of place or time." His critics argued that on his view the object of the intellect is the essence of a non-existing thing. Sensitive to this criticism, he supplemented his Platonic philosophy with a theology according to which God imprints "species directly upon the intellect. . . ." The upshot of the matter was that "he fell into philosophical skepticism but was saved by fideism."[61] Therewith medieval thought was apparently headed for "the theologism of Occam."[62]

In this crisis St. Thomas saved the day. He rehabilitated the sensible order, without for one moment derogating from "the rights of thought." He knew that truth "is the adequation of thing and intellect."[63] But this, he argued, must not lead us to a formal innatism. We must have a *moderate* realism, a realism that does full justice to thought and to sensible existence alike.

What, we ask, is the source of this moderate realism by which St. Thomas is supposed to bridge the chasm between abstract universals and unrelated particulars? Is St. Thomas doing virtually the same thing that Aristotle did when he bridged the gulf between Plato's wholly other world of ideas and the Sophist's world of pure change? According to Gilson, St. Thomas "never credits the Philosopher with the notion of creation."[64] It is Moses who gives us that idea. In giving us the idea of God as Creator "at one bound, and with no help from philosophy, the whole Greek contingency is left behind. . . ."[65]

How then, we ask, can the Greeks, not knowing creation and therefore admittedly having a totally mistaken notion of contingency, nonetheless give us the proper definition of truth? How can the heavens declare the glory of God and the firmament show forth his handiwork if pure matter be one of the ultimate explanatory principles of philosophy? On the other hand, if the human intellect is not that of man as created in the image of God, but rather is what it is because it participates in the nature of God, how can it look to any revelation above itself for truth? When pure form and pure matter are brought into interdependence with one another, how can there be any meaning to history and, in particular, how could there be any such thing as the incarnation of the Son of God?

How else can one who is conscious of his responsibility as a Chris-

tian thinker approach the Greek philosophy of things which comes
to its climax in the form-matter scheme of Aristotle, than with the
words employed by St. Paul? Paul asked the Greeks to repent of
their sin of thinking that they were not creatures of God but potentially
divine. Paul asked the Greeks to repent of their sin of concocting a
scheme of thought in which God is identical with an abstract form,
whose relationship to the world is one of correlativity to pure matter.

As noted, Gilson seems, from time to time, to see well enough the
contrast between the Christian and the Greek view of things. Yet he
thinks that the Greek scheme of things and the Christian scheme of
things can be brought into sympathetic relation to one another. The
Greek formulas, he contends, pointed toward the Christian God.
If this were not so, St. Thomas would not have found him there.[66]
It is only that the attributes of the Christian God overflow the attributes of Aristotle's in every direction.[67]

VIII. *Moderate Realism*

We see then that both Gilson and Maritain offer the moderate
realism of St. Thomas as the only effective remedy available for the
cure of "idealism" or modern subjectivism. They both hold that the
moderate realism of St. Thomas is the only effective escape from the
fatal dialectic between pure determinism and the pure indeterminism
as entertained by the Reformers.

According to both men, the Reformers cannot challenge the "natural man" to forsake his ways because, by means of their determinism,
they think of him as "essentially corrupt" and therefore as incapable
of redemption. The man of the Reformers does not, in any sense,
participate in being or in truth. Why preach to dead virtually non-
existent, men? Why tell them that they may be saved. As the man of
the Reformers is beneath the reach of God, so the God of the Reformers is above the reach of man. One never knows what God
will do.

On the other hand, the Reformers cannot challenge the "natural
man" to repentance because, by means of their determinism, they
think of God as having, from all eternity, already saved or damned all
men whatever they believe or do in the course of history. On their

doctrine of determinism, the Reformers lose their God in his own creation. His own creatures can claim the certainty of salvation because he has bound himself to give it to them no matter how wicked their lives may be.

One might say, I suppose, that in the opinion of Gilson and Maritain, the position of the Reformers is not unlike that of Matthew of Aquasparta, except for the fact that the Reformers really have no room in their scheme for philosophy at all. Their position is really an unintelligible fideism throughout. Thus Father O'Brien was right in saying that in the Protestant view each believer is his own Pope. The difference beween orthodox and liberal or modern Protestantism thus falls away. Again Mahoney was right in saying that the subjectivism of the Reformers is more deeply subjective than is the subjectivism of Descartes and his followers.

Insofar, then, as you are in agreement with these spokesmen for the church which I have discussed, you will have to call me to repentance from the subjectivism that I share with the followers of Descartes and Kant. And insofar as I may claim to belong to the "intellectuals," you will call upon me to follow the example of such intellectuals as John Henry Cardinal Newman, Monsignor Ronald Knox, and Dr. Cornelia J. De Vogel as they returned to the mother church. In it alone they said, did their intellectual striving and their faith come to rest.

IX. *I Cannot Return*

Yet, despite the evidently sincere and pleading voice with which the mother church, through her philosophical and theological spokesmen, speaks to me today, I cannot return to her bosom. Allow me then to state, as briefly as I can, this *apologia provita mea.*

I do indeed agree with my Catholic friends that subjectivism of the sort that confronts us in the Cartesian *Cogito* must be challenged with the assertion that man cannot know himself for what he is unless he sees himself from the first breath of his self-awareness, in relation to his ultimate environment. Self-awareness, such as Descartes would place at the foundation of his thought, is self-awareness in a vacuum.

The same is true of Kant's idea of self-awareness. Kant is not wrong in holding that self-awareness is awareness of freedom. But then, to find his true free self, Kant sets this self in negative relation to the world of logical relations. His true self, Kant holds, is found in the noumenal realm. Of this noumenal realm, he says, he can say nothing. Starting with this idea of self-awareness in the noumenal realm, Kant can find no God who can be of any help to man. To be of any help to man, his God, Kant realizes, must be *above* man. But Kant's God can be above him only if Kant projects him into greater opposition to the world of logical relations than he has already projected the self of man. If Kant can say nothing about himself, he can, if possible, say less about his God. Yet it is this God, of whom less than nothing can be said, who is supposed to save man. The incarnation of the Son is therefore, for Kant, the idea of the wholly other god coming into the phenomenal world in order to save man who is, so far as he is man, in the noumenal world already and does not need saving. Or, if he needs saving because he is in the phenomenal realm, then the God who must save him must himself become more deeply immersed in the phenomenal world than the man whom he must save. In that case God as above the phenomenal world will have to save God as immersed in the phenomenal world. All reality is a way downward and a way upward in a God of whom man knows nothing whatsoever.

In reality, the situation is even more complicated than this picture would indicate. In reality, the God of Kant must at the same time be *wholly above* and *wholly within* the world of phenomena. The same is true on Kant's view of every man. To be man at all, man must both be wholly known and wholly unknown to himself, wholly free and wholly determined, wholly in the world of the *noumena* and wholly in the world of the *phenomena*. No man therefore needs or could receive any help for the building up of his manhood from any other man, not even from the God-man. In fact, every man *is* a God-man by virtue of his dual citizenship in the world of *noumena* and in the world of *phenomena*. If this man, as God-man, speaks of making progress toward greater or more significant manhood in the future, he can do this only by way of a figure of speech. He already is everything he ever will be. He can never be any worse or any better than he already is. The difference between potentiality and actuality is meaningless on this view.

In other words, the Kantian scheme of thought involves the virtual rejection of the meaning of history in the Christian sense of the term. The modern theologians who, like Karl Barth, have built their theology upon an essentially Kantian view of man and his environment have thereby virtually made preaching of the gospel of grace unthinkable. Of course, many of them do not intend to do any such thing. But so far as their theology is composed of a combination of Kantian and biblical principles, thus far it is a monstrosity. Between Kantianism and Christianity there can be nothing but conflict to the death. Kantianism is subjectivism *pur sang*.

But how do my Catholic friends help me to escape from this pure subjectivism of Kant? Do I escape this subjectivism if I follow their advice and speak of human awareness as, from the start, "awareness of being"? More particularly, do I escape subjectivism if I am told that the being which I meet in my first breath of self-awareness is the *analogical* being of St. Thomas? I know what the analogical being of Aristotle is. I know that it is based on a supposed interaction of pure form and pure matter on a continuum of levels, a chain of being. I know that, with his idea of being as analogical, Aristotle tried to mediate between the abstract eternal essences of Plato's thought and the utterly unrelated particularism of Sophistic thought. I know that the effort of Aristotle, was a failure. His lowest species was still of the same nature as was the highest essence of Plato. For Aristotle, as well as for Plato, knowledge is of universals only. Aristotle's *concept* could do nothing but drift on a bottomless and shoreless ocean of chance that was pure matter. Holding firmly with Plato and with Parmenides to the adequation of thought and being, Aristotle was unable, for all his supposed empiricism, to attribute any significance to history and its individuality. The moderate realism of Aristotle, like the more extreme realism of Plato, could explain nothing in the world of change except by explaining it away.

It will be said, of course, that it is not the moderate realism of Aristotle but the moderate realism of St. Thomas, the Christian, that offers us escape from subjectivism. It is the God of Christianity, not

Thought-thinking-Itself, that saves us. But in what way, we ask, does the moderate realism of St. Thomas differ from that of Aristotle? It differs, of course, in that it is brought into relation with Christianity, with the teachings which the church has received from God through Christ. These teachings pertain to the triune God who has created the world; to man made in the image of this God; to man become sinner by keeping under the knowledge of God; to God becoming man in Christ Jesus, bearing for sinners the wrath of God and rising from the dead for their justification; gone to heaven to prepare a place for those he came to redeem, and about to return on the clouds of heaven to judge the living and the dead for their eternal weal or woe, according as they have or have not believed in him. Here, then, is a totality view of man and his environment, a view including every fact in the universe, involving them all in one grand drama of redemption or condemnation. This totality view stands totally over against the totality view which comes from the Greek spirit, the Form-Matter scheme, the Potentiality-Act scheme, the scheme of the four causes of Aristotle.

When Paul preached to the Greeks he asked them to substitute the Christian scheme for that on which they prided themselves. Paul asked them to repent and thus be saved from the wrath of God which is to come upon "all ungodliness and wickedness of those men who in wickedness hold back the truth of God" (Rom. 1:18, 19, C.V.). He asked them to believe in the Creator and Redeemer God revealed by Christ in his Word. He preached Christ and him crucified, Christ and his resurrection. All this was foolishness to the Greeks. Parmenides had told them that all reality can be only that which human conceptual thought says it can be. The human intellect, if capable of nothing else, is capable of making universal negatives. For him change could have no meaning. Heraclitus said that since change is real, *all* reality must be one flux. For him permanence could have no meaning. When Aristotle tried to combine the "truth" in the view of Parmenides with the "truth" in the view of Heraclitus, he still could give no genuine meaning to change and history. When, later, Plotinus gathered together the best of all Greek philosophy, he could only think of man as drawn downward toward extinction in pure non-being, or chance, and simultaneously drawn upward, toward absorption into the wholly unknowable One. Plotinus certainly could not think of man as a creature and a sinner receiving salvation through the God-man Jesus Christ. Dionysius the Areopagite and Scotus Erigena were both anxious to maintain the primacy of Christ and of his revelation in Scripture. Yet when they sought to harmonize this teaching of Scripture with the Plotinian scheme, the result was fatal for their Christianity. They presently reduced the biblical teachings with respect to creation, fall, and redemption to allegory. They did in those early days what the theologians of our day do when they explain Christian teachings by Kantian categories. As all is *mythus, symbol,* or *saga* now, so all was *allegory* then.

Now in thinking of such men as Maritain and Gilson we seem to have a sort of repetition of the type of combination between Christianity and Plotinian philosophy that we have in Dionysius and Scotus Erigena. Or, we may say, if their views can be said rightly to represent the great Schoolman, then St. Thomas must be said not to have led us out of the mire of anthropocentric humanism at all. I do not say that St. Thomas or Gilson or Maritain do not themselves seek to make Christ primary in their thinking. I am saying that in their *thinking*, as shown in what they have *written*, they have been unable to show us how we may do this.

I shall illustrate this by following Maritain in his way upward from man to God. Notice I say that we must follow him on his way *upward*. Unless Maritain has shown us that man *from the outset* of his self-awareness sees himself as a creature, as a sinner, and as saved from sin through the redemptive work of Christ in history, then his starting-point must be said to be *humanistic* in the unfavorable sense of the term. Over against "the dream of Descartes," he says that "everything depends on the natural intuition of being—on the intuition of that act of existing which is the act of every perfection, in which all the intelligible structures of reality have their definitive actualism, and which overflows in every activity in every being and in the intercommunication of all beings."[68] Now to say that man meets being when, as an adult, he thinks about himself and that thus he escapes subjectivism is an uncritical procedure. If man is to know himself, it is in relation to the triune God of Scripture, revealed in the Christ of Scripture, that he must know himself. In what sense does man know himself as self if he does not know that he is a creature of the Creator-God? Only the God of Scripture can and has identified himself in terms of himself, and has identified man in terms of his creation and redemption in Christ. Only the triune God of Scripture can tell man *that* he is because he alone knows *what* he is. To speak of the *existence* of God without speaking of the *nature* of God is meaningless. We cannot discuss the *that* of God as separable from the *what* of God. Hegel was not wrong when he said that the idea of being is by itself as empty a concept as is the idea of non-being. The idea of being as analogical does not escape this criticism. It has as one of its ingredient elements the notion of pure non-being, that is, of ultimate contingency. It was by the idea of pure contingency, i.e., pure non-being or pure matter, as correlative to pure being, that Aristotle sought to have the ultimate category for the explanation of all reality. When he said that pure being is pure act and pure non-being is potentiality, and when he then added that act precedes potentiality, he merely asserted his irrational belief in what Kant calls the "primacy of practical reason." For all the supposed objectivity of the Greeks, and particularly of the Aristotelian position as over against that of Kant, there is, we believe, no basic difference between the two. Both start with the assumption that man must somehow know *what* he is as well as *that* he is, without seeing himself from the outset as part of a created world, and himself particularly as created and redeemed by God in Christ, and without seeing that only God through Christ in Scripture can tell man what man is.

Moderate realism does not want a world of pure essence or form such as Plato had. It wants to deal with Socrates as a man of flesh and blood. But even Plato said that the Good, the pure essential form, tends to be inherently diffuse. Essence, he said, tends to reveal itself in the world of existence. But when it does so, it can do so only by itself intermingling with pure non-existence, the purely essential with the purely non-essential, the purely determinate with the purely indeterminate. But when the world of essence becomes incarnate in the world of existence, then this world of existence must *return* to the world of essence. And what is true of the world as a whole is true of each man in the world. Each man is separated from the world of essence by his participation in the world of non-being. But unless we *begin* with the Creator-creature distinction, participation in non-being is the only principle of individuation there is. Paul says that God reveals himself to man as his Creator. Man knows himself for what he really is only if he recognizes this fact. The fact of his creatureliness presses upon him everywhere and always. *Knowing God*, says Paul, i.e., *this* God, his Creator—man, as sinner, concocts schemes of thought whereby he assumes himself to be potentially divine. On the Greek view, as well as on the Kantian view, man, as participant in non-being, is inherently evil. But evil must not be allowed to prevail. True essence must be "victorious" over evil. And so men, with the world of essence as a whole, must be said to be on the way upward. So man must think of his freedom now as consisting in the *direction* of his absorption into the world of essence which never left its home in glory even while it was incarnate in the world of existence. Thus the whole of history is meaningless on the Greek as well as on the modern scheme.

When Aristotle expressed his views with respect to the relation of the world above to the world below, he used the potentiality-actuality scheme. This is, to all intents and purposes, the same as the more Platoninc picture we gave a moment ago. The Plotinian view of man's gradual rise from the material world to the spiritual, till at last he is absorbed in the pure super-intellectual *One*, brings to its climactic expression the Greek point of view of the relation between God and man.

Now it does not appear that Maritain has escaped from the coils of this essentially Plotinian point of view. Maritain's man seeks his freedom first in his nearness and his partial envelopment in non-being and then, and at the same time, also in being lifted above all space and time into participation with the being of the God who is above all knowledge which man can have of him. Logic is supposed to lie somewhere on the path between. Logic is said to be adequate to the grasping of being, but the being which the logic must grasp is utterly contingent at both the bottom and the top of its scale. And why should there be any scale of being at all?

Why should God be said to be *higher* than man if God is himself enveloped by pure contingency except so far as he *is* pure contingency? And in particular how could there be any difference between the Son of God who is the Son of man, namely, Jesus Christ, and all other men who are in principle sons of God already through the idea of the analogy of being?

Finally, how can Maritain or Gilson claim to offer us objectivity through a proper use of philosophy and theology if they start with virtually the same subjective view of man as does post-Kantian thought? Was Hans Küng then so wrong when he saw in the theology of the church essentially the same sort of primacy of Christ that he found in Barth's theology?

How can we call unbelieving man to repentance by belief in what Jesus Christ the Son of God and Son of man suffered on the cross of Calvary and through his resurrection from the dead, if we ourselves have first so largely emasculated our thinking by the very humanism from which we are seeking to save them?

How can I be expected to follow the example of those who returned to the mother church, when your leading theologians and philosophers join, as it were, modern post-Kantian thought in using the intellect only to *disprove* the possible existence of a *God who is the source of all possibility* while they *prove* the existence of a *God who only possibly exists,* and who, while doing so, bury the intellect in a bottomless ocean of chance? I know that I have accepted my position by faith in the absolute authority of God speaking through Christ in Scripture. But now I see more clearly than ever that unless I do this, I have no foundation on which to stand when I exercise my intellect and no object for my faith when I believe. Unless I do this there can be no theology, no philosophy, no science, no knowledge at all. All will be absurd. I see modern scholastic philosophy offering me an escape from "the dream of Descartes" by setting the human self from the outset of its awareness in a receptive attitude toward being as analogical, only to lead me back into a bottomless ocean of contingency. I see modern scholastic theology in conjunction with modern scholastic philosophy leading me to a God who, because he does not speak to me *at first*, can never speak to me at all. How can I, with intellectual self-respect, return to a philosophy which now, in virtual conjunction with modern irrationalism, crucifies the intellect of man, and to a church which offers me infallible authority but has committed itself to a view of being in which there *can* be no such thing as absolute authority in history at all? It is a sad day for me. I have lived to see the day when modern Protestantism has in effect returned to the bosom of the mother church even as the theologians of the church have in effect marched forward with the theologians of neo-Protestantism toward an alliance with modern subjective philosophy. May I now then, in the name of my Savior, withstand the temptation of the evil one and of my wicked heart to think that I myself need not repent from my desire to explain the mystery of the trinity and the mystery of the incarnation. As I would call you to return to the Christ of the Scriptures, I would first call myself to such a return. Let us now *together* turn unto Christ who has redeemed us, so that then we may preach the richness of his grace to men who are without God and without hope in the world.

NOTES

1. Hans Küng, *Rechtfertigung—Die Lehre Karl Barths Und Eine Katholische Besinnung*, Paderhon, p. 272, p. 12.
2. *Ibid.*, pp. 97-100.
3. *Ibid.*, p. 108.
4. *Ibid.*, p. 111.
5. *Ibid.*, p. 138.
6. *Ibid.*, p. 134.
7. *Ibid.*, p. 137.
8. *Ibid.*
9. *Ibid.*, p. 138.
10. *Ibid.*, p. 140.
11. *Ibid.*, p. 147.
12. *Ibid.*, p. 148.
13. *The Westminster Confession for Today*, 1960, p. 136.
14. *Ibid.*, p. 137
15. *Ibid.*, p. 131.
16. *Ibid.*, p. 122.
17. *Ibid.*, p. 131.
18. John S. Zybura, ed., *Present Day Thinking and the New Scholasticism* (St. Louis, 1926), p. 402.
19. John O'Brien, *The Faith of Millions* (Huntington, 1938), p. 22.
20. *Ibid.*
21. *Ibid.*
22. Jacques Maritain, *True Humanism* (London, 1939), pp. 19-20.

23. *Ibid.*, p. 8.
24. *Ibid.*, pp. 8-9.
25. *Ibid.*, p. 63.
26. *Ibid.*, p. 67.
27. Zybura, *op. cit.*, p. 133.
28. *Ibid.*, pp. 133-134.
29. *Ibid.*, p. 153.
30. O'Brien, *op. cit.*, p. 38.
31. *Ibid.*
32. *Ibid.*, p. 39.
33. *Ibid.*, p. 132.
34. *Ibid.*, p. 133.
35. *Ibid.*
36. *Ibid.*, p. 100.
37. Jacques Maritain, *The Degrees of Knowledge* (New York, 1938), p. 38.
38. *Ibid.*
39. *Ibid.*, p. 94.
40. Jacques Maritain, *A Preface to Metaphysics* (London, 1939), p. 18.
41. *Ibid.*, pp. 18-19.
42. *Ibid.*, p. 19.
43. *Ibid.*, p. 49.
44. Jacques Maritain, *The Range of Reason* (New York, 1952), p. 43.
45. *Ibid.*, p. 88.
46. *Ibid.*, p. 89.
47. Maritain, *The Degrees of Knowledge*, p. 130.
48. *Ibid.*, p. 132.
49. *Ibid.*, p. 141.
50. *Ibid.*, p. 277.
51. *Ibid.*, p. 291.
52. *Ibid.*, p. 297.
53. *Ibid.*
54. *Ibid.*, p. 314.
55. Maritain, *St. Thomas and the Problem of Evil*, p. 5.
56. Maritain, *Existence and the Existent*, pp. 96-97.
57. Maritain, *St. Thomas and the Problem of Evil*, p. 29.
58. *Ibid.*
59. Maritain, *Existence and the Existent*, pp. 117-125.
60. Etienne Gilson, *The Spirit of Medieval Philosophy*, p. 405.
61. *Ibid.*, p. 235.
62. *Ibid.*, p. 237.
63. *Ibid.*, p. 235.
64. *Ibid.*, p. 69.
65. *Ibid.*, p. 68.
66. *Ibid.*, p. 40.
67. *Ibid.*, p. 50.
68. Maritain, *Approaches to God*, 1965, p. 18.

Chapter VI

THE REFORMED PASTOR AND
ECUMENISM*

I. *Introduction*

The Reformed pastor cannot escape confrontation with the modern ecumenical movement. Many of his fellow ministers will chide him for his lack of enthusiasm for this trend. He may even be called in question for his loyalty to Christ by many evangelical clergymen who profess purely biblical motivations for their cooperative efforts with non-evangelicals. What positive presentation may the Reformed minister give of the biblical view of ecumenism? *Is* there such an ecumenism?

It is the purpose of this chapter to survey the ecumenism of the Bible and to set it over against the concept of ecumenism advanced by so many in the modern church.

The biblical foundation for ecumenism goes back at least as far as Abraham. In sovereign grace God called him out of Ur of the Chaldees and formally made his covenant of grace with him. "As for me, behold, my covenant is with thee, and thou shalt be a father of many nations" (Gen. 17:4). The world-church was founded in Abraham's tent. A "multitude, which no man could number, of all nations, and kindreds, and people, and tongues" will stand before the Lamb, "clothed with white robes, and palms in their hands," because, like Abraham, they have believed in him in whom Abraham believed.

The story of ecumenicity is the story of what happened and what will happen between that lonely tent of Abraham and the worshiping multitude of the Book of Revelation. "God so loved the world that he gave his only-begotten Son that whosoever believeth in him, should not perish, but have eternal life. For God sent not his Son into the

---

* The content of this chapter was given as an address at Drew University.

world to condemn the world; but that the world through him might be saved" (John 3:16, 17).

When he came into the world it was said of our Savior that he would "save his people from their sins" (Matt. 1:21). When he left the world he commanded his disciples to go "and teach all nations, baptizing them in the name of the Father, and of the Son, and of the Holy Ghost; teaching them to observe all things whatsoever I have commanded you: and, lo, I am with you alway, even unto the end of the world" (Matt. 28:19, 20). Nothing can hinder the realization of the ecumenical church of Christ.

How sadly his disciples at first misunderstood his mission. But he opened their understanding so that they might grasp the nature of what he had come to do. It "behoved Christ to suffer, and to rise from the dead the third day" (Luke 24:46). Having become one with Christ through faith in his death and resurrection, the disciples must go forth to preach "among all nations, beginning at Jerusalem," "repentance and remission of sins" (Luke 24:47).

II. *The Day of Small Beginnings*

Look forward then ye saints of God to the day when that great multitude will sing the song of Moses and the Lamb, and then, having sung that song, will finally sing creation's song: "Thou art worthy, O Lord, to receive glory and honor and power: for thou hast created all things, and for thy pleasure they are and were created" (Rev. 4: 11). But even as you look forward, look backward too. Whence came all this multitude? How did they learn to repent of their sins? The answer is that "the just shall live by faith" (Rom. 1:17). But whence then have they faith? Do men naturally have faith? They do not, you say. Men naturally, by virtue of their being made in the image of God, know him. But "when they knew God, they glorified him not as God . . ." (Rom. 1:21). Men "hold the truth in unrighteousness" (Rom. 1:18). They "changed the truth of God into a lie, and worshipped and served the creature more than the creator, who is blessed forever" (Rom. 1:25). "Wherefore as by one man sin entered into the world, and death by sin; and so death passed upon all men, for that all have sinned" (Rom. 5:12). Is it not true, therefore, that the "natural man receiveth not the things of the Spirit of God: for they are foolishness unto him: neither can he know them for they are spiritually discerned"(I Cor. 2:14)? And is it not true that "the god of this world hath blinded the minds of them which believe not, lest the light of the glorious gospel of Christ, who is the image of God, should shine unto them" (II Cor. 4:4)?

Well then, in a world in which Satan has blinded the hearts of men lest they should believe, in a world in which men are dead in trespasses and sins and of themselves cannot believe, how did Christ prepare for himself this host whom no man can number?

The answer lies, of course, in the grace of God—the triune God of Scripture. God the Father so loved the world that he sent his Son to save the world. God the Son gives himself a ransom for many. "For he hath made him to be sin for us who knew no sin; that we might be made the righteousness of God in him" (II Cor. 5:21). "Christ hath redeemed us from the curse of the law, being made a curse for us: for it is written, Cursed is every one that hangeth on a tree: that the blessing of Abraham might come on the Gentiles through Jesus Christ . . ." (Gal. 3:13, 14a). God the Spirit regenerated the hearts of sinners so that they might receive the salvation wrought for them by Christ.

III. *The Outworking of Grace in History*

But watch now the outworking of the grace of the triune God in the course of redemptive history. Christ plants and then protects the faith of Abraham even in spite of Abraham's own weakness and doubting. When he seeks for the fulfillment of the promise by means of human strategy, then Christ tells him that he will be the God of Isaac, not of Ishmael. True, upon Ishmael too there would be a blessing, but the promise was to Isaac, miraculously born. The ecumenical church is found only in the tent of Isaac as it had been found only in the tent of Abraham. The multitude that no man can number, from every nation, are born of Isaac as they are born of Abraham.

When through unbelief Abraham would use human strategy in order to become the father of many nations then he is told that Sarah, though old, shall have a son. When Abraham through unbelief would build his house upon Ishmael, then God told him to listen to Sarah and cast out the bondwoman with her son, "for in Isaac shall thy seed be called" (Gen. 21:12). God thus separates unto himself a people for his own possession. Those who have not the faith of Abraham are not the true seed of Abraham. They shall not be found among that numberless company of the redeemed.

Moreover, as God would be the God of Isaac, not of Ishmael, so he would be the God of Jacob, not of Esau. When Abraham wanted to build the ecumenical church on *physical* descent as such, then Christ points him to the fact that only those who by grace believe are in that church. So also, when Isaac in turn would bless Esau, his older son, then Christ points out that he will be called the God of Jacob, not the God of Esau. Jacob is not better than is Esau. It is God's electing grace alone that sets him apart in order that through him, rather than through Esau, the promises of God to Abraham are to be fulfilled.

It is the God of Abraham, of Isaac, and of Jacob, who gathers to himself a people for his own possession. It is the true seed of Abraham, those who have the faith of Abraham, who are gathered round the throne of the Lamb.

Moreover, as it was not Ishmael but Isaac, not Esau but Jacob, so it is not the descendants of Jacob as such which are the true seed of Abraham. To be sure, the physical descendants of Jacob were the people of God. When Moses saw the multitude about him about to enter the promised land he did see in them the beginning of the fulfillment of the promise of God to Abraham (Deut. 1:10). Even so, when parting from them he pointed out to them that only those who lived like Abraham, in the obedience, the patience, and the hope of faith, would finally be numbered with the people of God. There was to be no toleration of unbelievers in the midst of the covenant people. And if many, or most, of the physical children of Israel reveal themselves as not having the faith of Abraham then the wrath of God will rest upon them and destroy them (Deut. 28:62, 63). It is not the nation as such, it is the "remnant" who are covenant-keepers in whom the nations of the world shall be blessed. The others shall be dispersed. Those, and those only, who *repent* of their unbelief will God gather again from among the nations in order to make them more numerous than their fathers (Deut. 30: 2, 4, 5).

Neither the unbelief of the nations (Gen. 11) whom God permits to walk in their own ways, nor the unbelief of the descendants of Ishmael or of Esau, so near and yet so far from the covenant people, nor the unbelief of many of those who are the descendants of Isaac and of Jacob will prevent the Christ from gathering to himself his people whom he has come to save. Neither their common descent from Abraham nor their national heritage based on miraculous redemption from Egypt to Palestine, and in Palestine against the nations, was, as such, sufficient to furnish the binding power for the "people of God." Only the sovereign grace of God would prevail. The truly ecumenical work of Christ, the King of the church, cannot be stopped. For *he is* the seed of Abraham (Gal. 3:16). "For he is our peace, who hath made both one, and hath broken down the middle wall of partition between us" (Eph. 2:14). Those who "were without Christ, being aliens from the commonwealth of Israel, and strangers from the covenants of promise, having no hope, and without God in the world" (Eph. 2:12) are "made nigh by the blood of Christ" (Eph. 2:13). Those who were "by nature the children of wrath" (Eph. 2:3), those who were "dead in sins" God hath "quickened" "together with Christ." It is they, quickened together with Christ through his blood, who will be of that great host around the throne of the Lamb. Paul sums it up when he says: "For we are his workmanship, created in Christ Jesus unto good works, which God hath before ordained that we should walk in them" (Eph. 2:10). It is God himself through his Son, and the Son through his Spirit, "who hath delivered us from the power of darkness, and hath translated us into the kingdom of his dear Son: In whom we have redemption through his blood, even the forgiveness of sins: Who is the image of the invisible God, the firstborn of every creature: For by him were all things created, that are in heaven, and that are in earth, visible and invisible, whether they be thrones, or dominions, or principalities, or powers: all things were created by him, and for him: And he is before all things, and by him all things consist. And he is the head of the body, the church: who is the beginning, the firstborn from the dead; that in all things he might have the pre-eminence. For it pleased the Father that in him should all fulness dwell; And, having made peace through the blood of his cross, by him to reconcile all things unto himself; by him, I say, whether they be things in earth, or things in heaven" (Col. 1:13-20).

IV.   *Christ Gathers His Church*

This Christ gathers his church, so that through the church he may save the world. "Come unto me, all ye that labour and are heavy laden, and I will give you rest" (Matt. 11:28). The great Shepherd of the sheep gathers his sheep. He gathers them through the work of his apostles and disciples as they proclaim the gospel of his grace. "For the promise is unto you, and to your children, and to all that are afar off, even as many as the Lord our God shall call" (Acts 2:39). At the time of Pentecost "all they that believed were together" (Acts 2:44). "And the Lord added to the church daily such as should be saved" (Acts 2:47). In great amazement Peter beholds that "on the Gentiles also was poured out the gift of the Holy Ghost" (Acts 10: 45). And Paul, who could wish that he "were accursed from Christ" for the sake of his brethren, yet knows that "neither because they are the seed of Abraham, are they all children: but, In Isaac shall thy seed be called" (Rom. 9:7). Not "they which are the children of the flesh" but "the children of the promise are counted for the seed" (Rom. 9:8). "So then it is not of him that willeth, nor of him that runneth, but of God that sheweth mercy" (Rom. 9:16). Thus he magnifies his office as the apostle to the Gentiles. For by God's mercy they too have "attained the righteousness which is of faith" (Rom. 9:30).

When the apostle to the Gentiles, Paul, went out to preach the reconciliation of all things through the cross and resurrection of Christ, he soon met with opposition. He speaks of this opposition in his letter to the Galatians. The Judaizers were quite ready to accept the gospel Paul preached if only he would include Ishmael and Esau among the heirs of the covenant. Like the Sanhedrin before them they were willing to think of Jesus Christ as one of a class of

Saviors. Was not this true ecumenism? How can there be true ecumenism if some members of the covenant, professing to be the seed of Abraham, are excluded? Did they not bear the sign and the seal of the covenant in their flesh?

Paul's answer is unequivocal. He does not apologize for his exclusiveness. A true ecumenism requires the exclusion from the church of Christ of those who have not the faith of Abraham. Only they "who are of faith, the same are the children of Abraham" (Gal. 3:7). To have the external sign of membership in the covenant is itself no guarantee that one is a true child of Abraham. The Judaizers failed to realize that only they are Christ's who are Abraham's seed and heirs according to the promise (Gal. 3:29). "Christ hath redeemed us from the curse of the law, being made a curse for us" (Gal. 3:13). They who believe this for themselves are of the seed of Abraham. "So then, brethren, we are not children of the bond-woman but of the free" (Gal. 4:31). "Behold, I Paul say unto you, that if ye be circumcised, Christ shall profit you nothing" (Gal. 5:2).

The Judaizers represented an ecumenism not based exclusively upon the death and resurrection of Christ. This false ecumenism is in reality exclusivist and therefore sectarian. Says Paul: "They zealously affect you, but not well; yea they would exclude you, that you might affect them" (Gal. 4:17). The Judaizers first tempted the Galatian Christians with their message of tolerance. They would allow both those who believed in salvation through grace and those who believed in salvation through good works to be members in good and regular standing in the church. But after having attained equality of status for themselves, they tried to push out those who believed in salvation by grace.

There is nothing strange in this. Biblical ecumenism is based on salvation through grace alone. And if a church is truly a church that preaches salvation by grace alone, then it will of necessity not receive those who believe in salvation by works. This does not mean that a truly ecumenical-minded church will judge the hearts of men. It will judge only by the open confession of men. But when men deny that they expect a place in the great company of the redeemed at last *only* because they trust in Christ who bore their sins for them upon the accursed tree, then they exclude themselves and must be taken at their word.

On the other hand, non-biblical ecumenism is based upon the idea of salvation though human merit. And a church that is based upon the idea of salvation by human merit will, of necessity, exclude those who profess salvation by grace alone. The tolerance of non-biblical-minded ecumenism does not go so far as to allow for the inclusion of those who believe in salvation by grace alone. No doubt those who believe in salvation by grace alone would be tolerated in a church controlled by the non-biblical principle of ecumenism only if such people would keep silent. But those who believe in salvation by grace alone cannot keep silent. If they did keep silent, they would sin against their own deepest convictions. Paul the apostle was not silent in relation to the Judaizers. How then could those who trusted in circumcision, i.e., in salvation by works, tolerate one in their midst who would daily tell them that Christ would profit them nothing? How could they tolerate one who, in effect, told them that they have in the nature of the case denied Christ in the basic intent of his work of salvation for men?

The issue, then, would seem to be quite clear. No Christian can be opposed to ecumenism. Those for whom Christ died come from every nation and kindred and tribe. Those whose whole hope of escape from the eternal wrath to come and of entrance into the presence of Christ is the sovereign grace of God in Christ Jesus, are Christ's body. They are his people whom he came to redeem. He prayed for them before he left this earth: "They are not of the world, even as I am not of the world. Sanctify them through thy truth: thy word is truth. As thou hast sent me into the world, even so have I also sent them into the world" (John 17:16-18).

A. *The Early Church*

When the early church went out into the world, armed with the truth through which alone true unity could be effected, they, as well as Paul, met with opposition. From its earliest history the church was confronted with those who already had their own principle of unity. The natural man, anxious to repress the truth about himself lest he should have to confess his own guilt, hastens to construct his own principle of unity. According to this principle all "good people" everywhere manifest goodness and will receive at last whatever good Reality may contain. No one is under the wrath to come because no one has transgressed the law of love of his Creator.

Here, then, is non-biblical ecumenism. On its basis every man participates in the principle of ultimate of being, and ultimate being is good. Whatever falls short of this good may be called evil. This evil will, it is hoped, eventually fade away into non-being.

The Greek philosophers have given classic expression to this non-biblical ecumenism. Aristotle thought of God as an abstract, universal principle or form. Correlative to this idea of pure form was the idea of pure matter. All things in heaven and on earth, including man, were interpreted in terms of this form-matter scheme of thought. On this view there was no such thing as a creation of the world. On this view man was not created in the image of God and did not, because he could not, sin against God. So far as he had reality, man was participant in the universal principle of reality called God. So far as man had any individuality, he had derived it from the principle of pure matter, pure, meaningless contingency.

This form-matter scheme contains a basic dilemma. So far as man had any intelligible awareness of himself as an individual it was in terms of the principle of reality or rationality that devoured his individuality. The ethical separateness of men from one another was not, on this Greek form-matter scheme, a result of human sin but of human finitude. And their unity, if it was to be attained, had to be attained by their absorption into God as eternal being. Thus salvation or redemption was impossible for men. On the one hand they did not need it since they were not sinners. On the other hand, if they were redeemed or saved from sin, they could not be aware of it. For in that case their individuality would be lost in God.

By the grace of God the church did gradually learn to set the biblical idea of ecumencity over against the non-biblical one. Notably in the Chalcedon Creed those who believed in and worked with a non-biblical principle of ecumenicity were excluded from the church. Both the Eutychians and the Nestorians, working as they did with the Greek form-matter scheme, would, if they had been successful, have disfigured the face of Christ beyond recognition. But the church excluded them in order that the Christ, as true God and true man, might go forth in his church-gathering work.

B. *The Church Reformed*

As time went on, however, the church no longer loved God enough to exclude those who sought salvation by works. She sought for a synthesis between the biblical and the Greek principle of ecumenism. And having wrought out such a synthesis she excluded those who, like Paul, spoke out for salvation by grace alone. A non-biblical inclusivism led, in the case of the Church of Rome, to an equally unbiblical exclusivism.

The Christ of the Scriptures therefore continued his gathering together of his people through the Reformers and their followers. To be sure, in their midst too the principle of unbelief and therefore of schism and false separation continued to work. But, as has often been recalled, Calvin would have crossed seven seas in order to bring together all those who believed and trusted in the Christ of the Scriptures. Many of his followers down to the present would follow him in this respect. They think of all those who believe in salvation by grace alone through Christ's blood and righteousness as belonging to the church of Christ. They would call upon all their fellow Christians to join them to form the church according to the prescription of the Scriptures. They would be patient and tolerant of the many shortcomings and failures of all the children of God, remembering always that they are themselves greater sinners than are others. But they would, even so, always be mindful of the fact that the sacrament of the Lord must not be profaned by their own adoption of a non-biblical inclusivism. This is essentially the *Protestant* position on ecumenism, or perhaps we should say, the historic Protestant view of ecumenism.

And this historic Protestant conception of ecumenism may now be compared with the modern Protestant conception of ecumenism.

V. *Modern Protestant Ecumenism*

For purposes of comparison, we refer first to an article by Dr.

Adolf Visser't Hooft in the book entitled *A History of the Ecumenical Movement* on "The Word 'Ecumenical'—Its History and Use."[1] Dr. Visser't Hooft performed a genuine service for us all when in this article he described the various meanings of the word "ecumenical." We limit ourselves to the three meanings which, as Dr. Hooft says, "are modern developments." These three meanings are: (a) "those pertaining to the world-wide missionary outreach of the church," (b) "those pertaining to the relations between and unity of two or more Churches (or of Christians of various confessions)," and (c) "that quality or attitude which expresses the consciousness of and desire for Christian unity."[2]

Both the modern and the biblical forms of ecumenism naturally agree on the missionary responsibility of the church. They also agree on the fact that, so far as the principle of the gospel allows, various denominations should unite. And they agree that such union can come about only if there is a genuine desire for unity on the part of all the believers in Christ.

The difference between the two types of ecumenism makes its appearance, however, in mutually exclusive conceptions of the gospel. However difficult it is for us sinful men to do so, we must yet speak to one another of this difference. Let us by the grace of the Holy Spirit speak the truth but speak it in love. Christ our High Priest prayed for our sanctification but he prayed that it might take place by the Word and added "Thy Word is Truth."

As one who with the Reformers would follow Paul as Paul followed Christ, I cannot think that the modern ecumenical movement is based upon salvation by grace alone. Only a lengthy review of the development of modern thought, and, in particular, the development of the modern idea of the church, could fully substantiate this judgment. In the space available we can mention only a few of the high spots of this development.

A. *Immanuel Kant*

The modern Protestant ecumenical movement is, of course, based upon the modern view of the church. And this modern view of the church would seem to be a synthesis of the doctrine of grace with the freedom-nature scheme, as this has found its first major expression in the philosophy of Immanuel Kant. As Roman Catholicism sought for a synthesis between Christianity and the Greek form-matter scheme, so modern Protestantism seeks for a synthesis between Christianity and the modern nature-freedom scheme. This modern freedom-nature scheme is not essentially different from the ancient form-matter scheme. Both hold to a principle of unification of all men by virtue of human character, i.e., by good works. Therefore modern ecumenism has a non-biblical principle of inclusion and an equally non-biblical principle of exclusion. The modern ecumenical movement is indeed moved by the spirit of unity. It frequently recalls the prayer of Christ that all his followers might be one, but it tends to forget that Christ prayed only for oneness *in the truth.* Or, if the idea of truth is brought into the picture, it is forgotten that the truth is exisential in that it requires us to listen to Christ when he said: "He that eateth my flesh and drinketh my blood, dwelleth in me and I in him" (John 6:56). Those who implicitly or explicitly deny the substitutionary atonement of Christ in history should be given no place in his church.

It is almost too well known to need recounting that Kant reduced the biblical doctrine of Christ and his grace to a moralistic scheme in which man himself makes the ultimate distinctions between right and wrong. In Kant's total outlook on life there are no sinners who need grace and there is no Christ through whom grace has been given to man. For Kant God is a projection of the ideals that man, as autonomous, projects for himself. Man is said to know nothing of God. If man is to speak of God at all, he must do so in *ethical,* i.e., non-intellectual, terms. Man's independent moral consciousness may postulate a God who will, on the recommendation of man, effect a final triumph of right over wrong. And Jesus Christ is the archetype of of the right so far as the ideal of right has ever found expression in history.

B. *Friedrich Schleiermacher*

The reason for speaking of Kant is that he has largely influenced the movement of modern theology.

Friedrich Schleiermacher is the "father of modern theology." True, he did not like Kant's moralism. For Schleiermacher, in Christianity "everything is related to redemption accomplished by Jesus of Nazareth."[3] Schleiermacher wants to be truly Christological in his approach to all theology. But with Karl Barth he may assert: "Jesus of Nazareth fits desperately badly into this theology of the historical 'composite life' of humanity, a 'composite life' which is really after all fundamentally self-sufficient. . . ."[4] For Schleiermacher, our redemption is not based upon a transition from wrath to grace, effected for sinners in history through the death and resurrection of Jesus Christ. According to Schleiermacher, human nature has inherent within it the power of taking the divine restorative element into itself. Schleiermacher says that

> if only the *possibility* of this resides in human nature, so that the actual implanting therein of the divine element must be purely a divine and therefore an eternal act, nevertheless the temporal appearance of this act in one particular Person must at the same time be regarded as an action of human nature, grounded in its original constitution and prepared for by all its past history, and accordingly as the highest development of its spiritual power (even if we grant that we could never penetrate so deep into those innermost secrets of the universal spiritual life as to be able to develop this general conviction into a definite perception). Otherwise it could only be explained as an arbitrary divine act that the restorative divine element made its appearance precisely in Jesus, and not in some other person.[5]

Here, then, we have the foundation for Schleiermacher's idea of the ecumenical church. The personality-forming activity of human nature "wholly accounts for the personality of Jesus."[6] In a deeper sense even than is true in the case of Roman Catholic theology, the church is for Schleiermacher the continuation of the incarnation, and the Redeemer himself springs from the personality-forming activity of the cosmos. Therefore, according to Schleiermacher, all men are inherently in the church. All churches can readily unite on the basis of the ideals that human personality makes for itself, and the missionary task of the church is already accomplished in advance of the coming of the missionary to foreign soil.

C. Neo-Orthodoxy

Of even more importance for a comparison between the historic Protestant and the modern Protestant idea of ecumenism is neo-orthodoxy. Neo-orthodox theology has given great emphasis to the ecumenical movement. But we must be specific and speak more particularly of the theology of Karl Barth.

Basic to all that Barth teaches is the idea that in Christ God is wholly revealed and at the same time wholly hidden. In the Christ-event the full relation between God and man is expressed. If Schleiermacher's theology is Christological, Barth's theology is even more outspokenly so. But the question is whether the Christ of the Scriptures fits any better into Barth's theology than he does in that of Schleiermacher. And to ask this question is, in effect, to ask also whether Barth's theology is really a theology of grace, like that of the Reformers, or is a theology of salvation by character, like that of Schleiermacher.

One thing is clear, namely, that if Barth's theology is a theology of grace, then, on Barth's own estimate, the Reformers, and in particular Calvin, had no true theology of grace at all.

According to Barth grace is inherently both sovereign and universal. It is sovereign in that it is God's freedom in Christ to turn wholly into the opposite of himself, and as such enter into the realm of pure contingency with man. According to Barth, Calvin had no eye for this true, biblical idea of sovereignty, inasmuch as he believed that God is bound by his revelation in Jesus Christ as a direct and directly identifiable revelation of himself. According to Barth, Calvin had no eye for the fact that though revelation is historical, history can never be revelational.

Again, says Barth, as grace is inherently sovereign so it is inherently universal. The original relation of every man is that of grace which is his in Christ. Calvin had no eye for this true universality of grace as he had no eye for the sovereignty of grace. Calvin did not see that the highest attribute in God is that of grace. Therefore he did not see that man's offense against the holiness and righteousness of God can never separate him from the grace of God. According to Barth,

Calvin did not realize that reprobation is only the penultimate while election in grace is always the ultimate word of God to all men. Man's atonement precedes his existence in history. Thus Barth's "purified supralapsarianism" involves the "ontological impossibility" of sin.

On this view of grace, the empirical separation of churches is merely evidence of the fact that in history, human personality can never fully realize its own ideals. On this view the missionary task of the church is that of informing all men everywhere that they are in Christ because they have always been in Christ.

Perhaps we should now make contrast between the Christ of Schleiermacher and the Christ of Barth. Barth says that Christ has an uneasy place in the theology of Schleiermacher. But his remedy is to include all reality in Christ. For Barth the Christ-event as Act includes all reality. The unification of all things in Christ is of the essence of man as such. Ideally every member is a member of this unity even though empirically no one will ever fully be.

With Professor G. C. Berkouwer of the University of Amsterdam we must say that for Barth "a transition from wrath to grace in the historical sphere is no longer thinkable. It is clear that *this* transition is excluded. . . ."[7] Such a theology, as is obvious, wipes out all such boundaries as were made by Paul between those who believed in salvation by grace and those who believed in salvation by works.

The neo-orthodox view of the church is therefore not basically different from Schleiermacher's view of the church. Nor is it, as has been definitely shown by such theologians as Hans Urs von Balthasar and Hans Küng, basically different from the Roman Catholic idea of the church. The Roman Catholic synthesis of Aristotle, and Christ is not basically different from the Schleiermacher-Barth synthesis of Kant and Christ. And as G. Hoshino, the Buddhist philosopher, points out, the gospel as Barth interprets it is readily acceptable to his sect of Buddhism.[8] Why then should not the modern ecumenical movement, so far as it is informed and directed by neo-orthodox theology, proceed first to the unification of all "Protestant" churches, then to the unification of the Protestant and the Roman Catholic churches, in order finally to join forces with all men, of all religious convictions, to strive for the perfection of human personality according to a com-

mon ideal, in which such figures as Buddha and Christ may be thought
of as personifications?

An ecumenical movement thus initiated by a church in which there
is no transition from wrath to grace in history may expect to find
support from a "Christian historian" such as Arnold Toynbee.

According to Toynbee, history from time to time produces origi-
native and noble personalities. These originating personalities seek to
lead the human race to ever-higher heights of nobility and selfless
love. The passion of Christ was "the culminating and crowning experience of the suffering of human souls in successive failures in the
enterprise of secular civilization."[9] It was in Christianity that the
comprehensive character of the spiritual law "proclaimed by Aeschy-
lus" was realized, to the effect that "through suffering learning comes."
The "doctrine of redemption is the theological way of expressing the
revelation that God is love."[10]

Here then is the principle of self-sacrificial love, assumed to be
inherent in all men in greater or lesser degree, that seems to be that
which, in the eyes of present-day ecumenical theologians and historians
of culture, will eventually unite all things on heaven and on earth.
This God of love is the God of Ishmael and of Esau, no less than the
God of Isaac and of Jacob. All men are ideally one in this God by
virtue of their manhood. None of them will, because none of them
can, suffer the righteous indignation of God, for love or grace is
always higher than righteousness.

All men are welcome in this church, that is, all except those who
speak, because they must speak, of him who bore the wrath of God in
their place upon the cross.

Dr. Georgia Harkness calls such men "dissident fundamentalists."
Karl Barth tells them there *can* be no finished work of salvation
accomplished in history. Toynbee calls them to repentance from
their pride, in the name of the universal cosmic principle of love and
in the name of the sacred missionary task of true human personality.

> If Christianity is presented to people in that traditional arrogant
> spirit it will be rejected in the name of the sacredness of human
> personalities—a truth to which the whole human race is now
> awakening under the influence of modern western civilization,

which originally learned that truth from the Christianity that modern man has been rejecting.[11]

Yet those who follow Luther and Paul, seeking humility, knowing that what they have, they have received by grace alone, must, in their turn, call for repentance. They must call for repentance lest men abide forever, as now they are, under the wrath of the holy God. They must call for repentance so that men may have a true bond of fellowship with Christ through his righteousness freely imputed unto them and made manifest in his resurrection from the dead. They must call upon men not to forsake the ccumenical ideal, but to build it upon the transition from wrath to grace effected for sinners in the death and resurrection of Christ. Constrained by the love of Christ for lost sinners, they must proclaim redemption through Christ's blood and righteousness to all men everywhere. Only thus can the true and the whole body of Christ be built up, and that numberless host of the vision of John in the last book of Scripture be brought together. May God give all of us the grace to seek forgiveness for our sins through him who was made a curse for us and then enable us to engage in our true ecumenical task.

VI. *General Conclusion*

In this volume we have sought to give the Reformed pastor an insight into the main movements of modern philosophy and theology. This has, we trust, given him a deeper insight into the fact that no half-hearted apologetic will meet the need of the hour. The Arminian type of apologetics, so largely used, even by Reformed theologians, is unable to set off the full God and Christ-centered theology of Scripture over against the man-centered theology of liberalism and neo-orthodoxy. Only a fully biblical and therefore fully Reformed theology and apologetic can meet the need of the hour.

NOTES

1. "The Word 'Ecumenical'—Its History and Use," *A History of the Ecumenical Movement 1517–1948*, ed. Ruth Rouse and Stephen Charles Neill (London, 1954), p. 735.
2. *Ibid.*

3. *The Christian Faith* (Edinburgh, 1928), p. 52.
4. *Protestant Thought: From Rousseau to Ritschl* (New York, 1959), p. 313.
5. Schleiermacher, *op. cit.*, p. 64.
6. *Ibid.*, p. 401.
7. *The Triumph of Grace in the Theology of Karl Barth* (Grand Rapids, 1954), pp. 233-234.
8. *Antwort* (Zollison-Zürich: Evangelischer Verlag Ag., 1956).
9. Arnold Toynbee, *Christianity and Civilization* (London, 1940), p. 21.
10. *Ibid.*, p. 38.
11. *Christianity Among the Religions of the World* (New York, 1957), p. 99.